HARVARD HISTORICAL STUDIES

Published under the direction
of the Department of History
from the income of the Donald
Cope McKay Fund and of the
Henry Warren Torrey Fund

Volume XCI

The Election of 1827 in France

SHERMAN KENT

Harvard University Press

Cambridge, Massachusetts

and London, England

1975

Library of Congress Catalog Card Number: 75-3702
ISBN 0-674-24321-8
Printed in the United States of America

In Memory of My Masters

John M. S. Allison

Charles M. Andrews

K. Asakawa

Sidney K. Mitchell

Charles Seymour

George E. Woodbine

Acknowledgments

In all scholarly enterprises, the author incurs many debts of gratitude. First among my own are those owing my friend Marcel Baudot, gifted scholar and paragon of archivists, the recently retired inspector general of the French National Archives, whose wisdom, knowledge, and generosity of spirit was a continuing source of delight and helpfulness. To him and the former director, M. André Chamson, and their cheery and capable staff my warmest thanks. So too to the directors of the Archives Départementales and the remarkable men and women that surround them. As with all concerned with the history of France my gratitude goes yet once again to the staff of the Bibliothèque Nationale (with special thanks to M. Boudard) who do so much to make the institution's matchless collections available to scholars.

To André Tudesq, Adeline Daumard, and Odon de Saint Blanquat – the director of the municipal archives of Toulouse – my warmest thanks for a score of kind and helpful acts.

Among my American colleagues who share my interest in modern France I want to express my gratitude particularly to David Pinkney, Thomas Beck, William Pruitt, and Don Smith for their valued advice and assistance.

In the United States I have had the privilege of being able to use the Yale and Harvard University Libraries and the Library of Congress. I wish to thank the librarians and many of their co-workers for their help and guidance.

To my old friend Milton Venezky and my new one, Robert Baker, my deep appreciation for their expert work on the maps.

To my office-mates Bernard Drell, June Cassidy, John Scott, Betty Buffalow, and Edith Kelley who have furnished endless help in matters large and small, and to Edwin Gunberg, that most imaginative, deft, and generous of editors, more thanks than I can say. Blessed the retiree who still dwells among professional colleagues, twice blessed for this assortment of rare and sympathetic souls.

All gratitude goes to the Ford Foundation for a stipend which made possible a series of visits to almost every corner of France in my dipping into the archives of some threescore departments.

For the solution to the most vexatious of the logistic problems — namely, the penetration of the geographic mystery of French cities and their web of unfamiliar one-way streets — my deepest thanks to my wife who, with the *Guide Michelin* in her lap, and with skill and good cheer, was my flawless navigator and co-pilot on our motorized *tour de France.*

At the annual Congrès des Sociétés Savantes in 1971 I presented my findings with respect to the composition of the electorate and the corps of eligibles. I had hoped that my paper would appear in the publication of the French Ministère de l'Education Nationale: *Bulletin de la Section d'histoire moderne et contemporaine,* for 1973.

Meanwhile this book was in train. I hoped to submit it for publication sometime after the appearance of my article. In the book I could therefore confine myself to a short statement of principal conclusions about the electorate, leaving the article, to which I would refer, to carry the burden of the argumentation. Indeed, as is customary, I agreed to withhold publication of the substance of the article pending its issuance as a part of the *Bulletin.*

The French authorities have had their difficulties. They have been forced to delay publication of the *Bulletin* for the Congrès of 1971 well beyond the anticipated date. I have gone to them for guidance and they have graciously waived their prior right to the material and authorized its appearance as a part of this work. I deeply appreciate their kindness and their understanding.

And now a note of homage to two predecessors, Frederick Artz and that invaluable triad of scholars, Adolphe Robert, Edgar Bourloton, and Gaston Cougny who eight decades ago published their multi-volumed biographical dictionary of French legislators beginning with the members of the Estates General of 1789. Of the many services which this work has performed for countless readers, that of establishing some sort of norm for rendering the names of their biographees I rate among its most valuable. In a day when Adolphe Thiers's own newspaper could spell his name variously as Thier, Tier, Tiers, and finally Thiers; when a man with a complicated compound name like Dugué de la Fauconnerie might be placed in an alphabetical arrangement under Du- or Gu- or Dela- or La Fau- or Fauc-, the rendering of Robert and his colleagues – right or wrong – is there as a saving unity.

The debt to Frederick Artz is different. Back in the days when few of our fellow countrymen worked on any part of the history of France and few enough Frenchmen worked on the Restoration, Mr. Artz published a splendid article in the *Journal of Modern History* and a first chapter in his book, *France under the Bourbon Restoration,* which said a great many new, useful, and perceptive things about the elections of the Restoration. His is an enduring piece of work and I am well pleased to be associated with it as a latter-day supplementer.

My deep and lasting gratitude to Bonnie Klosnick, Sharon Bond, Suzanne Allen, Dorothy Cascioni, Alice-Marie Palluth, and Betty Naley, who have transmuted the obscurities of my longhand into beautiful typescript; to Mrs. Aida D. Donald, Editor for the Social Sciences, Harvard University Press; and especially to Mrs. Madeleine Gleason, Editor of the Harvard Historical Studies, whose limitless patience and great editorial skill added so much to this book.

Lastly, had Donald Cope McKay been living he would have been my indispensable critic and helper. A dear friend and stalwart colleage, he was one of the first of his generation to make modern France the focus of his scholarly interest. I am honored that this work has been published in part from the income of the fund which bears his name.

Contents

The Election of 1827 in France

Introduction

This is a book about elections in the period of the Restoration in France (1814–1830) and more especially about the most important of them, that of 1827.

I have focused on this election for a number of reasons: in the first place it resulted in the fall of the Villèle government whose tenure in office was one of the longest in modern French history. In the second, it elected a chamber of deputies whose majority carried the fight further on to that last desperate showdown with Charles X which led to his fall and the disappearance of the Bourbon dynasty. Furthermore, the influence of that chamber did not end with its dissolution in May of 1830. So great was the personal réclame of the men who made up its majority that practically all of them were returned to office in the subsequent elections of June and July 1830 – exactly contrary to the plan of Polignac and Charles. This, the successor chamber, which owed so much to the political doings of 1827, became *mutatis mutandis* the one which bridged the July Revolution of 1830 and played a pivotal role in the establishment of the July Monarchy.[1] Few indeed are the national elections which have had a more important and more variegated short-, middle-, and long-term influence. If one needs an excuse for putting forth a book's-worth of effort on so limited a subject matter, this is it.

But upon second glance the subject matter is not so limited. A simple examination of the election's outcome, an enumeration of the political orientations of the 430 winners, will show (in chapter 7, below) why the newly-elected chamber would not go on supporting Villèle and why Villèle could not live with it. But once these matters are explained other questions inevitably arise. It is hard to say which

1. See the admirable work of David H. Pinkney, *The French Revolution of 1830* (Princeton: Princeton University Press, [1972]), for which this book can serve as something of a political preface and an elaboration of one of the main themes of Mr. Pinkney's second chapter.

of several most insistently require an answer; there are however three which stand out.

The first of these is why was the election called in the first place. The sitting chamber of deputies had another three annual sessions to run before it would come to the end of its legal constitutional life. There may have been a dispute on this matter, but no disputant would have put the date earlier than the end of 1828. In other words, the decision to go to the country was a free choice and, in the light of the election's result, a dolorous one for the choosers. Could they have foreseen the outcome? Surely not with precision. But still there is evidence that some of them were beset by doubts. Who were these choosers – there were several of them – and when and why did they decide as they did? I have tried to answer these and other questions in chapter 2. My efforts have been greatly helped by the kindness of the present comtesse de Villèle who gave me access to the manuscript diary of comte Joseph de Villèle for the very year of the election, 1827. His testimony, originally written for his own eyes only, illuminates many of the tactical aspects of this subject.

But behind all tactical situations and tactical solutions, there lurks a complex of strategic factors. So here they lurked. They were complicated; but to avoid a discussion of them for that reason, or any other, would be to rob the tactical decision of its larger rationale. Chapter 1 accordingly is a discussion of this essential political background.

There is another pair of questions which asks for consideration, if not an answer. How did it come about that the oppositions (those of the left and of the far right) won this election; how did it come about that the government did not win it? Both sides made very great efforts. That the government should have done so is nothing to occasion surprise, for it possessed both the keenest sort of incentive in its desire to stay in control and a wealth of electioneering power. The ways in which the government exercised this power in the campaign is the subject of chapter 6.

The oppositions, for their part, lacked nothing in the way of incentive. They were fairly consumed in their distrust and dislike of Villèle and his government. To bring both down, and restore the Restoration, as many of the left opposition would have phrased it, was a matter of transcendent importance. That the oppositions also turned out to dispose the means and the political sagacity to reach and impress the electorate — and that in the teeth of the pervasive power of the government — does constitute a surprise. In fact some predecessor historians have treated it almost as a miracle. Be it said that in their terms — terms which ascribed virtually full credit to the brand new leftist electoral organization with the colorful name: the *Société, Aide-toi, le ciel t'aidera* — there was the stuff of miracles about it.

I have not seen it exactly thus. Without questioning the importance of the Aide-toi as an institution which accomplished much in the mobilization of the electorate, I felt that another and quite different organization, one established and guided by the great Chateaubriand — the *Société des amis de la liberté de la presse* (I will refer to them hereafter as the Friends) — was owing a considerable share of the honors. Indeed the surviving traces of this organization in today's documentary record are as rich or richer than those of the Aide-toi. Its name obscures the very function it performed most effectively. For however passionately Chateaubriand desired to unfetter the contemporary French press, the means he chose to accomplish his ends was the electoral: vote into power a legislature which would repeal the objectionable laws infringing the basic liberty of a free press.

The tireless and imaginative work of these two organizations cannot in itself account for the outcome of the 1827 election. It has seemed to me that the lessons of a number of elections between 1816 and 1824, and the work of prior opposition electoral organizations, national and local, was the basic stuff upon which the endeavors of a few months of 1827 rested.

For all these reasons I have taken two chapters (4 and 5) to discuss the electoral activities of the oppositions. The first takes up the Aide-toi, the Friends, and the historical background; the second, the campaign of 1827 as the oppositions conducted it.

Since relatively little of a systematic nature has been devoted to the institutional structure of Restoration elections I have devoted a chapter (chapter 3) to the electorate, the corps of eligibles, the nature of the electoral districts (post-1820), and the conduct of business in the electoral colleges. If one were to try to write of the campaign and its outcome without having first discussed these matters in a separate chapter, he would find himself covering them in a series of disparate parenthetical paragraphs thrust into the vitals of chapters devoted to other concerns. For this most obvious of reasons I have awarded these institutional matters their own chapter.

There is another reason too. In the French departmental archives, some sixty of which I visited in pursuit of another project,[2] I found among other treasures enough electoral lists to constitute a large sample of the electorate and to make possible an empirical analysis of its composition. I also found similar documents which permitted the same sort of analysis for the corps of eligibles. Furthermore in the national archives there survive a good number of documents which illuminate one of the major mysteries of electoral history of this period, namely the way in which one went about the delimiting of the electoral districts. In other words, the richness of these new materials constituted in itself a most urgent exhortation, and one not to go unheeded.

2. In its published form: "Electoral Lists of France's July Monarchy, 1830–1848," *French Historical Studies,* 7 (1971–1972), 117–127.

1 / Background to Trouble

This account, which concerns a small but important fragment of French history, begins in the autumn of 1826.

By this time the comte Joseph de Villèle, a central figure of the pages to come, had been minister of finance and almost simultaneously president of the council of ministers for something over four years. He had been Louis XVIII's choice for both of these positions as he became Charles's. He served these last two of the Bourbons with skill and exemplary devotion.

De Bertier de Sauvigny, citing some of Villèle's contemporaries, describes him "as a small man, thin and unprepossessing, with a prominent nose and a complexion marred by smallpox. His voice was sharp and nasal. But his lively and practical intelligence coupled to his enormous industry[1] permitted him a rapid mastery of all political questions, especially of those bearing upon public finance. He had a gift for expounding such matters with clarity and a wealth of illuminating detail." The warmth and compassion of his private life which glows through the meagre scratchings of his diary were not characteristics of Villèle, the high official. He had his enemies, and in bounty, for he was not a man to suffer fools: perhaps he lacked the temperament, surely he lacked the time.

As 1826 drew to a close, Villèle and his sovereign had had to conclude that if the rightward course of national policy[2] was to prevail they would have to cope with at least two trouble areas: that of the legislature and that of the periodical press.

There was to begin with the chamber of peers. Almost all of its members were the creation of Louis XVIII, and many of these at the motion of the liberal duc de Decazes.[3] Contrary to the tradition-

1. Villèle's diary reveals him on the job and hard at work almost every single day of 1827, including Christmas and Easter Sunday. For the diary, see the Bibliographical Note.

2. The rightward course usually associated with Charles had in fact begun under Louis XVIII in 1821 or earlier. For the background to this "Background" chapter see the admirable work of Guillaume de Bertier de Sauvigny, *La Restauration* (rev. ed., Paris: Flammarion, 1955), esp. pt. 2, chaps. 5 and 6, and pt. 4, chap. 1; quotation from p. 242.

3. In early 1819, Louis named 59 to the peerage. This infusion of liberals was more than enough to overpower the heretofore rightist majority.

al image of an upper house the peers were far more left-leaning than the chamber of deputies. The leaders of the faction which opposed the rightist policy of the crown were competent and resourceful parliamentarians – Broglie, Barante, Decazes, Siméon, Molé, inter alia – who had already achieved the defeat of important legislation dear to crown and ministry.[4] Obviously they could and probably would continue to obstruct. The constitutional remedy to the situation was simple and ready at hand. With the power to create new peers at will, the king had only to name enough new ones to assure a working majority and his legislative problems in that chamber, at least, would be over.

The matter was of course much more complicated. There was the large number that would be required (perhaps up to fourscore) and the problem of just who these new peers should be. The choosing would set in motion every cabal in the court, indeed in the upper social reaches of the kingdom; all manner of disturbing talk and intrigue would agitate the very group whose calm and undivided loyalty was most desired. There was perhaps the expense to the crown itself if the *majorat* – a sort of endowment for the holders of the title, *pair de France* – were to be invoked. Lastly, should a substantial number be chosen from the most competent parliamentarians among the deputies, would not the very effective leadership in the lower house be grievously weakened?

Thus not only was the question of packing the chamber of peers a vexed one in its own right, but it led inexorably to the equally difficult question of the deputies.

A few years back Villèle and his king, then Louis XVIII, had gone to the country. It was early in 1824. The timing was right and the electoral machinery well-oiled and skillfully manipulated. The election itself was a landslide in the government's favor. Of the 430 deputies chosen, probably fewer than 20 could be identified as ideological opponents of the ministry. Seldom has a prime minister had a more compliant and overwhelming majority in his lower house. But it was not to stay thus. With the passage of time the majority began to melt.

4. Adverse votes in the upper house had upset Villèle's first plan for the indemnification of the emigrés (June 1824), a bill to authorize the crown to reestablish religious orders for both men and women (late 1824), and a bill (April 1826) designed to impede the break-up of the landed estates of the most substantial landholders (called by its political enemies a return to primogeniture).

There had been in June of 1824 the unhappy and abrupt dismissal of Chateaubriand as minister of foreign affairs. This gifted and famous man took with him the loyalty and affection of the rightmost of the ultras who had given support to Villèle with something less than enthusiasm, but support nonetheless. From now on they would constitute a virulent parliamentary opposition of the extreme right. Known in earlier days as the *impatients,* they came to be called the counter-opposition or, pejoratively, the *défection* or the *pointus.* Their front runners in the chamber of deputies were men like La Bourdonnaye, Agier, and Hyde de Neuville. Their numerical strength in that house ran to two or threescore, depending somewhat upon the measure at issue.

Threats, though modest ones, also developed on Villèle's left. The parliamentary ranks of the true far left had not changed appreciably since the election of 1824, but Villèle's strong rightist orientation taken in combination with the absolutist inclinations of the king had caused concern among some of his one-time adherents. These were not akin to those pointus who had made common cause with Chateaubriand but were rather men who, having become bit by bit warm adherents of constitutional monarchy, had begun to harbor some justifiable doubts about the intentions of the high personages in charge. As these doubters contemplated changing the complexion of the peers by drawing upon the pool of attractive eligibles in the lower house, their concerns about that body grew.

That the problem of the peers was intertwined with that of the deputies is attested by at least one tangible and potent piece of direct evidence. It is found in the personal diary of Villèle for the year 1827. On 25 January of the new year he had had an audience with his sovereign. Villèle's note runs: "Was with the king with whom I spoke . . . *of the time of the dissolution of the chamber of deputies, of the augmentation of that of the peers, etc.* [sic; emphasis added]." All of it is illuminating (except that heart-breaking "etc."), especially the thought that they spoke not of whether to dissolve the deputies, but as if this had already been determined in the affirmative and what was left was the decision as to the propitious moment to do so. Furthermore, the close juxtaposition of the phrase about enlarging the chamber of peers strongly conveys a logical substantive connection.

Without scrambling too far afield, one may conclude the existence of a strategy which in a single two-pronged move would smother the liberal trend in the peers and reduce the power of the two oppositions within the deputies. With planning and luck a general election could rid the lower house of its schismatics of the extreme right and hold the strength of the left-wing opposition to that golden magnitude which would be too small to do hurt but large enough to frighten "royalist" dissenters and fence-sitters into a loyal and solid majority.[5]

Worry over recalcitrance within the two chambers was perhaps merely the first among many painful concerns. Near to it was the periodical press, especially the cluster of Parisian dailies which opposed every facet of the rightward policy and virtually every move made in its behalf. What this press chose to report, the way it did it plus the fact of its large nationwide readership filled the hearts of conservatives – starting with the king and Villèle – with consternation. The flavor and some of the substance of their concern is conveyed in a document of the day, ostensibly prepared for the consideration of the council of ministers.[6] "The Bourbons are deluding themselves," it says, "if they do not recognize the existence of subsurface ferment among the lower classes, which do not accept at face the ideological principles of the Restoration." It goes on to indicate that the institutions which are basic to the survival of the monarchy – the royal prerogative, the peerage, the property qualification for voting and eligibility for office, the place of the church, and so on – are under attack. The periodical press was, in the writer's view, the chief culprit in these destructive attitudes, and if not restrained in its abuse of its freedom would inevitably lead the country to a "political protestantism" which rejects all authority.

What the writer of this memorandum was voicing was something common to the thinking of the conservative masters of the kingdom. Whenever they reflected upon their pyramid of concerns, they were likely to do so in the context of a handful of Parisian newspapers,

5. I have borrowed this thought from something Villèle is reported by Guizot to have said later on in the year 1827 when he "promised the king, his colleagues, and his party a smashing victory: 'There will be sixty liberals, . . . I need them to rally the royalists.' " See the article, "Dix Brochures politiques publiées par la Société *Aide-toi, le Ciel t'aidera,*" first published anonymously in *La Revue Française,* No. 1 (January 1828), pp. 22–45, by François P. G. Guizot; reprinted under the title, "Des Élections et de la société *Aide-toi, le ciel t'aidera,* en 1827," in a collection of his essays: *Mélanges politiques et historiques* (Paris, 1869), pp. 435–466.

6. It reposes among the Villèle family papers. The document is devoted to the dangers of an uncontrolled periodical press and proposes a new scheme for censorship. The document is unsigned and undated. Context puts it close to the period under discussion.

led by the *Constitutionnel,* the *Courrier français,* and since the dismissal of Chateaubriand, by the *Journal des Débats.* With a readership considerably greater than all the pro-government papers combined and read throughout the country by many times more readers than subscribers, the opposition press was a bone in the government's throat.

For reason, it was regarded from the rightward end of the political spectrum as the fomenter of dissent if not outright treason. Although to a twentieth-century reader their columns seem mild indeed, to those contemporaries – still none too certain of the present and future, and aghast at the excesses of the Revolution and the costs of the adventurism of Napoleon – the utterances of the opposition periodical press brought fear and dread of a recurrence. From almost the earliest moment of the Restoration, the days in which the constitutional charter itself was being framed, the power of the press for evil was foreseen. Article 8 of that document reads, "Frenchmen have the right to speak out (*publier*) and to publish (*faire imprimer*) their opinions in conformity with the laws which are to repress the abuses of this liberty."[7] In consonance with the imperative of the article Restoration governments had time and again endeavored to write the sort of law which would in fact repress the abuses of a free press.

In the year 1826 the subject came up yet again. It is hard to explain what was attempted then without a look at what had gone before.

Among the Restoration's earliest statutes was the first press law, that of 21 October 1814. It ruled that a would-be newspaper publisher had to receive an authorization from the crown before he could begin putting out a paper. Furthermore, if his publication was to fill twenty or fewer *feuilles,* or printers' sheets, the law told him to submit it to a board of censors prior to publication.[8] The censors in their turn were instructed to deny publication to libelous

7. J. B. Duvergier, *Collection complète des lois, décrets, ordonnances, réglemens, avis du conseil-d'état,* 2nd ed. (31 vols., Paris, 1834–1838), XIX, 79. (Hereafter I will cite this compendium simply: Duvergier, *Lois.*)

8. This would mean censorship of everything from a newspaper of the day with its single feuille folded once (folio) to a book of 20 feuilles folded in eight (octavo) for 160 pages, or folded in 16° for 320 pages. This usage of the word "feuille" has not always been fully understood. Rendering it in English as "sheet" is not very helpful, and as "page" is wrong. See Robert Marquant, *Thiers et le baron Cotta* (Paris: Presses Universitaires de France, 1959), #75, p. 374: " . . . brochures . . . qui auront moins de 20 feuilles, c'est à dire moins de 320 pages, . . . " (Hereafter cited as Marquant, *Thiers et Cotta.*)

and defamatory writing and to that calculated to disturb the peace, endanger the constitution, or disrupt what was referred to as "bonnes moeurs."

For four and a half years – until the spring of 1819 – the press existed under this and similar legislation. The actual running of the censorship became, and was accepted as, a police function.[9] With the growth of the left of center in the chamber of deputies and with the departure of the occupying armies, the Decazes government sponsored a new initiative. The laws of 17 and 26 May 1819 took the press from under the police and censorship and put its regulation into the courts. The general thrust of these laws was to make the press an accomplice in crimes and serious misdemeanors which it was considered to have stimulated. The laws defined the sort of crime at issue and what was meant by defamation which became a serious offense; they also provided that the cases be tried in the assize courts before a jury. Two weeks later (9 June 1819) a third law imposed upon newspaper publishers the necessity to post bond (caution money) and rescinded the use of the jury.

With the murder of the duc de Berry in February 1820 came the three laws of exception, one of which put the press back on square one (law of 31 March 1820). Proclaiming on its face that the new censorship was a temporary measure to last only a few months it was extended by subsequent legislation to endure into 1822. Then in March of that year came a new approach, the law (17 March) of the *tendance*, as it was called – something which was neither censorship nor the formula of criminal liability attempted in the 1819 legislation. As Mrs. Collins has written,[10] the "novel feature which liberals denounced as the greatest threat to liberty of the press since 1814: [was] article 3 [which] provided that any journal whose general tendency seemed injurious to public peace or to the respect due to religion, to the king, and to the constitution, could be cited before the royal courts and suspended for a first or second offence and suppressed for a third. No specific words need be cited as in-

9. For a discussion of the details of press legislation, see the splendid book of Irene Fozzard Collins, *The Government and the Newspaper Press in France, 1814–1881* (London: Oxford University Press, 1959), chaps. 1–6. (Hereafter cited as Collins, *Government and the Newspaper Press.*)

10. *Ibid.*, p. 37.

dictable; a series of articles, each one legally inoffensive, could be judged as indicating a tendency towards libel."

Censorship was held out as a fall-back position; article 4 authorized the king to impose it by ordinance, "if in the interval between sessions of the legislature, special circumstances had . . . rendered . . . established measures inadequate."

Under the law of the tendance the government brought a good many actions and with very poor success. In mid-1825 it hailed the *Constitutionnel* and the *Courrier français* before the *cour royale* of Paris with a carefully prepared indictment based upon a cluster of ill-intentioned articles about certain orders of the regular clergy, especially the Jesuits.[11] In two separate judgments, handed down on 3 and 5 December 1825, the court found the defendants not guilty. The effect within the government went far beyond the chagrin at the outcome of the case. The principal one was to reinforce the doubts which the executive branch already entertained about the judicial, especially as a means of coping with the highly dangerous license of the press. If the courts as presently mandated could not or would not restrain the press by punishing violators of the law, then something would have to be done about either the judges, or the courts, or the legal procedures which obtained for this class of action: one of these or something wholly different.

The first remedy tried was surely new and different. Led into it by a court favorite, the fast-talking and irresponsible bearer of a great name, Sosthène de la Rochefoucauld, Villèle authorized a bold semi-clandestine operation. It involved literally the outright purchase of a controlling interest in the opposition newspaper press of Paris and the putting of individual papers under the thumb of an editor who would take his orders from the government. Not only did the scheme fail in that the important opposition papers proved not for sale, but also in that the papers actually bought and managed began costing a good deal more than was tolerable.[12]

11. Archives Nationales (hereafter cited as AN) carton F/7 6742 contains the printed version of the prosecutor's formal charges. See the Bibliographical Note for the explanation of my style in referring to cartons in the F series ("Administration générale de la France") of the AN.

12. Irene Fozzard [Mrs. Collins], "The Government and the Press in France, 1822 to 1827," *English Historical Review*, 66 (1951), 51–66, tells this most interesting story in great detail and with artistry and authority.

For the government the obvious course of action still open was a reimposition of the censorship. The first public notice of impending action came in the king's speech from the throne on 12 December 1826. The *Discours* was an annual event which formally reopened the new legislative session. It was drafted in the council of ministers on the basis of preliminary discussion with the king and delivered by him in person to the members of the chamber of peers and a delegation from the deputies. It contained the outline of the legislative program which the king would initiate through his ministers and, when appropriate, some general statements of policy.

Noteworthy in the 1826 utterance was one short paragraph devoted to the press.[13] The king said that he had wished that it were possible not to bring up the subject, but increased freedom of the press seemed to have produced new abuses which demanded wider and more effective countermeasures. His rationale was neatly put: "It is time to bring an end to these woeful scandals and to protect the liberty of the press from the perils of its own excesses. A bill will be submitted to you to achieve this end."

His next paragraph may have surprised a good many of his audience. "Imperfections have been noted with respect to the organization of the jury"; this was clearly one of the notable understatements of the year. "I am having presented to you a bill to remedy the situation and to give the jury a frame of rules appropriate to its function."

Here it was then. The government was about to take action against the press with the initiation of new legislation and, for reasons unclear at least to the public, simultaneously to reform the institution of the jury. At the time it is unlikely that the king and his ministers had an intimation as to how the fate of the two promised measures would affect the other two problems uppermost in mind: whether or not (or perhaps, when) to bring the chamber of peers to heel by a massive creation of new members; whether or not (or when) to dissolve the chamber of deputies and summon the electoral colleges in a general election. The point is that the journey of the two bills through the legislative mill turned out to have a most profound effect on the status of both peers and deputies and in a notable way contributed to the decision to go to the country and that, soon.

The comte de Peyronnet, the minister of justice, introduced both

13. For its text, see inter alia *Le Moniteur Universel,* 13 Dec. 1826, p. 1659. (Herafter cited as *Moniteur.*)

bills the same afternoon, Wednesday, 29 December 1826. He went first to the Luxembourg palace where he presented to the peers the government's bill relating to the jury and then on to the deputies where he presented the bill on the press.

The press bill was draconic.[14] To begin with, it relieved the courts of most of their duties vis-à-vis the press and shifted the responsibility to the executive. More specifically it held that no newspaper (*journal*) or periodic publication could be issued without the name of the owners and the printer, that no writing of twenty feuilles or less could be sold or distributed until five days after its formal filing with the *librairie* and the latter's authorization; for documents of more than twenty sheets the delay was to be ten days. Costs of administering the measure – or part of them – were to be borne by the publishers who were to pay a stamp duty of ten centimes for each average folio-sized page. Prosecution would be directed against the papers' owners, and the number of owners of any single paper was limited to five. Fines and prison sentences were lifted well beyond prior limits. This particular thrust of the bill was aimed at making maverick journalism costly beyond the means of would-be publishers. On top of all remained the additional risk of being charged as accomplice in any one of the subversive actions described in earlier press legislation.

After the presentation and first flurry of off-the-cuff comment the bill went into committee (of the deputies) for consideration.[15] It stayed there for six weeks while the Paris press fulminated and printers throughout the land, fearful for their livelihoods, memorialized the chamber in a deluge of petitions.[16] It was during this interval that the *Moniteur* carried two articles which endeavored to illuminate the government's position.[17] Generally believed to have been written by Peyronnet himself (they were unsigned) they were an elaboration of the thought in the king's speech. The idea was that the press itself in its excesses had destroyed its own freedom. The aim of the bill

14. The text of the government's bill as read by the minister of justice along with his preliminary remarks are in *ibid.*, 30 Dec. 1826, pp. 1728–1730.

15. Composed of nine members, one from each of the nine bureaux of the chamber: Dudon, Sainte-Marie, Miron de l'Espinay, Gautier, Bonnet, Maquillé, de Moustier, La Bourdonnaye, and Berbis. Most were strong defenders of the Villèle government and, Gautier and La Bourdonnaye aside, all would defend the bill.

16. The columns of the *Courrier français* and the *Constitutionnel* during January 1827 are full of news of these petitions.

17. *Moniteur*, 5 January 1827, p. 20, and 6 January 1827, pp. 23–24.

was a restoration of freedom which would flow from a salutory crack-down on licentious writers, editors, and publishers. The second paragraph of the first article began with the historic sentence, "La loi présente veut être une loi de justice et d'amour. . . ." This unhappy characterization became a watchword for all in opposition, a derisive bit of shorthand continuously cited by Villèle's enemies, the old ones and the new.

On 7 February Bonnet made the presentation for the committee, reporting the bill out favorably.[18] Its basic philosophy came through pristine.

Then began one of the great debates of French legislative history.[19] Seventy-five deputies, thirty-one in support[20] and forty-four opposed, signed the roster of would-be speakers. The discussion went almost unbroken between 8 February and 10 March; it fills more than one hundred pages of the *Moniteur.* More remarkable than the duration of the debate, or even than the lucidity and eloquence of Royer-Collard's great address of denunciation, was the line-up of spokesmen in opposition to the bill. It included prominent deputies of the left wing as one would anticipate: Constant, Dupont de l'Eure, Labbey de Pompières, Casimir Périer, Sébastiani, and Turckheim, among others; it included as well, and in solid alliance, the leaders of the counter-opposition of the far right such as Agier, Bacot de Romans, La Bourdonnaye, and Hyde de Neuville. Though in terms of social and political philosophy the two groups were poles apart, in their feelings about the importance of a free press and in their dislike of Villèle and his ministry which would bridle it, they had a deep community of interest.

The press issue, so sharply raised in this far-reaching bill, received added momentum during this legislative session by the introduction of two other related measures. One of these, presented at the opening of the session, provided for an increase in the costs which the postal services would charge for the handling and transport of news-

18. *Ibid.,* 8 February 1827, pp. 185–190. The last two pages present the government's bill and the committee's amendments in parallel columns.

19. There is a fine full-dress account of the debate in Achille de Vaulabelle, *Chute de l'Empire: Histoire des deux Restaurations jusqu'à la chute de Charles X,* 2nd ed. (8 vols., Paris, 1847–1856), VI, 452ff. (Hereafter cited as Vaulabelle, *Restaurations.*)

20. The loyalty of 7 of these 31 supporters of the government received its acknowledgment within the year. They were among the 36 deputies elevated to the peerage in the royal ordinance of 5 November 1827.

papers. Its motivation, readily perceived, was to raise the price of Paris papers to their widespread departmental readership and thus to inhibit the circulation of the opposition press. This bill passed with its contribution to the rancor of the two oppositions and with little other effect. Paris newspapers, practically all of which were sold via annual subscriptions, raised their price from 72 to 80 francs per year and suffered little if any damage to their circulation.[21]

The other measure presented to the deputies, almost certainly at Villèle's behest, brought about a considerable furore. La Boëssière, a man who stood high in court circles and one of Villèle's close associates, introduced it in mid-March, and it became known by his name. The bill would have created a commission of seven deputies which would have the power of oversight of the press's reporting of the doings of the legislature. In the event that it perceived erroneous or warped coverage of the debate it would signal the matter to the police for action.[22] To the oppositions the bill merely aimed to stifle honest reporting of the most important political news of the day; to the government it was a measure necessary to safeguard "the prerogatives of the chamber": Villèle's diary notes it in these terms.[23] With these differences of view the bill stimulated a considerable discussion which went on intermittently until late April when it passed the deputies. It died a quiet death in the gateway to the peers like its more eminent legislative associate, the law of "justice and love."

As for the latter, the peers received it from the deputies in much the same shape as the government's original, and the peers in accord with normal procedures a few days later chose a committee of five (Broglie, Portalis, Portal, Brissac, and Lévis) to deliberate and report it out.[24] It never emerged. Given the membership of the committee this was foreseeable and foreseen. The Villèle diary affords some glimpses of what happened: the entry for 24 March notes that a majority of the committee is "bad"; that for the next day has Villèle reporting as much to the king; that for a week later remarks

21. Collins, *Government and the Newspaper Press,* pp. 48–50.

22. *Moniteur,* 15 Mar. 1827, pp. 407–410.

23. Villèle diary, 15 Mar. 1827.

24. F. P. Lubis, *Histoire de la Restauration* (6 vols. in 8, Paris, 1848), VI, 182n. Of the multi-volume histories of the Restoration by writers who were close in time to the events, this one is seldom cited. It is worthy of a place among them. For example, I have not found the names of these committeemen elsewhere.

that the committee is ruining (*gâter*) the bill. During the first half of April the bad news continued, and on 14 April Villèle talked things over with Corbière and Peyronnet who were of a mind to ask the king to withdraw the bill. As it turned out he needed convincing, but on 17 April he had had enough and signed in council the ordinance which killed it. Peyronnet broke the news by a reading of the document to the peers. There was relief in both chambers and at an hour after midnight a shivaree in the streets with cries of "vive le roi, vive les pairs, à bas les ministres."[25]

During these very months while the press bill was having its ups and its final climactic down, the king and Villèle and his colleagues were receiving new cause for worry. Popular discontent and threatened disorder, particularly in Paris, which they inevitably linked to the seditious bearing of the opposition press, seemed to be growing. On the very day (25 January) that Villèle and the king spoke of doing something about the peers and deputies, Villèle's diary also notes that he had brought up "the present situation and the means to be employed if it worsens – above all the role (*du poids*) to be given the army." A few days later Villèle wrote, "was with the king who is worried about all the perturbations of spirit," and within a fortnight: "Public opinion (*les esprits*) continues to be much agitated; people seem to be working to frighten the king and at base to prepare a revolution. I do not believe that things are ready, but surely there is the wish and there is the hope for revolution." To cap this little mound of concerns Villèle noted that M. de Montholon told the king of a military conspiracy twice within the space of a few days.[26]

Although Villèle was clearly skeptical of these latter stories he or Corbière, in whom he likely confided all his and the king's concerns, instructed Franchet d'Esperey, the director of police, to memorialize the eighty-six prefects with a request for some national pulse-taking. The director followed through with a circular to the prefects (dated 22 February 1827) which asked each recipient to report forthwith, and once a month thereafter, on the "popular state of mind (*esprit publique*) in his departments: [attitudes] towards the king and his government; how the press (or any other

25. Villèle diary, 5, 9, 10, 11, 14, 15, 16, and 17 April 1827; quotation from *ibid.*, 17 April 1827.

26. *Ibid.*, 25 Jan. 1827; 2, 14, 15, and 20 Feb. 1827.

moving force, which [the prefect] should identify) would have contributed to the above; to what causes did the prefect attribute changes in the different classes of society? the magistracy? the army? commerce? industry? etc., etc. [sic]." It told him to classify his report confidential and send it in under seal.[27]

In other words, at the moment when the government and its adherents in the legislature were putting forth their best efforts to enact a measure to reduce the powers of the press for evil, the very evils they feared were seemingly present and growing.[28]

Looking back on the legislative history of the law of "justice and love" and that of the *proposition La Boëssière,* one perceives much that bore upon the future of the Villèle government and its end in the election of November 1827. There was, for example, the perhaps unexpected weight of opposition in the deputies. When the "justice and love" measure came to a vote, 63 of the 430 members were absent; of the 367 who voted 233 supported the bill, 134 opposed it. In the matter of the *proposition La Boëssière* the count was even more serious: the absentees numbered 122, up by 59; the supporters 164, down by 69; and those opposed 144, up by 10. In his long dealing with the lower house this was Villèle's worst showing. Where had his majority gone? If these measures had been before the deputies two years back, neither one would have stirred more than twoscore into determined opposition. What must have happened was that a "monstrous alliance" of the left and the extreme right, always at its firmest in matters affecting the press, had begun to attract supporters from the stronghold of the pro-Villèle right center. Was this the beginning of a larger and more ominous defection? Could it be possible that the presently constituted chamber of deputies would cease its support of right-wing governments?

What subsequently happened to the press bill in the peers was perhaps even worse than anticipated. It expired in the first skirmish in committee. This action doubly underscored the need for an infu-

27. AN F/7 6778 Doubs, 22 Feb. 1827. Copies of outgoing messages are something of a rarity.

28. With the death of the press bill there was no falling off in these causes for worry or in the government's attribution of blame to the press. There were demonstrations in Paris in front of the ministries of finance and justice, parades of students, noise and disorder, brought to an end only by the deployment of armed force (Villèle diary, 18 and 19 April). A week later the king dissolved the national guard of Paris in reprisal for the overt disrespect which some of its members showed for his ministers—notably his prime minister. This act in turn led to reverberations throughout the realm.

sion of new peers, men who would be more respectful of the legislative requirements of the king and the president of his council of ministers.

Lastly, the actions of the two chambers echoed the disapproval of a large segment of the nation. The press and its freedom were among the ideas most firmly planted by the Revolution; freedom of the press was among the most cherished of the fundamental liberties.[29] Those who would qualify it – particularly in the manner threatened by the law of "justice and love" – did so at their peril, for they not only ran counter to an ideological principle, but, in pragmatic terms, threatened the very livelihoods of publishers, editors, writers, and the practitioners of the printing craft itself. Whatever objection these could raise to the threat, they did repeatedly and with vigor and eloquence. As a result, few moves on the part of the government had received a noisier clamor of adverse publicity or reached a wider audience.

But what of the bill to reform the jury? Of what relevance is it to the substance of this chapter and this book? It is relevant because within the pool of mature and responsible male citizens which the law found suitable for jury duty a sizable proportion was made up of the men who had met the qualifications for the franchise and had become duly inscribed as members of the national electorate. A bill devoted to the jury unavoidably called attention to the electoral lists, and the mention of these lists in turn called attention to the need for altering the procedure of preparing them. This is just what happened, and the bill which began its life on 29 December 1826 as the government's bill to reform the jury ended with the king's signature on 2 May 1827 as something which might better have been known as the opposition's law on elections.[30] The relevance of this law to the decision to hold the election in the autumn of 1827 and the outcome of that election itself is, as the next chapter will show, very considerable.

29. See, for example, the leader in the *Constitutionnel* of 18 April 1827, which begins "Triomphe, . . . la loi . . . est retirée." It goes on: "The committee of the peers . . . has repulsed what was to destroy the first constitutional liberty of France. . . ."

30. *Moniteur* (5 May 1827, p. 717) gives the full text of the law showing that the king had in fact signed it. In the most grotesque typographical error of the decade, the signing king is Louis!—now dead two and a half years. A very red-faced *Moniteur* explained a bit later saying that the type-setters' custom of using what we would call slugs—as opposed to single letters from the font—was the way it came about. This particular slug had long outlived a normal life-expectancy hiding in the Charles box.

But a word about the jury and why it needed reforming.

The jury had come to French jurisprudence in the constitution of 1791 and in its operative legislation, the law of 16 September 1791. In the succeeding seventeen years it passed through many changes. It was jelled by Napoleon in his *Code d'instruction criminel* of 17 November 1808.[31] Whatever changes the succeeding decade and a half wrought in the society which the jury was to serve, the statutory definition of that body stayed still. Long before the autumn of 1826, the jury's need of an overhaul had been the subject of press comment and motions in the chamber of deputies. The old provisions were scarred by an anachronism, but more importantly the jury as an institution of justice was vulnerable to charges of the gravest sort: a susceptibility to being rigged.

Used only in criminal cases in the assize courts, any given jury consisted of twelve men who could find pro or con in something less than unanimity – between 1808 and 1831 by simple majority only. The twelve who sat on a case had been chosen by lot by the president of the court from a panel of thirty-six names which he had hand-picked from a larger panel of sixty names filed with him by the prefect. The prefect in his turn had himself hand-picked the list of sixty from the far larger pool of men eligible for jury duty. This pool was composed of male citizens thirty and older and drawn from eight categories, the most important of which was the first, the one consisting only of members of the electoral colleges.[32] The other seven included successful and usually well-paid men of the civil administration, business, and the liberal professions.

The often-reiterated complaint against the jury was not necessarily directed to the kind of man eligible to serve, but principally to the way in which juries were picked and above all to the timing of the selection process. As already noted both prefect and president of the court made their first selections of jurors (sixty by the prefect, of whom thirty-six were taken by the president) with their eyes open. Furthermore the selecting process did not begin until the date

31. For a quick historical sketch of the institution see Adrien Carpentier and G. F. DuSaint, *Repertoire générale alphabétique du droit français* (37 vols., Paris, 1886–1906), XXV, 600 ff. Firman Didot (Paris) published a text in 1824 which shows no changes. The section of the *Code* devoted to the jury is chapter V of title II, §§ 381–406 (pp. 79 ff.) in this edition. The Bibliothèque Nationale shows no edition closer to 1827.

32. A member of an electoral college in 1808 was one thing, a member in 1827 quite different. See Peter Campbell, *French Electoral Systems and Elections since 1789,* 2nd ed. (Hamden, Conn.: Archon, [1965]), pp. 55–56 and 57–60.

and docket of the assize court had been set. Thus it could be said, and often was, that prefect and president could tailor the matrix of juror material not only to fit the case which a given twelve jurors would hear, but perhaps as well to fit the sort of outcome that one or another (or both) of these individuals deemed appropriate. The seriousness of this sort of complaint took added weight from the fact that the ultimate choice by lot came too late in the procedure to be meaningful, and from the fact that both prosecution and defense were limited to only eight jury challenges.

In presenting the new bill to the peers, the government spokesman, Peyronnet, acknowledged the shortcomings of the reigning statute and went on to lay out the government's proposal for reform of the jury. Most of what he advanced need not concern us, for it has to do with the jury pure and simple. Two points concern us vitally; the first was the government's motion to alter the eight categories of men in the basic pool of potential jurors by throwing out all but the first. In the government's view jurors should be chosen exclusively from among the electors (the men thirty and older, with French citizenship and an established political domicile, who paid at least three hundred francs in direct taxes – the so-called electoral *cens*). The second involved the government's motion regarding the timing of the annual construction of the electoral lists or jury lists, however one wished to conceive them. To be sure there was in this latter area much to be tidied up, and government draftsmen had made the try.[33]

These were, of course, the motions which caught the eye of a number of the peers who had been told off as committeemen to study the government's bill and report it out to the full chamber. Study it they did and drastically amend it; their *rapporteur,* the comte Siméon, presented the detail of their findings about three weeks later.[34] It was the first overt move in the bill's passage through both chambers – a journey which was to transmute it from something which the government desired to something that the government wanted not at all.[35]

33. *Moniteur* (31 Dec. 1826, pp. 1751–1753) carries the introductory remarks of Peyronnet and the full text of the government's bill.

34. See text, and n.43, below.

35. There are a few cryptic entries in the Villèle diary which indicate his displeasure. That of 29 Jan. speaks of amendments which amount to the "loss" of the bill; that of 30 Jan. notes the rejection of a bad amendment put forward by Decazes; that of the next

Why had the government framed and introduced the bill in the first place? Why at this moment? A number of hypotheses come to mind.

The first is that the government took action for exactly the reasons given by Peyronnet, namely that existing law was seriously deficient and ought to be changed. Granting the weight that should be accorded this straightaway explanation, there are two counts against it. One is that, although the jury had needed reforming for many years, the Villèle government had done nothing about it – perhaps because Villèle, Corbière, and Peyronnet were not the kind of political leaders to bleed over complaints against the old code. The second is, why had the government reduced the code's fairly wide spectrum of men eligible for jury service to the narrow one consisting only of voters? This particular decision, whose defense seems to me the weakest part of Peyronnet's presentation, does run counter to generally accepted notions that a jury's impartiality should in part derive from the multiplicity of backgrounds of its members. It does, in fact, strongly suggest some ulterior motive.

A second hypothesis, based in a convoluted diabolism, totters a bit of its own weight. This was a proposition, put forward rather typically by the *Constitutionnel* and late in the game, which ran like this: jury duty is onerous to all that are called; it is economically a more difficult burden for the man of small means than for the rich; the man of small means will therefore evade jury duty with all his might; he would probably forego the right to vote if this would spare him service with the jury. Now it is from among these *petits propriétaires* that pro-government candidates find their greatest opposition at election times, hence it would be to the advantage of the government to give them an incentive to disenfranchise themselves. Prefects would simply forget to put them on the electoral lists, thus relieving them of their vote and the possibility of jury service. They in their turn would cheerfully refrain from actions aiming at reinstatement.[36] On the face of things all this sounds farfetched yet not wholly without merit. For if the government desired to purge both jury rolls and the electorate of petits propriétaires and, be it

day reports the adoption of "numerous amendments to the law regarding the jury which are ruining it"; and that of 3 Feb. reiterates the sentiment about the bill being spoiled by amendments.

36. *Constitutionnel,* 14 May 1827, p. 2.

said, also of the middling businessmen, this move might have helped. It seems dubious, however, that the government would have summoned the majesty of the national law-making process for such a devious end.

A third hypothesis – and this from the realm of practical politics – would explain the introduction of a bill to reform the jury as a sugarcoating to the bill which would assault the press. The government had a clear idea of the outcry that the latter would occasion; could it perhaps be damped down a bit by showing some humane concern in the area of criminal justice? Of course, things so obviously did not work out this way that it seems unlikely that even the most wishful officers of the government could have estimated the contrary.

A fourth hypothesis would connect the bill on the jury to some embryonic draft of the bill on the press. This is an attractive hypothesis for a number of reasons, but one which defies positive confirmation. This line of reasoning envisions Villèle, Corbière, Peyronnet, and others ever searching for a way of handling the periodic press without submitting its delinquencies to the lenient, even suspect, magistracy of the cour royale of Paris, or without reverting to the use of censorship and its attendant clamors of outrage. There was a possible middle position which would involve putting a range of press offenses back into the criminal courts and, as was done briefly in 1819, subject to trial in which the jury played a role. If something could be done to purge from the pool of men eligible for jury duty those who would normally be most sympathetic with the opposition newspaper press – the professional men (the scholars, doctors, lawyers, *notaires,* etc.), the businessmen, and certain of the small propriétaires perhaps – then juries, now in the new law to be chosen blindly and impartially, would still be composed of the sort of men likely to convict the errant press. Granted that this does seem to stretch credulity, one does wonder why, if not for this or some kindred reason, the government's bill on the jury excluded for the first time in decades the professionals and businessmen from jury duty.

The *Courrier français* was prompt to fancy a connection between the two bills, asserting that "the claimed reform of the jury amounted merely to new chains upon the press." Its demonstration of the charge does not spell things out as far as I have, but comes close.

"The bill against the press," it continues, "deals with crimes and misdemeanors, often imaginary, and levies against [the press] penalties out of all proportion in their severity. . . . [The] bill on the jury has as its aim the assurance that these penalties will be rigorously applied." It went on to make much of those whom the bill had excluded from jury duty as if a part of that assurance.[37]

There are some other pieces of evidence to show that while the government authorities were mulling over remedies for the press, the matter of finding a solution in the courts (though not necessarily linked to the jury in so many words) played a part in their thinking, their talking, and their writing of memoranda.

Duvergier de Hauranne, who was an active political participant in these days, wrote some years after the event: "Not only had the press bill been debated at length in the council of ministers, but [it] had been the subject of many private discussions. From each of these moments of testing it lost one or another of its more significant articles. Thus at one stage there had been the matter of authorizing the government to choose before which of the *cours royales* it would bring charges against such and such a writer. [But] this was dropped."[38]

Adolphe Thiers, who had not yet entered his long and fruitful political career but had already begun making his way in the circle of left-leaning newsmen of the capital, was acting inter alia as Paris correspondent for the foremost newspaper of Württemberg, *Die Augsburger Allegemeine Zeitung*. In his dispatch of 29 November 1826 to the editor, the baron Cotta, he reported a slightly different version of Duvergier de Hauranne's story and a bit more.[39] His information was to the effect that the government had decided not to use the weapon of censorship at all. By calculating the cash bond which the press had to deposit as an earnest of good behavior not in money but in terms of a newspaper's physical property, seizure

37. *Courrier français,* 1 Jan. 1827, pp. 2-3. The *Constitutionnel* of the same date (p. 3) links the two bills, though its indictment is less specific than that of the *Courrier français.*

38. Prosper Léon Duvergier de Hauranne, *Histoire du gouvernement parlementaire en France* (10 vols., Paris, 1857-1871), IX, 114-115. (Hereafter cited as Duvergier de Hauranne, *Gouvernement parlementaire.*) No source for this is revealed. However, because I have found things in Duvergier de Hauranne that I have found in Villèle's diary and not in the contemporary press, my respect for him as a historian has risen. With regard to the passage above I believe it came to him as worthy gossip from someone who had been close to the government.

39. Marquant, *Thiers et Cotta,* #75, pp. 372-375.

of which would ostensibly mean the loss of a building, printing presses, etc., the government intended to bridle the press by means of a powerful economic sanction. Going on to a new subject, Thiers wrote that, among other things,

> the most deplorable decision is this: In today's legislation [whereas] the *cour royale* of Paris alone has the power to prosecute a political article [in the press]; in the future all the courts of France can [so prosecute]. Since there is a mistrust of the *cour royale* of Paris, newspapers may now be judged before a 'safe' court (*dont on sera sûr*) in the provinces, and in such fashion the suppression of a newspaper will become the easiest thing in the world.

These two bits do suggest that in thrashing around for a solution to the problem of the press, the government had given serious thought to continuing to use the courts, but in a manner which would lessen the chances of what it considered demoralizing acquittals.

A third piece of evidence, the undated memorandum cited earlier in this chapter, suggests that the courts came into the debate in still another way.[40] The writer of the memo was on the pro-censorship side of the argument, but wise about the importance of a free press and cautious about the application of the censorship. After a score of longhand pages devoted to a philosophical consideration of the issues he advances a plan, and even a draft bill, which would have put the censorship under specially appointed panels of magistrates from the cours royales and other courts. They were to be appointed by the king, would be relieved of their normal judicial functions, would work eight to ten hours per day without vacation for a full year, and for their effort receive double compensation. Their task would be to pass immediately upon copy destined for the next day's paper. Editors who published without their sanction were eligible for progressively severe penalties presumably imposed by the panel, now acting more like judges than censors.

Could it be that, in these discussions of various possible uses of the courts and the magistrates, there had also come up the use of the jury? Could it be that the proponent of the jury idea had drafted up some legislation which would accomplish a twin result? It could be known as a law to *reform* the jury by eliminating the obnoxious phases of present law and, at the same time, be the means of assuring a pool of potential jurymen whose members would have little love

40. See above, text and n.6 of this chapter.

for those "implacable enemies of altar and throne," the composers of "insolent diatribes," and prophets of that dreaded "political protestantism."[41] Yes it could be possible; it must however, remain an interesting but unproven hypothesis.[42]

A last word about this scheme. Before it was jettisoned as a companion piece to a press law, so much thought and drafting had gone into its jury aspects that these may now have appeared as worth saving in their own right. In this case the government might have gone forward with the jury bill for one or all three of the first three reasons I have advanced, not perceiving the dangers inherent in some of the new text. These dangers lurked in the paragraph which reduced the former eight categories of men eligible for jury duty to the single category of elector.

It is almost certain that this very paragraph is what first caught the eyes of those peers chosen to study the bill in committee. When, three weeks later, their spokesman, the comte Siméon, reported the results of the committee's deliberation to the full chamber, it was apparent that the committee had spent as much attention upon the vexed question of electoral list-making as upon those other parts of the bill which dealt exclusively with the institution of the jury.[43] Significant as are these latter, I will skip them to focus upon my immediate concern, namely, how established legislation affecting the national electorate came to be altered in important respects. The greatest share of the responsibility is owing to the peers, some is however owing to the government – perhaps by inadvertence – and the rest to the chamber of deputies which chose to follow the lead of the upper house though given an option not to.[44]

41. These expressions are from the memorandum just cited.

42. Somewhere there is a Villèle diary for 1826 which may contain bits of information to help confirm or destroy this hypothesis. For years it reposed among the Villèle papers, but is no longer there.

43. *Moniteur,* 24 Jan. 1827, pp. 97–99. See also *ibid.,* 25 Jan. 1827, p. 103–a presentation in parallel columns, showing the original bill and the committee's amendments.

44. The government, mightily displeased with what the peers had done to its bill, attempted to get matters back on the track by a strange and rarely used device. It gave the chamber of deputies a chance to undo at a stroke all that the peers had accomplished by bringing to the deputies not merely the peers' amended text, but the original government bill as well. Peyronnet, again the government spokesman, invited the lower house to choose which of the two texts it would deliberate upon. Quite a debate followed in which ultras of the counter-opposition joined with the leftward ranks. When the matter came to a vote the deputies opted to accept the text from the peers. See the *Moniteur,* 15 Feb. 1827, p. 214.

At issue are three areas of the law: procedures for the preparation and posting of the electoral jury lists; procedures for the amendment of the first and later-published lists; and matters respecting the right of a man once inscribed on the list to stay on it without the trouble of annual reinscriptions.

It was article 2 of the government's bill which touched off the debate on the preparation and posting of the electoral lists. It is important to bear in mind, however, that the government was considering the list not necessarily for electoral, but for jury purposes only, and what it was urging was a measure to meet the classical complaint about jury selection. To this end the article proclaimed that, in conformity with prior law, the prefects of each department would prepare (*arrêter*) the list of men who met the conditions for the franchise. This would be done by 1 September at the latest. At some time, *not stipulated,* this list was to be posted in the *chef lieu* of each canton. The absence of a date for the posting of a jury list was, in this frame of reference, not a very serious matter, for no one was really keen to find out about his eligibility for that onerous service. On the other hand the omission of a posting date for this list, considered as an electoral list, was a very different thing. Whatever in the past had been done about jury lists, electoral lists had been handled in a manner to evoke loud criticism from the opposition.

Habitually when the crown announced, via royal ordinance, the coming of an election six to eight weeks ahead, the ordinance would provide that the electoral lists be posted only about four weeks in advance of the convocation of the electoral colleges, sometimes less. On top of this, prefects were sometimes dilatory within even this short time-span. Opposition spokesmen were bitter about the prefects' practice of sitting on the lists – guarding them in secrecy – to the last possible moment, for by this means a dishonest ("overzealous" was the word used by the government) prefect could cook up a list marred by omissions and mal-inscriptions, only a small portion of which could be rectified in the short time available.[45]

Incidentally, throughout the procedures in the deputies right and left oppositions made common cause. In referring to this union of forces Casimir Périer pointedly referred to it in the singular, the opposition of "the constitutional royalists" (*ibid.,* 15 Apr. 1827, p. 592). It may be that the use in opposition journalism of the word "constitutionnel" to mean a man of the "correct political attitude" dates from this utterance.

45. See, for example, the *Constitutionnel,* 15 Aug. 1819, pp. 3-4, and 29 Aug. 1819, pp. 3-4.

What was wanted was a regular annual date for the preparation of the electoral lists, a prompt public posting of the lists, and ample time for the disgruntled to seek relief.

Article 2 of the government's bill also opened the way for the peers, and later the deputies, to recast the text to cover these desiderata. By the time the document came to the king for signature, prefects would prepare (*dresser* is the verb this time) their electoral lists not by 1 September, but at least a month earlier, and would post (*afficher*) their first version by 15 August. Furthermore the lists were to be printed and posted not only in the chef lieu of the canton, but in every one of the communes of every department – all forty-odd thousand of them. Additional copies would be on file in the secretariats of the office of every mayor, subprefect, and prefect, and available to all comers.

The government's bill quite clearly regards the prefect's first list as a preliminary effort.[46] By reference to the electoral law of 5 February 1817 (article 5) it anticipated that there would be changes to come, and those within the short time span just noted. Formal application for a change could be made without recourse to the use of official "stamped paper" with its costs, small ones to be sure.

The peers and later the deputies gave a deal of precision to these matters. In their version the first list would be open to amendment

---

The royal ordinance for the 1819 election is dated 18 August; the election began on 11 September. The prefect of the Aisne posted his lists 28 August. According to the *Constitutionnel,* they were "full of inexactitudes" and were not packaged in a coordinated whole for the department.There were four, one for each of the arrondissements. Without literally traveling through the department a voter with taxable property in more than one arrondissement could not know for sure if he were getting the political credit for all of his tax payments.

46. The first two articles of the law under discussion (2 May 1827) distinguish between two "parts" of the jury list. The first "part" would comprise those men who qualified for jury duty because they were electors; the second "part" those who did not qualify as electors, but whose station in the community was such as to warrant their inclusion in the pool of potential jurymen (important civil administrators and successful businessmen and practitioners of the liberal professions). When the law came into effect jury lists were always composed with a "first part" (electors only) and a "second part" (all others–usually about 10% of the total). There is room for confusion in these terms with another aspect of these lists. In my subsequent discussion of the initial drafting and the initial posting of jury lists and of the periodic amendment of these initial lists, when I refer to the "first published lists" I mean those lists (both their "first" and "second" parts) posted on 15 August, the "second published lists" those posted on 25 August, etc. Thus my references to first lists, second lists, etc., should be construed as relating to the time of their publication, not their content, as distinguished from the "first *part*" or "second *part*" of the jury list.

for a clearly stipulated six weeks, that is from 15 August until midnight of 30 September. Men who had a grievance could table it with the prefect who was bound to consider it in the presence of his advisory council,[47] but his decision was not necessarily final. By action of the deputies – perhaps an unnecessary one – article 6 of the 1817 law[48] was brought up and restated here. This held that appeals beyond the prefect which involved civil or political rights would fall under the jurisdiction of the cours royales, those relating to the cens and political domicile under that of the counseil d'état.

Neither the government's bill nor the texts as they emerged from peers and deputies spelled out the periodic revision of the lists between the first posting (15 August) and official closure (midnight 30 September). Just why remains something of a mystery.

There was, however, on the books the royal ordinance of 4 September 1820 which the king had issued to cover the election of that year.[49] In each of the ordinances summoning subsequent elections (one in 1821, two in 1822, and one in 1824) this document of 4 September was cited in the preamble and corpus of the document as one of the governing texts; and in each of these elections the earlier ordinance was observed. It provided that every ten days after the lists were first posted the prefects would do some stock-taking of changes in the prior list and issue what came to be called "tables de rectification." It went on to direct the prefects – again in council – to go through a final review five days before the electoral colleges were scheduled to meet. They would then close the lists. From the opposition's point of view it was an improvement but no cure, for the ability of the administration to jigger the lists was not dramatically lessened.

At a guess, the chambers of 1827 must have anticipated a continuation of the old rules. Nor were they disappointed. Later in the year, as the government girded for list-making, the minister of the interior sent to the prefects a long and detailed circular of instruction which contained among other things an elaboration of the

47. Referred to variously as the *conseil de préfecture, conseil de département,* or *conseil général.* It comprised a group of prominent citizens who had been nominated by the prefect and appointed by the crown. Its members served without salary. Their functions were purely advisory. Final decisions had to be the prefects'.

48. Duvergier, *Lois,* XXI, 87.

49. *Ibid,* XXIII, 81.

message of the 4 September 1820 ordinance.[50] In other words, it may be that all concerned were satisfied with what they considered a final settlement of the issue and something which required no further tinkering.

As to making provision against actions on the part of the prefects and their subordinates which resulted in the unexplained erasure of duly inscribed voters from year to year, the government's bill touched upon the issue not at all. In the opinion of the peers, especially the duc de Decazes, this was a woeful omission.

To get one's self inscribed as a voter required the collection of official documentation which attested to date of birth, place of domicile, and payment of the cens. No matter the amount of effort involved, no one wanted to go through the process more than once. The trouble was that many of the voters had had to go through it a number of times; perhaps for good reason, perhaps not. Would it not be possible to give permanence to the lists?

The committee of the peers confronted the problem and tabled a paragraph to cover it in its amended bill. This caught the eye of the duc de Decazes, himself a former prime minister, who had had the experience of being inexplicably dropped from his electoral list. In addressing himself to a number of points in the committee's report he came down hard on this subject of the permanence of lists.[51] As a result new and stronger language was adopted by the peers and later the deputies. In the final text the new paragraph read, "No one may be erased from the list except by virtue of a decision for cause or by a judgment, against which . . . appeal [procedures] will have a suspensory effect."

This sort of phrasing was not going to satisfy men like Decazes who harbored a deep sense of grievance. On the other hand, if one deferred to common sense, the phrasing could not be cast with much more strength and precision.[52] Everyone must have perceived

50. The most important part of this circular appears in *ibid*, XXVII, 301–302. It bears the date 29 June 1827.

The original is a printed document which runs to more than 20 pp. The copy which I have examined is in AD, Ille-et-Vilaine (3 M 1/3). The bulk of the document left out of Duvergier consists of a series of forms which prefects were told to use in their list-making and list-correcting exercises.

51. See the *Moniteur,* 31 Jan. 1827, pp. 132–133. See also the *Courrier français,* 5 Feb. 1827, pp. 1–2.

52. However a year later under the Martignac ministry there was an attempt to push it further. This resulted in the law of 2 July 1828 (Duvergier, *Lois,* XXVIII, 227–240),

the folly of insisting, "once on the list, always on the list," irrespective of changes in fortune (with their relationship to the cens), not to mention changes of domicile, or that great final change from the living to the departed. But the mere fact that the problem had been aired, discussed, and ruled upon in peers and deputies had its effects, and those in large part in the favor of the man known for his opposition political views. Prefects still had the power to erase names from prior lists, but they would have to be circumspect and their decision was, of course, subject to appeal.

In summary then this law, which began its life as a measure devoted to jury reform, emerged from the legislative process as one which signally amended the matter of electoral list-making. Modest as these amendments were they had three profound effects. The first, in narrow construction, is the obvious one. Henceforth prefects had to make up electoral lists every year at a stipulated time and under conditions which very considerably reduced their ability to wheel freely. No more sitting on lists until so late that little could be done to correct their errors; no more posting of the lists in a single (and for the bulk of the voters) unhandy place or in illegible longhand;[53] no clear conscience for politically motivated or captious erasures from prior lists, certainly a lot less of the sort of erasure suffered by the duc de Decazes.

The second effect is less obvious and more important. The fact that the new legislation had occupied the peers and deputies for four full months, that its passage through the legislature had received a great deal of attention in the opposition press of Paris, that a large number of politically active citizens were aware of its fibres as woven into the positive law – these matters cast the whole realm of electoral politics in a new perspective. There is little that could more have starched up the opposition than telling it that its chances for effective political action had greatly improved,[54] and that those of the prefects to nullify this action had declined.[55] The invigora-

a well-known contribution to electoral legislation. One often forgets that it was the law of 2 May 1827 which first dealt with the problem.

53. It is worth noting that comparatively few official electoral lists prior to those of 1827 have survived in the departmental and national archives. This is almost certainly a function of their having existed probably in unique and often longhand copy. On the other hand a good number of lists printed in 1827, 1828, and 1829 survive.

54. The *Constitutionnel*, 1 Feb. 1827, p. 1, makes this point with eloquence.

55. In actual fact the law of 2 May 1827 did not by any means put an end to prefectoral monkey business, nor for that matter could any law except one that elaborately

tion of the opposition began to show itself soon after the passage of the law;[56] by June opposition leaders were already telling their supporters to ready themselves for the list-making which would take place that very summer and fall.

The last effect is the one that this chapter has been pointing at — the need for the government to do something about the composition of the peers and deputies. Clearly the peers were well out of hand. If their squelching of the government's efforts to bring the press into line was not sufficient demonstration, then that topped by their action on the jury bill was. From the point of view of Villèle and his colleagues, maybe even from that of the king, the main thrust of national policy as they wanted it would be at a standstill until the chamber of peers was considerably augmented and by the right kind of man. Villèle, of course, wished that the bulk of the new peers (perhaps as many as forty or fifty of the larger total) would be chosen from his following in the deputies. The price, he realized, would be appreciable; for not only would he lose valued friends in the lower house, but the empty seats would have to be filled in exactly that many by-elections. Taken in context of how strong the opposition vote had been with respect to the law of "justice and love" and the *proposition La Boëssière* this probably suggested the disadvantage of doing things by halves.

In other words, why not a general election and a wholesale reshuffle of the deputies? Following hard on this thought was one which highlighted the desirability of going for the reshuffle as speedily as feasible. Pro-government politicians were prompt to see that list-making under the provisions of the law of 2 May would result in some painful changes in constituencies heretofore safe for government candidates, that a general election under the new lists could be nothing like the golden year of 1824. Melancholy as were these prospects they may have seemed bright by comparison with what lay ahead. Any politician in full possession of his faculties had to

---

codified electoral procedure and exposed to criminal prosecution those who wilfully violated it. The last elections of the Restoration had their full panoply of sensational electoral irregularities, and so did all the elections of the successor monarchy. In the very last years of Louis Philippe the apostles of electoral reform were still pleading—and in vain—for this kind of remedial legislation.

56. The *Constitutionnel* (14 May 1827, p. 2) emphasized what the law required in the way of printing and posting the lists. Then it moved to the exhortation: "It is essential that you get on the list; by the fact of your inscription you will have the right to vote in your electoral college."

estimate that the effects of the new law would almost certainly grow with the passage of time and that if 1827 was not the ideal year for the government to go to the country it was probably better than the feasible alternative.

2 / The Decision

There was no legal compulsion to hold a general election in the year 1827. The chamber of deputies then sitting had at least one more year of constitutional life; at most, three years, depending upon how one read the law.[1] That a general election was called for the latter part of November 1827 was a free choice. The king, urged by Villèle and most of the council of ministers, made it. As things turned out, the decision brought a round of disasters – an immediate one to Villèle, a delayed one to the reigning monarch and the Bourbon family. Obviously these were not foreseen nor for that matter did anyone anticipate its opposite, another sensational victory at the polls. Though the men who were responsible nurtured the usual array of hopes for the best, probably all of them had doubts and misgivings. Why did they decide as they did and when they did? This chapter tries to give answers.

We are already aware of the need to augment the peers and that, to the extent that new peers were taken from among the deputies, the latter would have to be replaced via by-elections. In the event that Villèle had his way these might number as many as forty or fifty, or perhaps even more. We are also aware of the two oppositions in the deputies and the way they had eroded the ministry's majority from both left and right, and that as early as January Villèle and his king had talked about dissolving the chamber and going

1. The charter had given the deputies a maximum term of five years; it also accorded to the king the right to dissolve at any time of his choice short of five years. On the basis of the charter the chamber's fifth, and final, year would not be over until it had completed its session of 1828.

However the law of 9 June 1824, the so-called "septennalité," lengthened the term of office to seven years. In other words, if this law were construed as applying to the chamber elected in 1824, the latter's term would not run out before the end of the session of 1830. The language of the law (Duvergier, *Lois,* XXIV, 508): "La Chambre actuelle des députés et toutes celles qui la suivront seront renouvelées intégralement. Elles auront une durée de sept années à compter du jour où aura été rendue l'ordonnance de leur première convocation, à moins qu'elles ne soient dissoutes par le Roi," seems unequivocally to apply to the chamber elected in 1824 and still sitting in 1827. There were those who felt it did not. If indeed the matter had had to be adjudicated by the courts, the dissolution of the chamber in November 1827 rendered the question moot.

to the country. Events which followed this conversation must have recalled the subject many times.

There was, for example, the matter of how the law of 2 May 1827 was going to affect the composition of the electorate. All over France politically alert men who were also ideological opponents of the Villèle government knew that that very summer was going to offer them new and perhaps enhanced opportunities to get themselves and like-minded men inscribed on the voting rolls. If perchance their first realizations did not register with the government, their later and well-understood stirrings did. Had the law of 2 May made 1827 an inauspicious year to hold a general election? Of course no one could give a crisp answer, but most objective observers could see at a glance that the influence which the prefects could exercise over the composition of the electoral lists, and hence an election, had been materially reduced.

But if 1827 was going to be a difficult year, what about 1828? Could it be anything but worse? and 1829? and so on? In these circumstances might not one be forced to look upon 1827 as best in a choice of evils? In other words those who saw this far ahead knew that they had a bad problem and that in the near future they were going to have to do something about it.

My guess is that sometime while the peers were rewriting key paragraphs of the government's jury bill, Villèle, and perhaps Corbière, minister of interior, and Peyronnet, minister of justice, began to understand what was happening. They did what they could to stop it in the deputies, but to no avail. By the time the bill passed into law they may even have reached a decision in principle. On 3 and 4 May Villèle saw the king and noted in his diary for those days that there had been discussion "of measures to come" and "of measures to be taken after the closing of the [legislative] session [predictable for about mid-June]." Next day he had Corbière to dinner: "went with him to the bois de Boulogne, conferred with him about the situation and measures [to be taken] in the future" runs the diary entry.[2] Once again in May they had dinner, this time at Corbière's house, and once again Villèle talked "with him about things to be done before the [opening of] the next session of the legislature"[3]

2. The evening meal seems to have come in what we would call the late afternoon, maybe as early as 5 or 6 o'clock. Villèle diary, 5 May 1827.

3. *Ibid.,* 22 May 1827.

(normally the "next session" of the legislature would begin in, say, December of 1827 or the first months of 1828). A week later he noted that the king was very hesitant about things to be done in the area of domestic affairs.[4]

The decision which I think Villèle and his colleagues reached was to temporize. They seem to have decided neither definitely not to go for an election nor to call one. Rather what seems to have been in their minds was a plan to get all in readiness for an election and reserve final judgment until they could see how things went during the six summer weeks when the electoral lists would be refashioned. By early October the prefects would have gained some clear insights into how pro-government candidates would fare in their departments; on the basis of their estimates the final decision could then be taken. The important thing to note is that the government, at a minimum, did decide to do all in its power to see that these estimates would be justifiably optimistic. It would use its time to its best political advantage.

It seems almost certain that the king was fully apprised of this gambit, for Villèle was not the man to play games behind his sovereign's back. Not only would his deep-rooted loyalty have forbidden it, but his sense for the practical made it out of the question. After all it was the king's prerogative, not that of the prime minister, to call an election, and Villèle knew well that the king would sign no ordinance on his minister's simple say-so. He would insist that not only the council of ministers be heavily in favor but, more important, the dauphin, the dauphine, and a lot of high-born members of the court too. In these terms it was imperative that the king be brought into ministerial thinking as soon as it had advanced to an appropriate state of maturity. I feel certain that he was.[5]

As things turned out, Villèle and his colleagues began to get some

4. *Ibid.,* 28 May, 1827. This cryptic remark of course need not refer to the matter of dissolution, though the king was seised of the problem.

5. In a first draft of this chapter, my reasoning pretty well left out the king. I had fancied that the decision was largely that of Villèle and Corbière. A reading of the Villèle diary has definitely changed my mind. This document shows Villèle in almost daily contact with the king about the full range of important matters of state and the king himself taking them under advisement and discussing them with his son, his daughter-in-law, and others, like Polignac, who had access to the presence. There can be no doubt of Villèle's power to influence the king and no doubt that it was just this kind of power. It had to be exercised with delicacy and in constant awareness that the king was the man in charge.

premonitions as to how their electoral chances were shaping up long before the prefects had completed work on the new electoral lists. Early on there was some disquieting news from the old electorate or, better, a sample of it. Death, which had dealt lightly with the sitting chamber of deputies (it had taken only six members in the years 1824, 1825, and 1826), rapidly claimed seven in as many months: one towards the end of 1826 and six more in the first half of 1827.[6] Four of the seven had sat to the right of center and supported the Villèle government,[7] the other three were among its opponents.[8]

To fill the vacancies the king convoked the appropriate electoral colleges, and the first six of the by-elections took place between 5 March and 21 June of 1827. Five of them went to enemies of the government; all five men were of national prominence. Laisné de Villevêque (Orléans) had served seven years in the deputies (1817-1824) and on the left center and lost to a government candidate in the 1824 election. Jacques Laffitte (Bayonne) was already a rich and famous banker whose anti-Villèle political views were well known. Louis Bignon (Rouen) had served in the deputies (1817-1822) where he had made quite a mark as leader of the movement to press the withdrawal of foreign occupying forces. He was known as a constitutional leftist. André Dupin (Mamers) – always called "Dupin aîné," to distinguish him from his brother Charles, his junior by a single year – was a young lawyer, famous for his defense of Marshal Ney and other Napoleonic generals and later as successful advocate for Parisian newspapers which had tangled with the press laws. It went without saying that no friend of the opposition press could be a friend of Villèle.

The last of the five was none other than Lafayette (Meaux), the marquis himself, who had been intimately associated with dangerous manoeuvres and plots against the crown in the early 1820's and who was the standout among figures of the radical left. Villèle's diary

6. One of these died on 4 Dec. 1826. The by-election to replace him came after the New Year.

7. These were: Crignon d'Ouzouer of the electoral arrondissement of Orléans (Loiret), d. 4 Dec. 1826; Lizot of Bernay (Eure), d. winter 1827; Regnoust Duchesnay of Mamers (Sarthe), d. 29 Mar. 1827; and Descordes of Angoulême (Charente), d. spring 1827.

8. These were: Basterreche of the electoral arrondissement of Bayonne (Basses-Pyrénées), d. 5 Jan. 1827; Stanislas de Girardin of Rouen (Seine-Inférieure), d. 27 Feb. 1827; and Pinteville de Cernon of Meaux (Seine-et-Marne), d. 2 April 1827.

notes the election, a distinction he accorded but one other of the series.[9]

The only election in which the government scored was that in the heretofore relatively safe electoral district of Bernay (Eure). Even there Bignon, running a month before his win at Rouen, came within a few votes of beating the Villèlist candidate.[10]

The loss of two or three of these by-elections would have meant little in itself; the loss of five and a close squeak in the sixth could not but have focused thought on the mood of the electorate and its probable attitude in days to come. Could it not be that the simple passage of time was partly responsible for the change that seemed to have developed since the election of 1824? Could it not be that the gradual decline in numbers of voters who were twenty years or older in 1789 and the increase in voters who were younger in that year had something to do with the matter?

Charles Dupin, André's younger brother and a man of many scholarly interests, said, yes. In a remarkable study devoted in the main to the economic life in the departments of the northerly half of France, the author moved from a concern with capital goods, productive resources, to labor, and then to people – that is, exclusively French people – in general.[11] It was in his long introduction that he presented his thoughts upon the aging of a segment of the French nation and its social and political effects. He took the year 1789 as a watershed and had a look at the men who were then twenty or older. He looked again at this group in 1827 (thirty-eight years later) and, surely not to anyone's surprise, saw that their ranks were depleted. The element of surprise came when Dupin turned his attention specifically to the electorate and gave his demographic findings a political twist.

Assuming that the Restoration electorate numbered 100,000, he estimated its composition in 1823 to have been 53,300 of the "older" men (those of twenty or more years in 1789) and 46,700 of the "younger"; its composition in 1824 as about 50,000 of each; and in 1827 some 40,000 "old" as against 60,000 "young." The falling-off of the "old" progressed more rapidly with the ensuing

9. Villèle diary, 23 June 1827.

10. He got 155 of 335 votes cast (*Constitutionnel*, 4 Apr. 1827, p. 2).

11. Charles Dupin, *Forces productives et commerciales de la France* (2 vols., Paris, 1827). (Hereafter cited as Dupin, *Forces productives.*) In the introduction the author tells how he began the book in September 1826 and finished it in July 1827.

years. He went on to make the unproven, but nevertheless unsettling, assertion that the class of his "young" was more amenable to the ideological bequests of the Revolution and Napoleon than the "old" and was finding its political niche among those in opposition to the established order. To people who were impressed by his figures and his reasoning – and there was much to recommend both – this merely meant that the conservative, not to say the reactionary, elements of the nation were passing on and that the sort of thing that the Villèle government stood for was doomed – and in pretty short order.[12] Dupin was careful not to use names, but his general meaning was clear as clear.

If these findings had had to await the publication of that book,[13] they probably would have had less effect upon the thinking of the government than they actually did. But Dupin had composed his principal findings about the electorate and youth's wave of the future earlier in the year and made them available in a separate brochure. This of course came to the attention of the young editors of the *Globe,* that sheet put out by and for intellectuals, whose columns rarely touched upon political issues. Left-leaning in their muted political sympathies, they found the Dupin brochure well suited to their purposes. By giving prominence to a review of this non-political dissertation they could, without risk of direct involvement, strike a blow for their own political proclivities. Accordingly they devoted almost their whole edition of 3 May 1827 to the publication, reproducing its tabular findings and much of its explanatory text. Two key sentences ran: The lesson to be drawn from the figures is that "today [1827] the effective existence of geographic power, of domestic national power, and of electoral power is lost for the old generation. Since 1825 the majority has gradually passed to the side of the new. . . . This is the generation whose eyes are fixed on the material advantages of a livelihood in commerce."

Of course one cannot say what effect the results of the spring by-elections and the publication of the Dupin pamphlet had upon the thinking of Villèle and his close associates. One can say, however, that if they considered these matters at all – and there is some

12. *Ibid.,* I, xxvii–xxviii.

13. This probably took place in early August. The *Globe* of 11 Aug. 1827 noted its availability.

evidence that they did[14] – their fears that time was running against them must have been reenforced. Even so, the final decision did not have to be made at once; they could keep their options open and await the prefects' views as to how that summer's list-making would affect the electorate.

The very fact, however, that a general election was being contemplated as a possible course of action was something to be confined to the smallest feasible group of insiders. Graveyard secrecy had to be one of the essences of the grand political strategy. The chancellor, Pasquier, has told of the great secrecy which attended meetings of the council of ministers where the matter was presumably discussed and gratuitously remarks that subordinate officials talked outside and loosely.[15] Doubtful it is that they were the principal culprits, for there were already many officials who had to be on the inside – some of them were charged with important operational tasks to assure the success of the decision, should it be in favor of an election that year. The optimistic hope of holding things close was just ludicrous.

What happened to this secret is what has happened to many another; it leaked, and leaked so widely that it eventually broke through into parliamentary debate and was printed in the *Moniteur*. On 1 June 1827, the last active day of the session for the chamber of deputies,[16] the vicomte de Lézardière, an opponent of Villèle from the right, warned of rumors to the effect that the ministry contemplated creating enough new peers to alter the political complexion of the upper house. He continued that it was also being said that the bulk of the new creations would be from among the ministry's adherents in the chamber of deputies, and that this body in turn would be dissolved. He did not mention a new election, though this was implicit. His remarks drew a defensive comment from a Villèle supporter, which in turn moved Hyde de Neuville, one of

14. In the Villèle diary (21 July 1827) there is a note which indicates that Dupin was not unknown in high circles of the government. It runs: "Eu conseil à St. Cloud. M. le dauphin m'a demandé l'agrément de donner copie de ma lettre sur son ouvrage à M. Dupin."

15. Duc d'Audiffret-Pasquier, ed., *Mémoires du Chancellier Pasquier*, 2nd ed. (6 vols., Paris, 1893–1895), VI, 94.

16. The lower chamber completed its business on this day. It did not meet again, although formally still in session until the peers wound up their business three weeks later. Then both houses were adjourned.

the chamber's famous men and a member of the right-wing opposition, to speak to Lézardière's point and give it added emphasis.[17] The little contretemps served to publicize the rumors.

A few weeks later the baron d'Haussez, the prefect of the Gironde and deputy from the neighboring department of the Landes, wrote Villèle: "The rumor spreads of an imminent dissolution of the chamber and receives a sort of confirmation in certain official journals. I do not seek to penetrate secrets of the government, but I feel it is my duty to inform you of the situation in my department [Gironde]." He goes on to say that if an election should soon take place a maximum of four (possibly as few as two) pro-government deputies (out of eight) would win. In short, to hold an election would be an error for, he urged, what is now above all needed is a period of calm to let things cool off. He ends with the assurance of his loyalty, but begs that he be given ample time for preparation if the king should decide to go for an election in the near term.[18]

In short, by June's end, and still months before the final official decision to have the election, a large number of people thought the matter an all-but-foregone conclusion. Irrespective of reliability of the source and without regard to the inconsistency between story and story, the political leaders of the opposition could afford to do no other than to give heed to the general drift of the rumors. The alert ones realized the possibility that no election would be called; they also realized that if one were, the matter would be kept secret to the last possible moment. Hence for them there was really only a single logical course of action: get ready for the worst case; do those things which should be done if a general election were a dead certainty.

The government, holding its options open, had plenty to do to forward its own strategy. One thing it might have done even if it had not contemplated the possibility of an election was to impose the censorship on the periodical press. As has been noted there was a law on the books which authorized the king to impose censorship during the adjournment of the legislature by the mere issuance of a royal ordinance.[19] Whether or not to invoke this power, and at

17. *Moniteur,* 2 June 1827, p. 902.

18. Personal letter, Haussez to Villèle, 28 June 1827, in the Villèle papers.

19. Article 4, law of 17 March 1822 (Duvergier, *Lois,* XXIII, 479–480).

this time, was an agonizing decision for Charles;[20] almost certainly with Villèle and Corbière in favor of the move he finally signed the ordinance on 24 June. It goes without saying that to the men on the government side of things there were always plenty of reasons to stop the press's dangerous clamor. The matter of a possible election was a new and special one. Well they knew of the immense power that the *Constitutionnel* alone had exercised in earlier elections, how it had told its left-leaning readers what had to be done, who was doing it, and how they were going about it. Well too they knew of its successes.[21] This year they realized that the *Constitutionnel* would be joined by the *Courrier français* and the *Journal des Débats* in behalf of left-center and leftist electoral activities and by the *Quotidienne* in behalf of those of the counter-opposition over on the distant right. To still these voices for the next few months would be highly desirable.

What the king ultimately signed was the principal ordinance which clamped on the muzzle, and three supporting ones: The first of these latter established the bureau of censorship for Paris and named its director and secretary, cited the prior press legislation (the laws of 31 March 1820 and 26 July 1821) which was to be considered in force, instructed the eighty-six prefects to make what provisions were necessary to censor the periodical press of their respective departments, and established a top-level council of surveillance in Paris empowered to recommend to the minister of justice the suspension or actual suppression of an offending journal. The limits of censorable substance were defined by reference. In bald terms the ordinance obliged publishers to submit copy prior to publication to their local board of censors and to observe the latter's injunctions not to print on peril of jail, fine, or even going out of business. Considered censorable were the wide range of matters stipulated in the earlier press legislation; the power of interpretation was vested in the first instance, of course, in the censors them-

20. The Villèle diary entries for 1, 3, 8, 12, 16, 21, and 22 June 1827, show the king originally opposed to the idea of the censorship, then "tormented" about it, and gradually coming around to it in spite of the opposition of the dauphin and Chabrol de Crouzol, minister of the navy. The diary is mute as to the rationale for the censorship and what convinced the king.

21. See chapter 4, below, for the role of the opposition press, especially the *Constitutionnel,* in these early elections.

selves.[22] The next two ordinances gave the names and titles of the full membership of the council of surveillance and board of censors for Paris.[23]

Just how the board of censors sitting in Paris worked to further the electoral strategy of the government comes through in a revealing document now in the Archives Nationales.[24] It is undated as to year, but its addressees, its dating by month and day, its signers, and above all its content identify it beyond all shadow of doubt as a report of Paris's working censors during a summer week of 1827. Their attitude toward articles relating to matters electoral comes through clearly in this single week's work. On 23 July they suppressed an article submitted by the *Constitutionnel* which in their view asserted the government's intention to dissolve the chamber and go to the country. They suppressed another which told how the authorities had refused to give a would-be voter a receipt testifying to his having filed with them the assortment of documents necessary to achieve his inscription on the electoral list. In the entry for 25 July they note that they had permitted the press to advertise the publication of Victor Guichard – an instruction to jurors and voters – but not to allow reprinting of certain passages "injurious to the administration."

In rough parallel, on 27 July they reported that the *Constitutionnel* had presented an article containing information of use to jurors and electors. With a bit of self-conscious deference to their masters, and perhaps with an eye to some historian of the future, they go on to say that while applauding the press in its efforts to enlighten people about the exercise of political rights (i.e., how to get inscribed) they felt obliged, for example, to suppress text which misled public

22. Duvergier, *Lois*, XXVII, 290; for the earlier laws, see *ibid.*, XXII, 409–410, and XXIII, 293.

23. *Ibid.*, XXVII, 290–291. Bonald was the chairman of the council. Among the other eight members were the deputies Frénilly, Ollivier, and Maquillé who had been prominent on the government's side on the great debate over the press law. All three received peerages in November 1827.

24. AN F/7 6772 Seine. The document's outside page bears the heading "Rapport/ sur les operations du bureau/de censure de Paris (5e semaine)." It is addressed to "Messieurs les membres de la Commission de surveillance" and signed by the members of the bureau of censorship for Paris: Lourdoueix, the director; Deliège, the secretary; Levacher-Duplessis, Lévêque, Sillans, Berchoux, and Pain, members. The "5th week" of censorship is the week 22–29 July, confirmed by the dating of entries within the document.

Mrs. Collins (*Government and the Newspaper Press*, p. 52, n. 1) reports the existence of similar documents in AN BB/30 268–269.

opinion and presented the administration as ceaselessly scheming to deny the franchise to a whole class.

In the light of what the censors are known to have excluded from the press as from the evidence above, and what one senses to have been suppressed, as one looks in vain for coverage of opposition electoral activity, one must conclude that the imposition of the censorship in the first place, and what the censors kept out of print in the second, were dictated in some important way by the unannounced political strategy of the Villèle government. Nothing else will explain why, from the end of June until the beginning of November, the Paris press of both oppositions and the departmental press — what I have seen of it — contain virtually no news of partisan politics. Nothing else will explain the absence of all reference to the existence of two opposition electoral groups — the Société, Aide-toi, le ciel t'aidera and Chateaubriand's equally effective and half-misnamed Société des amis de la liberté de la presse — all reference to their founding fathers, their organization in Paris and in the departments, their methods and, above all, their goals. How else explain the wholly neutral tone of the advice to would-be electors that was printed?[25] The sort of article at issue here appeared with regularity, wholly bereft of partisan pleadings; they read as if the *Constitutionnel* or the *Courrier français,* for example, were equally keen to advise and incite to action potential voters of every political stripe!

In such fashion were the oppositions denied the single handiest and most useful medium to work for the inscription of the opposition voter and to publicize the names of possible candidates of their choice.[26] And in such fashion the government took a first step to impede the sort of political climate within the electorate which, should it develop, would qualify the government's freedom of choice later on.

25. See, for example, the *Courrier français,* 11 July, p. 2: reprint of the ordinance *re* the formation of electoral lists; 17 July, p. 1: notice of the publication of the Guichard brochure, *re* problems of inscription; 21 July, pp. 1 and 2: more instructions *re* getting inscribed; 22 July, p. 2: about a problem of inscription in Paris; 28 July, p. 2: more of the same; and this sort of thing for almost every day of August and a number of days in September. The master work of Isambert, *Instruction aux citoyens français pour la reconnaissance de leurs droits d'électeurs et de jurés* (Paris, 1827) BN Le/8.18, is cited inter alia 30 Aug., p. 1, and 26 Sept., p. 3.

26. It is important to underline that the censorship was applicable only to the periodical press and did not apply to pamphlets or books which had no set times of publication. Both oppositions, and the government side as well, made extensive use of the pamphlet in lieu of the periodic newspaper press. See below, chapters 4, 5, and 6.

The second step was to instruct local officials – the prefects and other administrative officers, the finance officers, and the officers of the courts – in all the ins and outs of electoral list-making under the old legislation (where still relevant) and especially under the new. It was a matter of great importance that these functions be promptly and accurately carried out. On 29 June the ministry of interior sent out a detailed circular of instructions with an appendix running to twenty-odd pages.[27] A second circular went out on 19 July. The ministry of justice told *its* people of their duties regarding jury lists in its own circular of 30 June[28] – the first part of the jury list, one will recall, was the list of voters. These three documents were public and their thrust was to tell the list-makers exactly what the law required of them. One thing the ministry wanted to avoid was a well-founded public outcry against alleged electoral fraud on the part of its departmental officers. There would be enough of this even if everyone scrupulously observed the law.

The last and by all odds the most important task of the government in the pursuit of its strategy was the intelligence task. Just what was the temper of the country and what the composition of the electorate and its probable voting choice? By mid-October at the latest (two weeks after the list-making business was over) and much earlier, if possible, the government had to know. If things looked auspicious, the final decision could then be made; if not, the election could be put off a year or more. The best way – in fact the only practical way – for the government in Paris to gather the intelligence necessary to an informed decision was to call upon the prefects and their subordinates. There were risks in going to the prefects for this sort of information, for any blunt statement of the requirement at this early stage of affairs would be both unnecessary and dangerous.

So as a starter early in July the director of police in the ministry of the interior reissued the circular message of 22 February 1827: the one requesting the prefects' confidential views on the esprit publique and a number of its important component phenomena.[29]

27. Duvergier, *Lois,* XXVII, 301-302. The appendix is not in Duvergier. I found it in AD Ille-et-Vilaine, 3 M 1/3, which also contains the circular of 19 July.

28. Duvergier, *Lois,* XXVII, 303. For these circular messages, see below, p. 131, n. 1.

29. See above, chap. 1, text and n.27. Although the date of the outgoing messages to the 86 prefects is sometimes 3, 4, or 5 July, the issuer, in follow-up correspondence, refers to it for an unknown reason as his "message of 6 July 1827."

He wanted the prefects to send in their first reports promptly and to continue to send them in each month thereafter. Although nothing in the outgoing message suggested the matter of an election, many prefects had had the word over the rumor network and began incorporating in their replies some general comments on the outlook for elections should they occur. Whatever it was that set the rumors in motion, there could be no secret about what nurtured them.

As early as the end of June, and in response to Corbière's open circular about list-making, forward-looking and responsible prefects began composing the electoral lists that they had to post on 15 August in each commune of their departments. This involved a goading first of the departmental tax collectors to tally up men who paid enough direct taxes to vote, and then of the subprefects and mayors to come forward with certifications of appropriate age and domicile. As a foundation for the prefectoral labors, there were the lists which had served in 1824 but which had not received a systematic and critical review for almost three and a half years.[30] Obligations to revise and inscribe *de novo* begot correspondence[31] and correspondence begot talk among the bureaucrats which was overheard and did not stop there. The politically conscious citizenry was already astir when news of the seventh and last of the by-elections electrified them, the bureaucracy, and the government itself. Moreover, it lent a new urgency to the government's intelligence-gathering task.

The place of this seventh and last by-election was that arrondissement of the Charente which bears the name of the department's chef lieu – the provincial city of Angoulême; the time, mid-July. Pierre Jean-Baptiste Descordes, a Villèle supporter, had vacated his seat.[32] Three candidates came forward, one a Villèle supporter and two anything but. The two, who would vie for the left-opposition vote, were Gellibert des Seguins, an esteemed medical doctor of

30. A confidential circular of 14 July 1827 signed by Corbière contains a sentence which strongly suggests this. "I presume that in general it will be convenient to reproduce provisionally on your 15 August list the old inscriptions, after erasing those which you judge to have become invalid since 1824. . . ."

In the next pages I will refer again to this and other related circular messages. My principal use of them will come in chapter 6. For full references, see the Bibliographical Note.

31. The voluminous nature of this correspondence is treated in chapter 7.

32. Probably he resigned his deputyship towards the end of the session. The record is incomplete.

Angoulême; and Chauvelin, a well-known man of many talents. As if two opposition contestants were not already too many, came a third, Delalot – well to the right of the others (perhaps far enough to be associated with the counter-opposition), in all events a dedicated enemy of Villèle. Since each of the three had his own band of followers, it did not take a very bright observer to realize that in dividing the vote of the two oppositions – and that in three pieces – the government candidate had an assured free ride to victory. The Paris censors permitted the *Constitutionnel* to say as much in muted tones.[33]

Sometime before the meeting of the electoral college Chauvelin got the word and withdrew his candidacy. This left Dr. Gellibert and Delalot to fight it out when the first balloting took place. They did and they neatly divided the vote; neither of them received enough ballots to win, nor, for that matter, did the government candidate. It was at this point that Gellibert himself withdrew and urged his left-wing followers to swallow their politics and vote for Delalot, whose opposition to the government was rooted in a different substance. On the second ballot Delalot won.

To the government the outcome was a stunner: the loss of a seat was another worrisome omen, but that its loss had come as a result of the union of the two oppositions was trebly so. The shock waves traveled upwards to the king himself, whom Villèle reported to be "grievously pained at portents of the election of M. Delalot."[34] The principal and most ominous threat to the king and his ministers was the possibility of an understanding between leftist leaders and those of the counter-opposition to forego internecine battle and join forces. If from such there arose a solid political alliance it would significantly hurt the chances of pro-government candidates in perhaps upwards of threescore electoral districts. In short, the by-election in Angoulême brought an important new ingredient into the problem of whether or not to go for a general election that very autumn. More than ever the government would have to know how the electoral lists would be shaping up from the earliest moment.

Less than a week after Delalot's victory, out to the prefects went the first of a new series of circular messages. These are not

33. *Constitutionnel,* 7 July 1827, p. 2.

34. Villèle diary, 13 July 1827. An entry for the next day indicates a wider adverse effect: "La nomination de M. [De] Lalot fait un mauvais effet et ôte confiance aux amis du ministère."

to be confused with the two which were sent out earlier (22 February and 5 July 1827) by Franchet d'Esperey, director of police, asking about the state of the esprit publique. The new circulars were sent out by the minister of the interior, Corbière, and in his absence by his august stand-in, Villèle himself. They dealt squarely with the business of electoral list-making. Most of them were classified "confidential" and asked that the replies be handled through special channels, "eyes-only," direct to the minister. The first, which went out on 14 July, was principally an expression of the ministry's concern with the lists and an injunction not to miss the inscription of any pro-government voter. Four other messages in this series followed in August and September – one signed by Corbière, three by Villèle – asking each recipient prefect to report on the probable political complexion of his electoral list.[35]

In response to these queries and to the earlier appeal of Franchet d'Esperey, two streams of information began flowing into the ministry of the interior in Paris.

The archival record of messages to the police in answer to the director's broadside query of 5 July is full. In the relevant cartons of the Archives Nationales[36] are 179 communications from 81 different prefects which contain enough substantive information to be worthy of note. They differ widely from prefect to prefect in their periodicity, the range of things covered, and in the perceptiveness of the author. Certain prefects sent in highly informative reports almost fortnightly (those of the Gironde, Loire-Inférieure, and Pyrénées-Orientales, for example); many others skimped (those of the Aisne, Cantal, Loiret, Lot, and Marne, for example). These and some 30 others are represented in today's archives by only a single report each. The best of the reports are as wide-ranging as the director's request and wider. Many prefects lunged beyond to volunteer their views on the matter of an election.[37] From these reports some fairly pointed generalizations emerge. If these were fully communi-

35. I will come back to these messages and some of their post-September fellows, and in detail, in chapter 7.

36. AN F/7 6767–6772. See the Bibliographical Note for the contents of the cartons by departments.

37. No question but that in their reply to the police certain harrassed prefects incorporated answers to the more precise questions about electoral matters posed in the ministerial circulars and hoped that a single report would satisfy the two masters in Paris. In a few cases this is just what was done and acknowledgedly so.

cated and understood they would have quite definitely chilled any optimism about the outcome of an election in the autumn of 1827.

Among even the earliest replies were words of deep concern. As prefectoral reporting fell off somewhat in quantity when the administration swung into the demanding business of list-making (perhaps also as a function of time's having blunted the urgency of the director's needle) the message of worry, even alarm, abated not. Three points among many stand out: first, adherents of the government, usually referred to as "royalists," were not taking seriously their responsibility of getting themselves inscribed on the lists; they were showing themselves apathetic to political issues and insouciant to their political obligations; those who did care were divided among themselves and squabbling. Secondly, men of the opposition, on the other hand – sometimes both the counter-opposition and the *libéraux* were showing the qualities that go with an acute and determined political leadership.[38] Well before they began receiving the requests for essentially electoral information sent out by Corbière and Villèle, certain prefects were offering their advance views on the subject, and melancholy ones they were.[39]

Their incoming messages were read and analyzed by some subordinate in the office of the director of police. A rough draft of his work survives in the archives. Addressed to the baron Capelle, the interior ministry's top official concerned with matters affecting the departments, it is dated "August," which is lined through, and "September" added. Its covering note reads, "The director of police has the honor to address to baron Capelle a series of opinions relative to the elections, extracted from the [confidential *lined-out*] monthly reports from the prefects."

There follows in highly abstract form the central thought of

38. See Ardèche, 30 July; Aude, 20 July; Aveyron, 10 Aug.; Calvados, 3 June, 30 Sept.; Charente, 4 Sept.; Côtes-du-Nord, 18 July; Doubs, 6 Oct.; Hérault, 29 Nov. (the prefect here is looking back); Ille-et-Vilaine, 6 July; Jura, 27 Aug.; Loire-Inférieure, 1 Aug., 5 Feb. 1828 (another retrospective report); Mayenne, 24 Oct.; Meuse, 22 July; Hautes-Pyrénées, 14 July; Sarthe, 8 July; Deux-Sèvres, 16 Sept.; Somme, 3 Sept.; Var, 1 Sept.; Vaucluse, 12 July; Haute-Vienne, 5 Oct.

Most of the remarks about the stance of the opposition is included in the messages just cited, where royalist efforts are compared unfavorably. But see also Eure-et-Loir, 5 Aug.; Finistère, 9 July; Rhône, 6 July.

39. See Ardennes, 9 July; Creuse, 30 Aug.; Eure-et-Loir, 8 July; Haute-Garonne, 9 July; and Haut-Rhin, 4 Oct.

twenty-seven reports, almost all of which are gloomy.[40] If by chance this memo was done up in clean draft and sent on to Capelle and if he knew no more about this particular reporting from the field than what he learned here, he was not getting the full story. For this memorandum is a very poor piece of analysis. It does not take into account seven pessimistic reports which had all but certainly arrived in Paris before the end of August and three more which probably arrived in the first few days of September. The choice of departments actually reported upon could not have been dictated by bad news from hitherto safe departments nor by a decision to check on the prospects in departments which had had a reputation of strong electoral opposition.[41] One is left with the feeling that the choice of departments was largely a matter of whim, or what documents happened to be on top of the stack. Doing things this way conveyed the impression of a lively political opposition in the countryside, but probably short of what things were really like at the time and certainly short of what they were a month later.

The second stream of information – that in response to the ministerial circulars of August and September – probably came directly to Capelle's own office. From some samples one knows it was voluminous: the prefect of the Tarn sent in sixteen reports and the prefect of the Var, more than forty.[42] Christophe de Villeneuve-Bargemont, prefect of the Bouches-du-Rhône, wrote at least five which run to several thousand words.[43] The sample also reveals that the prefects were doing their best to tell their masters how their electoral lists were shaping up. They reported the total number of voters inscribed to date and their best estimates as to how many

40. For the parent document, see AN F/7 6741. Of the 27 reports it abstracts, 24 still exist in the AN F/7 6767–6772 cartons. This datum, almost incredible, does much to establish one's faith in the probable degree of completeness of this particular official record.

41. In the 1827 elections there were 41 departments which sent strong opposition delegations to the chamber. Only 16 of these appear in this list of 27.

The handful of opposition candidates who won elections in 1824 came from 12 departments. Only 4 of these 12 departments figure among the 27 of the memo under discussion.

42. These (Tarn 4 and Var 4) and others in this series are in the cartons of AN F/1c/III group. See the Bibliographical Note.

43. Those which I have seen are drafts. They are in the AD Bouches-du-Rhône M/2(III)–9. I found none of them in the AN.

would support candidates of the counter-opposition and left opposition as well as the number of doubtful and unknown political leanings. The most conscientious prefects sent in such estimates at fortnightly intervals or even oftener. In many cases the "doubtful" or "unknown" column contained large numbers, which of course made impossible any confident estimate as to how an election would actually come out.

On the basis of these reports, Capelle or someone in his office apparently tried from time to time to put together the broad picture. As is generally the case in such endeavors, the analysts passed on their conclusions in tables of discrete numbers, a technique which obscured the fears, doubts, and hopes that had done service for gaps in the basic data. Even so, as will be shown later, all but the last of these summaries designed for the enlightenment of the crown and the ministry paralleled the cheerless outlook conveyed by the other stream of information. One might add that if the high-level readers of these summaries had also had time to read the oftentimes wordy reports from the prefects which defied quantification and especially the ones which came in late in the game, they would have been even more impressed at the somber prospects for the outcome of a general election.

In a way some of the bad news carried its own neutralizer. This was to the effect that if 1827 was inauspicious another year was no better. As the prefect of one of the solid pro-government departments and Villèle's home department, the Haute-Garonne, put it (he was writing in the context of opposition electoral activity), "Next year we will not [be able to escape the registration of] a single liberal elector."[44] He had previously written that it would be a grievous error to consider that eligibility for jury service would inhibit the effort of any liberal voter to get on the list.[45] Jordan, the prefect of the Haut-Rhin, was fuller and more alarmingly explicit. "It is above all among the businessmen [*patentables*] that these efforts are to be noted. They have been seconded by ultra liberal lawyers. . . . The law of 2 May is at the bottom of all this. I fear that in each year of our era the results will be the same, for, more sensible than the royalists, the liberal opposition will never be

44. AN F/7 6769 Haute-Garonne, 4 Sept. 1827.
45. *Ibid.*, 9 July 1827.

divided within itself, nor will it ever pass up a good opportunity."[46] This sort of reminder from the field intensified ministerial concern about the best time to hold the election. These particular ones seemed to reenforce the notion that the sooner the better.

But should it be sooner? Should it be in the autumn of that very year and soon after the final lists were posted, or should it be in 1828 or later? This question engulfed a good part of the thinking time of the ministry and the court. Its importance was widely understood and by none with greater clarity than by Villèle. He was well aware that his continuance in office might depend upon avoiding the bad choice; others with far less of a personal stake than he were equally fearful of consequences of an election which went strongly against the "in" group. What would follow none could foresee and this uncertainty was doubly unsettling in the light of the long incumbency of the sitting government.

Before a final decision about the general election could be taken, at least two men had to agree: the king and Villèle. Villèle, of course, could not make the decision on his own authority and the king, who did have the power, almost certainly would not have exercised it against the man who had served him so loyally for so long and for whose judgment he had so high a regard. But even though the two held between them the power of decision, neither was wholly free. Villèle had his colleagues of his ministry; those closest to him, Corbière and Peyronnet (especially Corbière), probably shared his hopes and fears and the general thrust of his thinking. But there were others – notably Chabrol de Crouzol, the minister of the navy, and Clermont-Tonnerre, the minister of war – who did not. Nor was the king free from advisers beyond the ministry. He had his son and the dauphine with whom he was in close touch, and he had the members of the court.

Thus the little circle of two became a much larger circle at the remove of a single echelon and a much much larger at two echelons; all members of all the circles were likely to hold strong views on one side of the debate or the other – views which they longed to communicate upwards, and did whenever they had the chance. For

46. AN F/7 6771 Haut-Rhin, 4 Oct. 1827. Note the use of "patentables" as a synonym for the group in the electorate most feared by the government. Jordan, the author of this, I rate as hands down the most perceptive and articulate prefect of the 86.

weeks the principals to the great decision were the recipients of this welter of commentary and advice.

From the vantage point of the Villèle diary, it seems as if the prime minister held a steady course. Surely he had not made up his mind not to urge his master to go for the election; he continued to hold the options open awaiting news from the prefects and their list-making. But the victory of Delalot in Angoulême and the chance that it presaged a wide-spread alliance of the two oppositions had shaken him. Was there a way to neutralize this particular threat? Thrice he had received important men from the right end of the spectrum – Michoud and Berryer, Clausel de Coussergues, and Berryer *fils* – each conveying a possible though distasteful solution. They had urged that he take the initiative to make peace with the counter-opposition: Michoud and Berryer indicated the desirability of a "partial change" in the government – no names are mentioned in the diary; Clausel de Coussergues suggested adding Polignac to the cabinet as minister without portfolio; and Berryer *fils* came in with the same proposition and included Portalis with Polignac.[47] Through such a measure the dangerous alliance might be reversed, uniting once again all so-called royalists and leaving the left to find comfort solely within itself. The unspecified urgency for such a course was in all likelihood a belief that elections had already been decided upon. Of course they had not. In any case nothing seems to have been done to bring Polignac into the cabinet.

Villèle had many other visitors during July and August and other intimations of doubt and danger. He saw delegations of deputies three different times, and of one group which waited upon him he noted, "saw a number of stalwart deputies [who were] fearful and discouraged at the evil turn of public opinion towards both themselves and us." Earlier in the month he had confided to his diary, "There is forever talk about the difficulties of the course to be followed by the ministry and about the danger of elections." An evening with Bonald and others produced the unhelpful conclusion that something had to be done, but nobody knew what. If Villèle had a plan of campaign other than to wait and see, he almost certainly told no one beyond Corbière. However, the king had urged him to confer with the dauphin about possible new peers and the ques-

47. Villèle diary, 10, 23, 24 Aug. 1827.

tion of the election and also to get his views as to the proper time to bring the questions before the full council of ministers.[48] In other words whatever talk was buzzing through the government was up to this point at least strictly unofficial.

But Corbière was obviously a special case. One evening early in July he had talked with Villèle until near midnight and confided his thoughts about the peers, the deputies, and some of the prefects. Then, until the end of August, the diary is mute about Corbière; but on the twenty-eighth it tells of how they had come back together from a meeting of the council with the king at St. Cloud. They spoke of the forthcoming trip of the king and of Corbière's accompanying him; Corbière recalled the desperate illness of his son and his desire to resign should the boy succumb, his desire that Villèle should direct the ministry of the interior in his absence on the trip. Tacked on the end of the ambling sentence which touches several subjects comes: Corbière "thinks that in spite of all the difficulties, it would be better to go down than temporize."[49] Although there is no referent to identify the seat of the dilemma, the one that makes the most sense seems inescapably to be the election. Thus one is led to guess that Corbière, at least, was coming down solidly to hold it in 1827 no matter the consequences.

On 3 September the king departed his capital for the royal progress to the north, taking with him Corbière, a considerable retinue, and 220,000 francs for expenses and to give away as royal largesse.[50] Back in Paris Villèle was in charge and almost at once received the first dismal news from the prefects. Perhaps what he saw was the memorandum prepared in the office of the director of police which has been noted earlier, perhaps it was the full collection of prefects' reports upon which the memorandum was based. In all events, the documents which he read concerned the prospects for an election and made the point that almost everyone was opposing it as burdened too heavily with danger. When he next saw the dauphin and dauphine he brought them up to date on the situation with the perhaps predictable result that the dauphine bespoke her own fears

48. *Ibid.,* 16 Aug., 1 Aug., 15 Aug., 31 July 1827.

49. *Ibid.,* 9 July, 28 Aug. 1827: "il vaut mieux fondre que temporiser."

50. *Ibid.,* 30 Aug. 1827. The king asked Villèle for 120,000. Villèle and Corbière thought this was too little. Next day (31 Aug. 1827) Villèle wrote the king a note "pour l'engager de prendre 100 mille francs de plus pour donner dans son voyage."

for the future and her great concern about an election. This and other news spread through the court and disapproval of holding an election became general; Villèle's characterization of the attitude of mind at St. Cloud was that "everyone is crying down [the thought] of dissolution [of the present chamber of deputies]."[51]

But the "everyone" did not include the king himself. Just as he had agonized over the decision to impose the censorship, so he was agonizing over this one, and for a longer time. In mid-July Villèle had found him at St. Cloud sad in mood and unresolved about what to do. The trip to the provinces and the warm reception he received had cheered him, but not to the point of leading him to make up his mind. Even the glum atmosphere of the court had not convinced him to drop further consideration of the election. When Villèle saw him towards the end of September he was pleasant enough but still undecided.[52]

Villèle, uninformed as to how the prefects would evaluate their final lists, apparently made up his own mind at about this time and in favor of holding the election. The evidence comes in two pieces, both from Villèle himself. He noted in his diary (27 September) that the king had instructed him to talk to Chabrol, whose opposing views were well known, and try to win him over to Villèle's side with respect "to the peers and the election." On the very same day Villèle signed a long circular message to the prefects in which, among other things, he warns them to avoid certain provocative action, "for this would be to announce the coming elections."[53]

Then followed two highly disturbing weeks. News from the prefects indicated that things were going no better for the government and that throughout the countryside there was a turmoil of mind about the elections. A few days later another batch of reports seemed to show that the "new electoral lists were not bad,"[54] but then in a short interval came a correction: "learned that the news from the departments is less good than that of the past." A reading of

51. *Ibid.*, 3, 5, 23 Sept. 1827.

52. *Ibid.*, 17 July and 25 Sept. 1827.

53. Villèle signed the circular message as acting minister of the interior.

54. Villèle diary, 1 and 4 Oct. 1827. The passage quoted is followed by: "C'est plutôt l'opinion qu'a varié que les nombres dans les colleges." Exactly what this meant to Villèle is something of a puzzle. Taken in context it probably means that there was significant opposition to the government among voters, but probably that the number of opposing voters had not grown as much as Villèle had feared.

those prefects' reports which survive today confirms this, for in general there was a distinct change, and in the direction of gloom, that entered their evaluations of early October. On the eleventh Villèle talked things over with Corbière, who next day brought back some cheer: his first numerical estimate as to the probable wins and losses in the event of an election. Corbière had figures which indicated that of 249 seats in 58 departments "163 royalistes, 43 libéraux, 43 pointus" would win. "In this count," adds Villèle, "we would have [a majority] of 80 votes against the two oppositions."[55]

This estimate had its impact upon the king, for the very next day Villèle wrote in his diary that the king had been "very agreeable to me and favorably inclined to the dissolution [of the chamber of deputies] and the [matter of the] peers, seeing things in a very reasonable light."[56] But not for long; new reports were again laden with gloomy forecasts[57] which threw the king once more into indecision.[58] This time, in irked awareness of the disarray within the council of ministers, he yielded to an unusual impulse. He instructed Villèle to summon his colleagues apart from the royal presence and to beat out an agreed position.[59] It was almost as if the king were taking comfort from the existence of indecision elsewhere in high places and saying half-aloud, "Why should I make up my mind if you, my own council, cannot make up yours?"

The very day that the king told Villèle to convene the council (16 October) there was bad news and good. Poor Corbière, whose son had died only recently, came down with a fever which incapacitated him for weeks; someone in his ministry sent on to Villèle a final and optimistic estimate about the probable outcome of an election. The meeting of the council which was to take place at Corbière's house had to be postponed. It met on the eighteenth at Villèle's house where both issues – whom the council should recom-

55. *Ibid.*, 8, 11, and esp. 12 Oct. 1827. Note that 249 seats was only something more than half the total.

56. *Ibid.*, 13 Oct. 1827.

57. *Ibid.*, 14 Oct. 1827: "Reçu beaucoup d'observations contre la dissolution" is the naked phrase.

58. *Ibid.*, 15 Oct. 1827: "le roi qui m'a gardé fort longtemps et est assez indécis sur la grande mesure à prendre." One guesses from the next line that one of the courtiers, the duc de Rivière, tutor to the king's seven-year-old grandson, the duc de Bordeaux, had spoken long with the king in opposition to the election.

59. *Ibid.*, 16 Oct. 1827.

mend for the peerage, and whether to dissolve the chamber of deputies — were canvassed. Despite the cheering estimate, Chabrol and Clermont-Tonnerre alone continued to harbor doubts. Villèle reported as much to the king who in turn, talking things over with the dauphin, seemed disposed to Villèle's view.[60] But still no firm decision.

What of the new estimate and its good news? It held that of 427 deputies (out of 430) 254 "royalists" would be elected and only 109 "liberals" and 64 "pointus" of the counter-opposition. As Villèle should have known, and probably did, everything in this estimate depended upon exactly who had been bracketed into the "royalist" category. As he knew well, there were many kinds of royalists — a broad spectrum of men devoted to the king, the charter, and the principal tenets of constitutional monarchy. The word could designate some, politically perhaps even a bit to Villèle's right, who would have continued to support him. It could also stand for a good number to his left who could not have endured another minute of his leadership. Good royalists though these may have been, their opposition to the incumbent ministry would have been swift, unqualified, and remorseless.

But this crashing dissonance the estimate obscured by not rising to a higher level of enquiry and neglecting to refine on the word "royalist." There was however no reason for the council of ministers to have been so uncritical. In fact it is hard to believe that its leading members were; it is hard to believe that they did not see that the chances for a victory for the ministry were indeed slim irrespective of wishful definitions of this key word. But this did not mean that the chances were zero; there was still room for hope. And however faint the hope it was nourished by a contemplation of the alternatives.

Here in mid-October things had gone so far in the direction of holding an election with so many important men so fully aware, that to draw back now would be akin to the government's giving itself a vote of no-confidence. Villèle's waning majority in the old chamber might disappear forthwith. But this was only a possibility of the immediate future. Further ahead the evil prospects seemed both more evil and more certain. First there would be the old chamber — sadly weakened, plundered of perhaps threescore Villèlist

60. *Ibid.*, 16 and 18 Oct. 1827.

supporters to fatten the peers.[61] Then there would be the by-elections to replace these deputies. Could they be guaranteed to give good returns? Further, there would be the list-making of 1828 and the augmentation of left-wing voters as the wisest prefects foresaw. A general election in the autumn of 1828 would be more hazardous than today.

But could not 1828 be passed over in favor, say, of 1829? Perhaps not without at least a large number of by-elections deriving from a threatened mass resignation. This had been promised by a group of deputies led by the baron Turckheim who said they would refuse to accept the sixth and seventh year of the seven-year term vouchsafed by the law of the *septennalité*. Pointing to the five-year term defined in the charter they asserted that the law of 1824 was unconstitutional and that they would not hold office beyond the stipulated years of the charter.[62]

Putting to one side for the moment the threat of Turckheim and his followers, what about 1829? Surely there was nothing there to fill the heart with cheer. The same disadvantages, perhaps augmented by the passage of time, would hold as for 1828. Perhaps even, there would be a new one. For the closer one came to 1830, the closer to the general election made mandatory by law; thus if the try for tactical surprise had turned out badly in 1827, how much worse it would turn out the closer to 1830.

At moments like these, impossible decisions get made and this one was. Perhaps on the false optimism of the last numerical estimate, more likely on the bleak outlook for the future, Chabrol and Cler-

61. Villèle and Corbière, working over the list of new creations, nominated for the king's consideration no less than 57 deputies plus 33 "notables" of the departments and 5 archbishops for the peerage (Villèle diary, 19 Oct. 1827). The king whittled back on the figure 57 and ultimately named only 36 deputies to the peerage out of the total of 76 so elevated.

62. Turckheim, a rich and respected businessman of Alsace, known to all smokers of the region as the manufacturer of their favorite tobacco, was a pillar of the constitutional left opposition. The idea of self-immolation at the end of five years seems to have made quite an appeal to his colleagues, at least while the due-date was still a year or more away.

See the *Constitutionnel*, 24 June 1827, p. 2: a lead article entitled "Que-feront les ministres?" The subject matter had obviously had much discussion before the publication of this piece.

During the summer at least 3 prefects reported on the possibility of mass resignations from the chamber at the end of its fifth year and that the thought had the approval of numbers of citizens who were anti-government in their political views. See AN F/7 6767 Ardennes, 31 Aug.; 6769 Haute-Loire, 15 Aug.; and 6771 Saône-et-Loire, 9 July.

mont-Tonnerre caved in. In a second meeting of the council in Villèle's house they rallied to the majority view and Villèle informed the king by letter. Next day, 21 October, a Sunday, the king met with the council, and because of the absence of two of the ministers he deferred the final formal decision. But he was committed. He told Villèle, whose impatience must have reached the flash point, to go ahead and notify the prefects that the ordinance which would dissolve the chambers and convoke the electoral colleges would be signed and issued on 5 November.[63]

The formal decision, duly taken by the king in council, came on Wednesday, the twenty-fourth.[64] The temporizing was over, now for "the going down."[65]

63. Villèle diary, 20 and 21 Oct. 1827. The prefects received the alert in the circular message which Corbière signed the next day (22 Oct. 1827).

64. *Ibid.,* 24 Oct. 1827.

65. The account above of the way in which the final decision was reached rests almost wholly, as the reader has observed, upon the Villèle diary. Before I had the good fortune to see it, I had composed a draft on the basis of other, and be it said highly conflicting, contemporary sources. For those who wish to see for themselves, I note: Duvergier de Hauranne, *Gouvernement parlementaire,* IX, 325–326; Vaulabelle, *Restaurations* (cited above, chap. 1, n.19), VI, 494ff.; Lubis, *Histoire de la Restauration,* VI, 195; also *Mémoires du baron d'Haussez,* . . . publiés par son arrière-petite-fille, la duchesse d'Almazan (2 vols., Paris, 1896–1897), II, chap. 2; Duc d'Audiffret-Pasquier, *Mémoires du chancellier Pasquier,* VI, 85–94; and Claude de Barante, *Souvenirs du baron de Barante . . . 1782–1866* (8 vols., Paris, 1890–1901), III, 386.

3 / Electors, Eligibles, the Electoral Districts, and the Electoral Colleges

Whatever the web of circumstance that resulted in the convocation of the electoral colleges and whatever the play that engaged the politically-minded citizenry, the thing at the heart of the matter was the electorate — in fact two electorates. It is proper to begin this chapter with a close look at both.

All members of the electorate had at least five things in common: they were French citizens, they were male, they were thirty or older, they had an established political domicile, and they paid at least three hundred francs in direct taxes.[1] As of 15 August 1827, the date of the publication of the initial list, the prefects had counted something over 70,000 of them, and six weeks later, on 30 September when they closed the lists, the number of electors had grown by 25 percent to almost exactly 88,000.

1. The age and property qualification were stipulated in art. 40 of the constitutional charter (Duvergier, *Lois,* XIX, 67).

The direct taxes were four: (1) the *contribution foncière* (the tax on real estate—both land and buildings); (2) the *contribution personnelle et mobilière* (a nominal poll tax plus a tax computed upon the rent of the dwelling); (3) the *contribution des portes et fenêtres* (a tax on the doors and windows of the dwelling); and (4) the *impôt des patentes* (a sort of license tax for carrying on an industrial or commercial enterprise). See my *Electoral Procedure under Louis Philippe* (New Haven: Yale University Press, 1937), chap. 2, for a full discussion of the direct taxes.

It would be impossible to say with any precision what the payment of the 300 francs cens meant in terms of income and wealth. I have found a score or more scattered references (mostly in the ADs) which indicate that the direct taxes amounted to about 12% of most censeurs' incomes: in my tiny sample the rate varied from 8% to 20%. In his *Forces productives* (I, 140–142) Charles Dupin describes a hypothetical "average" department based upon his study of 32 northerly departments. The total direct taxes in his model would be about 16% of total income. If he had extended his study to include the less favored departments of the south, the percentage would probably have been smaller. These figures merely reinforce what is already clear: a man paying 300 francs in direct taxes was well off; one paying 1,000 francs (the cens of those eligible to run for office) was among the rich. There were a few voters who did not themselves pay the full 300 franc cens. These were the sons, grandsons, or sons-in-law of widows who were authorized to *delegate* the political credit attached to their payment of the contribution foncière. See art. 5 of the law of 29 June 1820 (Duvergier, *Lois,* XXIII, 15 [14]), and below, chap. 5, text and notes 12–13.

This was the first of two electorates. It would assemble in the arrondissemental and "special colleges"[2] to elect 265 deputies to the chamber.

The second electorate was an elite fraction of the first. It dated from the electoral law of 29 June 1820 which held that the most highly taxed 25 percent of the regular voters of each department were to assemble in the so-called departmental colleges where they could cast a second vote. Altogether these men who were the beneficiaries of the double vote elected a total of 165 more deputies.

Let us look at the first electorate first.

Most notable of course is the relative smallness of its size. France's population in 1827 was some 32 million. Thus one person in about 360 had the vote, and among adult males about one in fifty to sixty. In rural areas there were many communes without a single voter and where even the cantonal clusters of communes produced no more than a handful.[3] Good-sized towns like Troyes (the Aube's chef lieu) had fewer than 200, and provincial centers like Dijon and Grenoble had fewer than 400 and 300 respectively. Paris with almost a million people was overwhelmingly the best represented city. It had something over 8,000 voters, and here as in all other matters was truly a special case.

Next most notable was the way that the electorate had diminished in size since the elections of the early Restoration. George-Denis Weil estimates that the electorate of 1817 numbered some 110,000, that of 1820 some 105,000.[4] An official count put that of 1822 at 101,612.[5] My estimate of the electorate of 1824 is between 96,000 and 99,000.[6] Weil asserts that the diminution was a function of the lowering of the sums collected annually in the contribution foncière, and the figures, of course, bear him out.[7] The continuing decline in registration between 1824 and 1827 is largely ascribable

2. The "special colleges" will be discussed later in this chapter.

3. To illustrate the point, in 1828 the cantons of Rocroy, Rumingy, Rancourt, and Marchault of the Ardennes had 5, 7, 11, and 4 electors respectively (AN F/1c/III Ardennes 4).

4. Georges-Denis Weil, *Les Elections législatives depuis 1789 . . .* (Paris, 1895), p. 97.

5. AN F/1c/II 52.

6. Both of these figures derive from official documents. The first is from the many procès verbaux of the 1824 elections (AN, cartons of the F/1c/III series); the second from a document clearly official in nature, in the AN carton F/1c/II 52, simply headed, "Nombre des électeurs 1824 et 1827."

7. Between 1816 and 1824, the yield of the contribution foncière declined from an estimated 300 million (my estimate) francs to 253.1 million (15.6%); total direct taxes

to the same cause: the contribution foncière fell off some 6 percent in those years.[8]

The very low figure (70,000) on the first published lists of 1827 – those posted on 15 August – cannot be accounted for in terms of lowered taxes alone. In all likelihood the prefects, who were wholly on their own in constructing these first lists, made a point of erring on the side of caution. They were certain to have dropped the names of men who had voted in 1824 when they knew that the latter had died or moved out of the department or suffered dramatic changes of fortune. They may also have failed to reinscribe voters whom they knew to hold political views hostile to the government. They were under no legal obligation to do so if the man had not already filed the official documents attesting to his age, domicile, and payment of the cens.[9]

As noted earlier, this first published list went through four periods of revision, each lasting ten days, and a fifth period lasting five. At the end of each period the prefects posted a table of rectification; at the end of the fifth (midnight of 30 September) they closed the lists and posted the final and definitive rectification as soon thereafter as possible. In 1827 this six weeks of activity resulted in adding some 18,000 names to the first published lists. In nine departments, generally the most important and prosperous, the final lists showed increases over the first ranging from 50 to 250 percent, while in nine other departments they were smaller than the first. Closer to the average were the sixty-eight departments in which the increase was between 1 and 46 percent.[10]

declined from 402.1 million to 344.1 million (14.4%). These figures are from *Documents statistiques sur la France,* publiés par le ministère du commerce (Paris, 1835), ser. 1, vol. I, pp. 117–119. Budget figures in appropriate volumes of the *Bulletin des lois* vary considerably from the above, nevertheless they too show a similar downward trend.

8. In the two years after 1827 the electorate grew a bit, probably as a result of the small increase in the contribution foncière and because the law of 2 July 1828 made it more difficult for the prefects to make arbitrary erasures. The text of this law is in Duvergier, *Lois,* XXVIII, 227–240. The electorate as of 1 Oct. 1828 was about 93,000, and as of 1 Oct. 1829 something over 95,000. The first of these figures is probably close to the fact, the second may be low. Both came from documents in AN F/1c/II 52. The 95,000 of October 1829 was substantially the electorate which re-returned the 221 in the elections of June and July 1830.

9. This action on the part of prefects purged the lists of many who had voted in 1824. For example, in the Haute-Vienne there were over 300; in the Rhône more than 1,100; in the Isère almost 700; in the Aisne and the Calvados some 400.

10. Between the first and last published lists registered voters increased in the: Indre-et-Loire 50%, Loire-Inférieure 64%, Gard 77%, Seine 79%, Seine-Inférieure 79%, Seine-et-Oise 82%, Isère 92%, Rhône 97%, and Haute-Vienne 250% (see the table in chap. 5, below).

What may be said of the 88,000 Frenchmen who comprised the general electorate?

In age, they were all over thirty; this we can assert. But how many of them were how much over thirty cannot be known, for the electoral lists of the Restoration contain no indication of date of birth. One can make an educated guess that the median age was probably within the 53–55 bracket.[11]

As to distribution between the great cities and major towns on the one hand and the small towns and countryside on the other, it is possible to count the voters of the four largest cities – Paris, Lyon, Lille, and Marseille.[12] About one eighth of the voters were clustered here; about a tenth in Paris alone. There is more difficulty in trying to establish how many voters came from the middle-sized towns. If you were to count all the voters from the electoral districts which had at their hearts the towns which constituted the chefs lieux of the eighty-two departments (leaving out the Seine, Rhône, Nord, and Bouches-du-Rhône), you would have about 31,000 individuals or some 35 percent of the whole electorate. But in fact probably about one half of these men lived in the urban centers themselves; the rest would have come from the multitude of smaller communes which fell within the electoral district. Thus the registered vote for the four great cities plus the middle-sized cities and the provincial towns which were also chefs lieux de département would probably amount to between 25 and 30 percent of the electorate.

The northern part of the realm had more voters and more deputies per unit of area, population, and payment of direct taxes than the rest of the country. The thirty-two departments lying to the north of a line from Cherbourg to Geneva (but including the Manche)[13] had almost one half the electorate (43,000) and 43 percent of the deputies, though they comprised only 25 percent of the total area, had 37 percent of the population, and paid only 30 percent of the direct taxes.

11. Electoral lists of the July Monarchy do contain the year of birth of each voter. The median age was probably between 45 and 50. But in this era the age of qualification for the franchise was five years lower (25) and the cens 100 francs lower (200). These provisions made for an electorate twice as large as that of the Restoration and a younger median age.

12. Electoral lists exist for these cities.

13. This is the group of departments studied by Charles Dupin in his *Forces productives*. The "line" is his line.

As to the make-up of the electorate according to occupation, one may hazard some estimates based upon the stuff of the electoral lists. I have had the good fortune to find a score of such lists, some in the departmental archives, some in the Bibliothèque Nationale. Twelve are full official electoral lists, four are full unofficial lists, and four are fragments of official and unofficial lists.[14]

Now a short prefatory word about this group of lists, and a longer one on electoral lists in general.

My group of lists is, of course, a sample. In one sense it is a large one. It represents more than one fifth of the departments of the realm and almost one third of the electorate. But it is what it is from the accident of my collecting successes. These may have produced something with a built-in geographical skew. A different sample of the same size or a complete set of lists might have a significant effect upon my findings.[15]

About electoral lists in general: First, an electoral list and its tables of rectification will contain the names of all the voters of a given department. It is subdivided according to electoral arrondissement or district and within each district further broken down alphabetically according to canton. Within each canton the voters appear in alphabetical order.

For each voter the list gives his full name, occupation, commune of political domicile, and the details of his cens (how many francs he paid in each of the four direct taxes). Unofficial lists usually give a lump sum for the cens without the tax-by-tax details. The data of most interest in a study of the make-up of the electorate according to occupation are of course those under the "occupation" heading and those, where available, which show whether or not a man paid a sum in the *impôt des patentes* (which would confirm his occupation in the category of business) and how large a tax he paid

14. The departments covered in full or in part are the: Ain, Aisne, Bouches-du-Rhône, Côte-d'Or, Doubs, Drôme, Hérault, Isère, Lot, Nord, Pas-de-Calais, Pyrénées-Orientales, Haut-Rhin, Rhône, Seine, Seine-Inférieure, Seine-et-Oise, Vendée, and Vienne. See the Bibliographical Note. Unofficial lists were the product of some private enterpriser. Sometimes they were included as a section of the departmental almanac, sometimes put out as a separate publication. One is probably justified in the belief that their content derived from the official lists.

15. I think that it would be all but impossible to assemble a complete set of official lists. However I know of one fragment not in my collection (two electoral districts of the Aube) and I would guess that a canvass of all departmental almanacs for the years 1827–1830 would produce a number of other unofficial lists.

in the *contribution foncière* (which would indicate the magnitude of his holdings of real property).

Even with data of this sort there still remain considerable difficulties in making a meaningful determination of a voter's occupation. In the first place, within any group of lists there will be many more than a hundred different "occupations" cited. Some of these will be precise and useful in my kind of analysis; others are useless, as will appear shortly. In all events nothing but confusion would result from using the multitude of callings; in the interest of common sense one must generalize them into a few. In this respect I have followed the example of my predecessors (most notably Adeline Daumard) and adopted four major categories: Public Service, Propriétaire, Business, Profession. With the number of callings greatly reduced and broadened there still remain methodological difficulties. The chief one arises from the individual quirks of the registrars. All probably would have used the same nomenclature for a doctor, or an innkeeper, or an ironmaster, a brewer, or a magistrate. We can be reasonably sure that a consistent usage runs through these professional and business designators. The trouble begins with the landed notables. Some prefects called them "propriétaires" irrespective of other claims to fame. Other prefects were deferential to titles and entered in the occupation column such things as "member of the legion of honor," "chevalier of St. Louis," or upon many an occasion baron, marquis, or comte. The trouble grows with the prefects' deference to those titles which denoted an unsalaried and largely honorific position in the administration, such as member of the conseil général, conseil d'arrondissement, and conseil municipal. No matter that the true source of these men's livelihoods, like those of most others designated as mayor and deputy mayor (*adjoint*) — also for the great part unsalaried positions — was elsewhere, the occupation column of course shows it not.[16] Equally disturbing is the very considerable difference in the frequency of employment of these titles between department and department. It appears that who received these designators of occupation depended largely upon the taste of the given registrar.[17]

16. Although many of these men received money compensation, probably in the form of a stipend from the crown, it would be hard to class them as salaried career officers of the administration.

17. An unofficial list for the Pas-de-Calais recognizes 281 men holding unsalaried government positions. This is to be contrasted with 80 in the Côte-d'Or, 30 in the Doubs, about 100 for the Hérault.

It is thus in the area of the categories of the propriétaire and unsalaried public service that I have made my most significant departures from the literal notations in the occupation column of the electoral lists. In Appendix I I discuss the methodology at greater length; here let me say that I counted as propriétaires all unsalaried officials and other men identified only by title unless they paid a patent tax. If they did and the payment was significant, I counted them in the business category.

In the great cities there were so few unsalaried officials on the lists that the adjustments were minimal. But the use of the lists for France's four largest cities – Paris, Lyon, Lille, and Marseille (and Rouen, though not necessarily the fifth in rank) – does require some special treatment which I will discuss later.

Composition of the Electorate (percentages rounded)

	Public Service	Propriétaires	Business	Professions
16 departments, ex Marseille and Lyon	12	60	20	8
5 large cities: Paris, Lyon, Lille, Marseille, Rouen	6	32	53	9
National (estimated)	11	56	25	8
Beneficiaries of the double vote and voting in the departmental colleges	15	61	18	6
Composition of the corps of eligibles	11	73	11	5

The accompanying table sets out the composition of the electorate by occupation. In the analysis of sixteen departments minus the great cities of Marseille and Lyon, which fell in two of the departments, the percentages for the business and professions categories are very close to the raw count; those for the public service and propriétaire categories derive from the adjustments I have noted above. I have not made that adjustment for the electorate of the five large cities where all but a tiny fraction of the men of the public service group were salaried officials. Here the percentage of the business group is, of course, much higher than in the electorates of the sixteen departments. Finally, by combining these first two sets of figures, with the city electorates of necessity counted once and only once, one may hazard an estimate of the make-up of the 88,000-man national electorate which voted in the arrondissemental and "special" colleges.[18] The magnitude of the business percentage in this composite figure is to me the noteworthy element. It is possible that the group of departments which comprise my sample has more than its share of middle-sized cities and, in consequence, more than its share of businessmen. Even allowing for this, I do not see how the business category within the national electorate could possibly drop below 20 percent.[19]

The lists of departmental college voters from twenty-one departments provide the figures for an adjusted analysis of this, the electorate of the elite.[20] Here the decrease in the business and professional groups and the concomitant increase in salaried public servants and propriétaires is notable, but not surprising.

There remains one last facet of this general subject which can be similarly analyzed: the composition of the corps of eligibles. What about the men eligible to run for the office of deputy, for which the qualifications were even steeper than those required of departmental college voters? The eligible candidate had to pay a cens of one thousand francs and be at least forty years of age.[21] My sample of lists of eligibles involves those of twenty-two depart-

18. See Appendix II for the methodology of this joining procedure.

19. Those familiar with a theoretical calculation I once made of the composition of the electorate of the July Monarchy, without benefit of electoral lists (*Electoral Procedure*, chap. 2, esp. pp. 53–54), will probably compare those conclusions with the ones above (I assure you that I did) and conclude that I must have considerably underestimated the size of the businessman's vote and that of the professions.

20. These colleges – and the AD call numbers for the relevant departmental lists which I found – were the Aisne, Allier, Aube (M 47 A), Bouches-du-Rhône, Côte-d'Or, Creuse (3 M 37), Haute-Garonne (2 M 24), Hérault, Isère, Lot, Marne (4 M 2), Haute-Marne (27 M 14), Mayenne (M 434), Moselle (16 M 1 bis), Pas-de-Calais, Bas-Rhin (II M 16), Haut-Rhin, Rhône, Seine-et-Oise, Deux-Sèvres (3 M 11/11), Vendée. For the ADs not detailed here, see n.14, above, and the Bibliographical Note.

21. The constitutional charter, art. 39, ruled that "if in a department there were not fifty men of the age indicated (40) who paid at least 1,000 francs in direct taxes, the number (50) would be made up of the next most highly taxed – below 1,000 francs, and these latter may be elected along with the [1,000 franc censeurs]" (Duvergier, *Lois*, XIX, 67). These are the so-called complimentary eligibles. Comparatively few departments were obliged to raise their quota of eligibles in this fashion. Corsica was the outstanding example, indeed the number of *voters* in Corsica was often less than 50.

ments and contains 3,243 names.[22] Four times this number for the whole country would probably not be far wrong.

The actual number of men who were interested in being a deputy and who could bear the expense of living in Paris without compensation (deputies received no salary) considerably reduced the real list of eligibles. For men opposed to the government, the absence of a salary could mean much, for they were highly unlikely to be awarded a government sinecure; the opposite often obtained for men who devotedly served the ministry. The net of all this was a screening-out process which affected both the quantity and the quality of the men who could seek and actually sought the office of deputy.

Before we leave this general subject of voters and eligibles whom I have treated in the mass, consider for a moment the voter as an individual. Some were, of course, among the highest stratum of the society and the richest, and moved in lonely orbits among the elite. Their views – political, social, and economic – were likely to lie towards the conservative, even reactionary, end of the spectrum, and their isolation from the ferment of the day made them relatively unaware of the disquiet which prevailed a few notches down the social ladder. One perceives this fact most glaringly in the reports of high-born and affluent prefects. When they took notice of such things as the hatred of Villèle, distrust of the crown, strong distaste for the censorship, and the economic woe of the depressed years, they showed little comprehension and, naturally, no sympathy with these live, deep, and widely-felt grievances. Nor did they give evidence of understanding the strength of anti-clericalism. So was it probably with their social equals whose political sentiments have left no such track.

Below this elite was the bulk of the electorate. These were economically secure civil servants, landholders, businessmen, and professionals who moved freely with their peers most of whom had not paid quite enough taxes to gain the vote. They must have met at the same cafés, belonged to many of the same *cercles* and *sociétés*

22. The sample includes 15 lists of eligibles for the June-July elections of 1830 (discussed in my *Electoral Procedure,* pp. 14–15) and 7 new lists (4 for 1827 and 3 for 1830). Both groups of lists are in the AN F/1c/III cartons. The 15 lists are from the Hautes-Alpes, Aude, Cantal, Charente, Cher, Côtes-du-Nord, Drôme, Jura, Landes, Loire, Loire-Inférieure, Lozère, Manche, Morbihan, and Rhône. The 7 new lists are from the Basses-Alpes, Ariège, Aube, Aveyron, Calvados, Indre, and Haute-Marne. I have made adjustments here as with the non-great-city electorates.

for the promotion of almost every cause or calling under the sun, and discussed with their unenfranchised fellows the issues of the day. The point is that they could not be, and I warrant were not, immune to the ferment that surrounded them; in fact, in a small commune where they were a mere handful the influences playing upon them were certain to have made their impress. In these circumstances there is no reason to think that all members of an electorate at three hundred francs were parts of an insensitive group living in a social and economic vacuum. The outcome of the general elections of 1827 and 1830 and the by-elections in between lend substance to this thought.

Article 2 of the law of the double vote (29 June 1820) had brought in its wake a new concept to the matter of delineating the electoral districts. The principal thrust of the law was the creation of the so-called departmental colleges and the award of a second vote to the most highly taxed 25 percent of the voters. Since these colleges were to elect between one and four deputies *at large* for the whole department, it became necessary to change the conditions of the election of the remaining deputies by the non-double voters of the full electorate.

Up until this moment, these deputies themselves had been elected at large when *all* of the voters of a given department had assembled in a single electoral college.[23] Seemingly this made too many at large

23. One of the most tedious occupational hazards involved in the discussion of French electoral legislation is the way one is impelled to move chronologically backward. Start with 1820, and if you can resist the call to '89 you cannot avoid some reference at least to the way in which earlier Restoration governments coped with the business of districting representation to the chamber of deputies.

The following derives in part from Peter Campbell's *French Electoral Systems* (Hamden, Conn.: Archon, [1965]), pp. 57–59. Mr. Campbell's short treatment is appealing and useful, and in this case gratifyingly incomplete.

The first chamber of the Restoration, the *chambre introuvable,* elected in 1815, had 395 members. The basic electoral district was the administrative arrondissement. Each arrondissemental college elected the number of deputies which would later represent the department. Once this had occurred, a second or departmental college met and made one half of its final selection from among the arrondissemental nominees. The other half it chose from among the eligibles at large. However elected, the deputy had a *nominal* expectation of serving for five years. But since one fifth of all the deputyships had to be turned over each year, some of the deputies in the early years of the Restoration would serve only a single year, some two, some three, some four, and only one fifth of them would serve the full five years (see art. 37 of the Constitutional Charter, Duvergier, *Lois,* XIX, 67).

When Louis XVIII tired of the reactionary nature of the *chambre introuvable,* he

elections, and accordingly the first move to create single-deputy constituencies came alive. The two relevant paragraphs, both in article 2 of the 1820 law, read as follows:

> The election of the present 258 deputies is [hereby] attributed to arrondissemental colleges to be formed in each department [certain exceptions noted which I will discuss later] . . . . These [arrondissemental] colleges will each elect one deputy. They are to be composed of all the electors who have their political domicile in one of the communes which lie within each electoral arrondissement. [The geographical boundaries of such arrondissement] will be set provisionally by royal ordinance upon the advice of the general coun-cil[s] of the departments. The provisional boundaries will be submitted for legislative approval at the new [legislative] session.[24]

Exactly this two-step procedure took place.

Look at step one. In each of the departments affected, the council met in early August. Among a given group of councillors there seems to have been an understanding of the desirability of dividing the department into electoral districts which would be, if not identical, at least roughly comparable. Furthermore, within most councils there was an awareness of the political implications of what they were about to do and an alertness to the need to delimit districts, which would not prejudice the electoral chances of conservative

dissolved it by ordinance and by the same action changed the ground rules for the election of its successor. The famous ordinance of 5 September 1816 retained the two-step election and the electoral roles previously assigned to arrondissements and departments, but it reduced the total number of deputies to 258 – a matter which required a reallocation of seats among the departments. Some were awarded a single deputy (e.g., the Hautes-Alpes and Corsica), others got as many as eight (the Seine and the Nord). The rest got two to seven.

Both the total number of seats and the way in which they were distributed among the departments derived from a Napoleonic arrangement (a Senatus Consultum of 16 Thermidor of the year X) which was in effect at the time of Louis's return. Louis had put it aside for his first election and went back to it for his second. This arrangement had allowed about one deputy per 100,000 population. The ratio held in most cases, but there were some quite startling departures. The Lot, for example, with 272,000 people got four deputies. More startling, this inequity was never fully corrected.

Aware that his unilateral alteration of the electoral law had put noses out of joint, Louis initiated a proper electoral bill which emerged as the law of 5 February 1817. It left the number of seats at 258, but moved away from the two-step election. Henceforward the department alone was the representational unit; all voters of the department came to the chef lieu and in a scrutin de liste procedure elected the department's quota of deputies at large. The law continued the practice of the five-year term for deputies, one fifth of whom had to seek reelection each year. This is the way things stayed until the law of the double vote in 1820.

24. Duvergier, *Lois,* XXIII, 13.

candidates. In this regard they could count upon the support of their prefect.

Although the statute does not specifically assign any role to the prefects, the sharpest of them had done their homework in advance in the hope of influencing the deliberations of their councils. Needless to say, they too were well aware how the new districts should be roughly equal and they probably cared about the matter. But what they cared about much more was the political complexion of the new districts. Accordingly, when the councils assembled, a number of prefects were ready with tentative solutions, the supporting data, and a sales talk.[25]

However much or little the prefects intruded themselves into the task, the councils did their work with exemplary speed and forwarded their results to the ministry of the interior. There, without substantive amendment, they were packaged for the royal signature and, receiving it, emerged as the ordinance of 30 August 1820.[26] The electoral districts there defined became exactly those which served in the elections of early November for the arrondissemental colleges of the fourth series.[27] That they did not also serve for subsequent elections does detract somewhat from their significance. Yet there can be little question that they constituted an important influence upon the configuration of the final districts as these were defined in the subsequent law of 16 May 1821. More important is that the archival record of how the councillors, with and without prefectoral prompting, delimited the new electoral districts is astonishingly full. Here, in the only instance in my experience, are laid out the details of the way in which electoral districts were drawn in a *régime censitaire.*

What fairly leaps out of the archival record is not a single methodology for the delimiting of electoral districts but almost as many

25. Excellent examples of a prefect's busying himself in advance of the gathering of his conseil are in the AN F/1c/III cartons. See for example Lot-et-Garonne 4, pref. to min. int., 11 Aug. 1820, where the prefect attempted the creation of three electoral districts which would be identical in population, in payment of direct taxes, and in the number of voters. By carrying his subdivision down to individual communes, he came close to his goal.

26. Calendar only in Duvergier, *Lois,* XXIII, 80; text in *ibid.,* 1st ed., XXIII, 97–114.

27. This would be the group of departments, roughly one fifth of the total, whose turn it was to renew its delegation in the annual "partial" elections. The practice of the partial elections ended with the electoral law of 1824.

different ones as there were conseils and prefects concerned. Some councils began with the administrative arrondissements, combining two to make a single electoral district or shuffling cantons around the arrondissemental matrices.[28] Other councils seem to have begun with the department as a whole and to have cut it up with only slight regard to its arrondissemental lines. Rather they endeavored to carve out electoral districts which would be roughly comparable[29] in population or in the amount of direct taxes assessed and paid, or in the number of voters, or in the distance voters would have to travel from their homes to the polling place, or in some combination of these things.[30]

Still another methodology emerged in deference to special travel problems of the voters. In the cases of the Loir-et-Cher and the Lot, two departments cut in twain by rivers (the broad Loire and the intractable Lot) which had to be crossed at established bridges and ferries, the conseils chose to draw districts which necessitated a minimum of river-crossing.[31]

It is hard to believe that a last methodology, that of the stark political gerrymander, did not in some way also color all the others suggested above. It probably did, but not as a final determinant – as in the Moselle where the conseil followed the prefect's recommendation and as much as gave the electoral district of Sarreguemines to the opposition in order to make sure that the other three would be solid for the government. Any other arrangement, he argued, might cost two seats.[32] The same sort of debate attended the decision in the Haute-Marne, the Rhône, and the Tarn-et-Garonne,[33] where decisions were greatly influenced by simple political considerations.

The most pointed and heated discussion took place in the Haute-Loire, the home department of Lafayette *fils*, who bore a gallicized version of his godfather's name: Georges Louis Gilbert Washington. The main issue before the conseil was the division of three administrative arrondissements into two electoral districts, and the special

28. For cases where the administrative arrondissemental lines were important determinants, see AN F/1c/III Hérault 4, Manche 4, Morbihan 5, Nord 5, Oise 6, Puy-de-Dôme 4.

29. For discussions of the issue of comparability, see *ibid.*, Pas-de-Calais 5, and Tarn 4.

30. *Ibid.*, Haute-Saône 4, Vaucluse 4, Bas-Rhin 4, Meurthe 5.

31. *Ibid.*, Loir-et-Cher 3, Lot 4.

32. *Ibid.*, Moselle 5, pref. to min. int., 8 Aug. 1820.

33. *Ibid.*, Haute-Marne 3, Rhône 3, Tarn-et-Garonne 2.

problem: which of the three arrondissements was to be split and divided up. In normal circumstances this would not be the arrondissement which surrounded and bore the name of its famous city, Le Puy, which was also the departmental seat. The arrondissements of both Brioude and Yssingeaux were likelier candidates for partition. But, reasoned the members of the conseil from Brioude, if voters of Le Puy were not distributed they would, in concentration, be numerous enough to elect the feared and distrusted leftist Georges Lafayette. So strongly did they feel about this that they refused to sign the document which left Le Puy in one piece. They filed a separate report with the ministry in Paris.[34]

So much for step one, the step which resulted in the "provisional" delimitation of the electoral districts. There was still ahead step two, which would involve a final delimitation and its incorporation into formal law. This began in the ministry of the interior soon after the returns were in from the general councils. There can be little doubt that the spectrum of forces which had had its influence upon the prefects and councillors continued to be operative upon the officers of the ministry who began preparing the bill which would go to the chamber of deputies. They had at hand the councils' reports of August and the afterthoughts of a number of prefects.[35] When their work was done it went to that committee of the deputies whose task it was to consider it, amend it, and report it out. The record of what happened from this point on is barren of the detail furnished in the reports from the councils and the prefects. One must guess that, if available, it would provide little additional enlightenment. Given the extraordinary difficulty of the problem one should not be surprised at the multiplicity of methods suggested nor the incongruities of the result. The plain fact is that the 247 electoral districts as they were delimited in the law of 1821 showed in their wide and dramatic divergences the tortured nature of their origin.

So they did in 1821, so they did in 1827, the year of the election of our concern. For example, there was one electoral district (Agen,

34. *Ibid.*, Haute-Loire 3. There is a dossier of a dozen documents on the case. The way it came out was that Le Puy was split up and Georges Lafayette defeated.

35. See for example *ibid.*, Ille-et-Vilaine 5, pref. to min. int., 10 Jan. 1820, where the prefect takes issue with the earlier recommendations of his conseil. He feels that voters whose cens is above 700 francs are royalist, that those whose cens is between 300 and 600 francs are likely to be of the opposition. He suggests to the minister a new pattern of districting which would assure a predominance of the higher censeurs in each district. There are other late prefectoral comments.

Lot-et-Garonne) that had almost five times more population per deputy than one other (Nantes, Loire-Inférieure); there was one electoral district (Benfeld, Bas-Rhin) that had some thirty-two times more population per elector than one other (the second electoral district of Paris); there was one electoral district (the first of Bordeaux, Gironde) that had seventeen times more electors per deputy than one other (Epinal, Vosges). Discrepancies in these ratios were only slightly less dramatic for whole departments.

That this sort of thing happened is perhaps less notable than that it stimulated so little comment. To be sure, some of the conseils généraux appended to their reports to the ministry their gripes about their departments' quota of deputies in the light of quotas of other departments,[36] but so far as I found there were practically no popular reverberations. The only traces I have come across are the fair-sized pamphlet of P. Flaugergues and an anonymous author's reply. Both concern the principle of representation and suggest different ways by which the elected chamber might be made more truly representative of the diverse social and economic interests of the country.[37]

There is another trace — this one to the effect that the government itself was in some way concerned. In 1822 and again in 1828 it asked the prefects to examine the ratios of deputies to population and of electors to population within each of 247 arrondissemental electoral districts and in the departments of the special colleges. When the returns were in, someone in the ministry of interior pulled them together in a single memorandum where the insiders could see at a glance the full range of dramatic disparities.[38] No one seems to have had the stomach to change things.

36. *Ibid.*, Eure 6: a complaint against the 1820 districting of the department filed in 1829; *ibid.*, Meurthe 5, 9 Aug. 1820: the conseil wanted it known that it felt that the Meurthe was under-represented in comparison with the Moselle and the Vosges; *ibid.*, Rhône 3: the prefect points out (29 Dec. 1820) that his department is under-represented notably in comparison with the Lot; *ibid.*, Deux-Sèvres 3: the conseil was hopping mad about the representation of its department in comparison with that of the Vendée and the Vienne.

37. *De la Représentation nationale, et principes sur la matière des élections* (Paris, 1820) BN Lb/48.1409, and Anon., *Un mot sur la représentation des intérêts dans la chambre des députés* (Paris, [1820]) BN Lb/48.1422.

See the Bibliographical Note for reference to the BN and Lb and Le series of pamphlets and for the explanation of my style in referring to them.

38. The single summarizing document for 1822 is in AN F/1c/II 52. The material for 1828 is scattered through the cartons of the AN F/1c/III series.

The law of 29 June 1820 created three categories of electoral colleges. We are already familiar with two of them, the arrondissemental and the departmental. The third, for lack of a more precise term, I will call the category of the "special colleges."

The law provided for this group of colleges to handle elections in those departments where the population and number of qualified voters was small and where in most cases the number of deputies to be chosen was minimal. In departments of this category, there were neither arrondissemental nor departmental colleges. To the single special college came all of the voters on that department's electoral list. They met in a single assembly and chose two or more candidates at large as the department's delegation to the chamber. That was the end of it. No matter how high the cens of the most highly taxed voters, they did not enjoy the *cachet* of the double vote, as did their brothers in the neighboring departments.

Article 1 of the 1820 law held that special colleges would obtain in departments which fulfilled any one of the three following conditions: (1) they had been represented by only a single deputy according to the representational allocations of the ordinance of 5 September 1816 and sanctioned by the electoral law of 5 February 1817 (this meant the Basses- and Hautes-Alpes, Lozère, and Pyrénées-Orientales); (2) irrespective of representational allocations, they had mustered fewer than three hundred voters (this applied to Corsica and the Hautes-Pyrénées); or (3), again irrespective of the number of deputies to be chosen, they were divided into five *administrative* arrondissements and mustered fewer than four hundred voters (this did in fact apply to the Basses-Pyrénées and, in the election of 1827, should have applied to the Vosges, but did not. More of this case in the last chapter). The total number of deputies involved was 18.[39]

This means that regardless of the time-honored numbers – 258 deputies from arrondissemental colleges and 172 from departmental – and even though these very numbers are used in the law of 1820, they were never correct. A fiction persisted that of the eighteen elected in the special colleges eleven were to be thought of as arrondissemental deputies and seven as departmentals; the fact was that

39. Two each from the Basses- and Hautes-Alpes, Corsica, Lozère, and Pyrénées-Orientales; three from the Hautes-Pyrénées; and five from the Basses-Pyrénées. If the law had not been disregarded in the case of the Vosges, it would have had five.

they were not. Rather they were chosen by an arrondissemental type of electorate and in a procedure (scrutin de liste) characteristic of the departmentals. In short, they were an institutional hybrid which richly deserves the "special" label.

Colleges of all three categories met in cities or towns designated by the crown. As a general proposition the departmental and special colleges met in the departmental seat and the arrondissemental colleges in a chef lieu d'arrondissement. This happened not only as a matter of the dictates of good sense but legally because the king so ordained.[40] Seldom if ever did he alter the meeting place of the departmentals and specials. There was, however, a certain amount of change with respect to the arrondissementals. The preliminaries to the election of 1827, for example, brought about at least five. There was of course no official explanation, but the citizens who approved the changes ascribed them to the greater convenience for the greater number of voters and those who did not, to bare-knuckle politics.

It is difficult indeed to discern any motive other than political for moving one of the colleges of the Gers from Condom, a fair-sized town and arrondissemental seat, to the obscure commune of Eauze. In all justice to the crown, I have found no evidence that would indicate that a pro-government candidate would do better in Eauze than in Condom, but to harbor this suspicion as one reason for the change seems permissible. A comparable change made in the Lot in 1827 might be equally suspect.

The actual physical premises — the prefecture, the town hall, a courtroom, or whatever — were matters of choice for the local administrative officials. The voter learned exactly where to go via an official communication from the mayor of his commune. It was a sort of ticket of admission which had been prepared in the prefect's office and which told the voter where he should report at 8 a.m. on the opening day of the meeting. The card was, more importantly, his authorized credential certifying him to the officers of the college and guaranteeing him entrance to the hall.[41]

40. See art. 8, law of 5 Feb. 1817 (Duvergier, *Lois,* XXI, 88).

41. A few of these tickets, more properly "*carte(s) d'électeur,*" survive in the ADs. I found one in AD Haut-Rhin (Liasse 11712). If the voter did not receive his card, or if he lost it, his registration at the college sometimes occasioned difficulties. There are cases where voters claimed that a willful mishandling of their cards had resulted in their disenfranchisement.

The principal officer of the college was the president. He was most often a local notable – sometimes a pair de France, sometimes a famous military man or magistrate, often the incumbent pro-ministry deputy, or a man who had the government's blessing as an aspiring candidate. Generally picked from a slate which the prefect had furnished on request, he was in every case an appointee of the crown and, as such, a prestigious figure. He put things in motion by appointing what was known as the provisional bureau. This was a group composed of four ballot-counters and a secretary, and they served only until their permanent replacements were chosen by the members of the college.[42]

In the election of 1827, as in its predecessors and successors, the election of the permanent bureau was the first piece of business to engage the voters.[43] As their names were called they came forward, took the oath of allegiance to king and charter, and voted for the five members of the permanent bureau.[44] When all present had voted, the president closed the proceedings, ordered the opening of the ballots and an out-loud reading and tally. Candidates with a majority of those voting were the winners. The college recessed.

The make-up of the temporary and particularly of the permanent bureaux was upon occasion a matter of great political importance. When irregularities occurred in a college, the members of the bureau

42. The list of college presidents, and vice-presidents where necessary (see below), was issued as a royal ordinance close to the time of the ordinance which convoked the electoral colleges. In 1827, both ordinances were issued the same day, i.e., 5 November 1827.

Article 9 of the law of 5 February 1817 set a limit of 600 as the largest number of voters permitted to gather in a single college. Thus if an electoral district's roster of registered voters was 601 the college would have to assemble in two sections, one of 300 and one of 301; if 800, then 400 and 400, etc. Each section was in the charge of a vice-president, who like the president was a royal appointee. When the votes of his section were counted he passed his tally to the president, who made up a consolidated report to the ministry in Paris.

For formal rules of procedure within the electoral college, see arts. 10 and 11, law of 5 Feb. 1817 (Duvergier, *Lois,* XXI, 88); a royal ordinance of 20 Aug. 1817 (*ibid.,* pp.200–203); and art. 410 of a royal ordinance of 11 Oct. 1820 (*Bulletin des Lois*).

43. The business of electoral colleges was the same for all three categories, except as members of the arrondissemental colleges voted invariably for single candidates. The accounts of what went on are contained in the procès verbaux, scores of which survive in the F/1c/III cartons of the AN.

44. The names were called from a document called the *liste de votants* which prefects and subprefects had had prepared in advance. It contained the names of voters in alphabetical order, their occupation, the commune of their political domicile, but nothing about their cens, and blank spaces where officers of the college could indicate that they had voted for members of the permanent bureau and candidates for the office of deputy.

became a sort of court of first instance. Consider, for example, the counting of ballots which had been inscribed in an irregular fashion. A friendly bureau in the Aisne in 1824 counted in behalf of Sébastien Maximilien Foy ballots variously inscribed "foy," "Foy," "General Foy" and "foy foy." He would have lost the election had they been nullified. An unfriendly bureau in the Sarthe would not count in behalf of André Marie Jean Jacques Dupin a group of ballots inscribed "Dupin aîné" – the name by which he was known to thousands. Without these votes he lost the election.

The secretary of the bureau was the man who drafted the procès verbal which, when signed by the president, went to the ministry of the interior and ultimately to the chamber.

One readily perceives why political sophisticates put such store by having their friends sit on the permanent bureaux, or as few of their enemies as possible.

The day after the permanent bureau was chosen – and the second day of the college – the actual balloting for candidates for the deputyship began. In 1827 it was Sunday, 18 November. Deferring to the solemnity of the occasion many a president disregarded the stipulation of the law and enjoined the voters to attend mass before gathering one hour late. Much the same procedure as the day before followed: voters who had missed the Saturday oath-taking took it this day when they came forward to vote for their candidate.

Notable, of course, was the complete absence of nominating speeches, indeed of any public nominations at all.[45] Most voters came to the college knowing exactly whom they would vote for. Those who did not, or who were in general innocence of the identities of the front-running candidates, received a speedy education outside the polling place either in man-to-man encounters or in informal caucuses. Balloting took place as each voter came forward, wrote a single name on a piece of paper, folded it and handed it to the president, who dropped it into the box. With the last vote in, the president called for the count.[46] To win on this, the first ballot,

45. Art. 8 of the law of 5 Feb. 1817 states that the electoral colleges must confine themselves strictly to the business of electing deputies, that all discussion, all deliberation was forbidden. The rule was not construed as forbidding presidents of the colleges the right to make tedious speeches at the opening of the proceedings.

46. Art. 13 of the law of 5 Feb. 1817 states that the working session of the college should last six hours and that the voting was to cease at 3 p.m. However, a ministerial circular of 1 Nov. 1820 (Duvergier, *Lois,* XXIII, 182) gave presidents the license to keep a college in session until every voter had had an opportunity to vote.

or the second which would take place the next day, a candidate had to receive votes representing one third of the inscribed voters and a majority of those present and voting.[47] In cases where a third ballot was necessary the race would be narrowed to the two leaders and decided by simple majority.[48]

The normal calm of voting could be dramatically upset as for example in Bourbon Vendée, when opposition voters felt that the secrecy of the ballot was being jeopardized by the fact that members of the bureau were close enough to read the name that a voter wrote. They offered a loud complaint and a request that a box be put on the table to shield the ballot from wandering official eyes. The president suggested that those who felt a want of privacy should shield their ballots with their hats. This caused a redoubling of the uproar, particularly on the part of those who feared that civil servants who wished to vote against the ministerial candidate would give themselves away in the hat manoeuvre.

At this point the prefect, the comte de Suleau, entered the room, caught the drift of the argument about the hat and, all unknowing who had suggested it in the first place, is reported to have cried, "c'est une infamie. . . ." When he learned of his unintended affront to the president, who happened to be the department's top-ranking magistrate, he tried to quiet things. Voting was finally resumed but not terminated at the legal hour of 3 p.m. Finally, there was the noise of a carriage outside and the hurried entry of two late voters. There were objections to these votes being cast beyond the hour of closure, at which the president declared it was not yet three and made the grievous error of pulling out his watch to prove it. Those nearby saw that the hands of the watch stood at 3:15 and said as much. Then followed the day's real turmoil causing the president to threaten to clear the premises by armed force. There came relative calm and a counting of ballots with a majority going to the ministerial candidate, Boscal de Réals.[49]

47. Art. 7 of the law of 29 June 1820 (*ibid.*, 15).

48. Art. 14 of the law of 5 Feb. 1817, borrowed from legislation of Napoleon's day. Some races, still tied at the end of the third ballot, continued day after day until someone came out on top.

49. AN F/1c/III Vendée 3. See the procès verbal which in a measured and stilted way makes clear that the proceedings were something other than routine. See also the indignant letter of the bishop of Luçon to min. int., 18 Nov. 1827, and the more temperate report of a captain of gendarmes of 19 Nov. A fulsome account occurs in the pamphlet by Un Electeur, *Détails sur ce qui s'est passé . . . Bourbon-Vendée* (Paris, n.d.) BN Le/54.338.

It is probable that lesser ructions of this sort took place more frequently than the procès verbaux would lead one to suspect, but who knows?

For most colleges, two or three sessions sufficed, and their returns were dispatched to Paris by the speediest means at hand.[50] Thus by Wednesday or Thursday the results of a good many of the arrondissemental and special elections were appearing in the Paris press. The outcome of the elections of the large colleges where a single balloting might have required more than six hours and of those in some of the remote arrondissements were not known until the end of the week.[51]

Then starting again on Saturday, 24 November, the whole process began again, this time in the chefs lieux of the departments for the benefit of the departmental voters. Where these colleges had more than a single deputy to elect they used the scrutin de liste procedures. Otherwise, business was conducted as in the arrondissemental colleges and terminated in about the same time interval. Upon rare occasion the freedom of the departmental voters to choose whomever they wanted from among the eligibles was curtailed. Article 42 of the charter held that one half of the deputies from a given department had to be residents of that department. Sometimes the arrondissemental colleges of this given department used up the quota of "out-of-department" deputies in their elections, thus forcing the departmental voters to choose among local residents only.

Just who would qualify as a local resident was merely one of the multitude of data which prefects and their subordinates had assembled in preparation for the election. For example, they had passed through the ardors of list-making. This had heavily involved the officers who assessed and collected the direct taxes. These men had had to scour their tax records to calculate the cens of would-be voters. It had also involved clerks in the prefecture and the subprefectures in massive correspondence with distant officials, in an

50. Circular messages went out from the ministry of the interior in the second week of November 1827 telling those prefects who were on the telegraph (semaphore) line to use it, those who were near it to send their returns by special courier to a neighboring prefect who did have access to the telegraph, etc. AD Bouches-du-Rhône M/2(III)-9, min. int. to pref., 12 Nov. 1827.

51. Communications with Corsica were so slow that the election there was not even called for the 17 November date. When the prefect of Corsica got the ordinance of 5 Nov. 1827, he was probably relieved to learn that his election would not come until January 1828.

effort to turn up out-of-department tax payments or certificates of birth (usually for favored voters, to be sure). The mechanics of readying the lists for the printer, and the rectification tables, and the cards of admission for every voter; the seeing to the proper distribution of such documents and the preparation of the final liste de votants — these were duties over and above the normal chores of office.

As the first day of the election approached there was the array of tedious little housekeeping duties to be performed. The meeting place of the college had to have a dais, the president's table and chair, places for the members of the bureau, a place for the voter to write out his ballot, paper, pens and ink, and so on. The details come down to us in a little clutch of documents in Vesoul which are the account of petty expenditures required of the subprefect of the arrondissement of Gray and the mayor of Vesoul.[52] The entries convey across the years the message of trivia which occupied the attention of these two fairly important officials.

Owing to the subprefect, for example, was a total of 461 francs, the greater part to go to a printer for printing up the last rectification table, the royal ordinance, a broadside about the election, and the election cards. Other items were a charge of 4 francs to move a platform from storage to the proper room in the *mairie* and 10 francs to move it back, 4 more francs for a wooden plank to augment its size, 15 francs for stove wood to heat the room, small sums for paper, quill pens, pen knives, and an ink well (at 6 francs!), 10 francs for extra cleaning and sweeping of the room before, during, and after the electoral sessions, and 24 francs to the sieur Jobard, the bell ringer, for having tolled the great bell four times at each of the two college meetings *à trois francs par coup.*

52. AD Haute-Saône 7 M 7.

4 / The Campaign of the Oppositions (I)

Almost a half a year before the sieur Jobard had first tolled his bell in Vesoul, those opposing the Villèle government began mobilizing forces for a political campaign. As usual Paris was the birthplace. These two groups came to life around leaders of the opposition's right and left wings: one around the charismatic figure of François René, the vicomte de Chateaubriand, the other around the young men of the *Globe.*

Chateaubriand was in many ways the ideal man to rally that part of the opposition composed of ultras and more moderate royalists who had a personal aversion to the Villèle government. He was a man of impeccable credentials, one whose devotion to crown and charter could no more be doubted than his unswerving profession of the faith, a man who had held high diplomatic posts (Stockholm, Berlin, London, and chief of the French delegation to the Congress of Verona), and who had served as foreign minister under Villèle. From his position as editor of the *Conservateur* he had attacked the governments of Richelieu and Decazes, and had gained a well-deserved reputation as a journalist. He was a thoughtful and articulate political philosopher who put freedom of the press high on his list of attributes of the good society.

By no means least in the array of qualities fitting him for the new role was his bitter enmity for Villèle, who, under royal instructions, had dropped him from his cabinet post (6 June 1824). Thence he had joined the staff of the *Journal des Débats* in whose columns, with Bertin de Vaux, the owner, he led the anti-Villèle vendetta.

The ordinance of 24 June 1827 which reimposed the censorship upon the periodic press brought his anger to a new pitch and triggered an action which went far beyond his immediate concern over the censorship. Early in the second half of July he published a pamphlet which bears the title, *Marche et effets de la censure.*[1] At the top of the title page are the words "Amis de la liberté de la presse."

1. (Paris, 1827) BN Lb/49.629, 32 pp. This was the second pamphlet which Chateaubriand wrote on the censorship.

The first, *Du Rétablissement de la censure . . .* (available in most collected works, see,

The pamphlet begins with the matter of the censorship. For twenty-three pages it sticks closely to the point, then charges off in a new direction – politics, and the election which may be around the corner. To paraphrase: if we do not wish to have censorship as a permanent way of life let us watch the enemies of our liberties, let us act together. The elections which we expect to be coming can be our salvation. Reflect on the recent by-election and the defeat of the government's candidate; censorship did not save him.[2] Reflect also upon the excellent new law on the jury, remember that the jury lists are electoral lists. "Realize that no one will come to your home to alert you to your opportunity to be inscribed as a voter; surely the authorities will not, and the press under the yoke of the censorship will have to keep still. The first of October will arrive and if the chamber of deputies is dissolved what will you do?" In such fashion did an organization whose reason for being was the concept and fact of censorship of the press slip over into the area of political action.

Organization? Yes. Sometime probably in the first two weeks of July some sort of organization seems to have crystalized around the full name, *Société des amis de la liberté de la presse* – a title which bespoke yet another incarnation of a society which during earlier years of the Restoration had had two or three brief existences. With those, however, it had little in common except the name: Where they had been formed and run by men of the moderate and far left, this was made up of "royalists and ministers out of office";[3] where the former focused their attention on the iniquity of censorship and the plight of journalists and editors in trouble with the law, this took on the political mission of electing a chamber of deputies which would make future censorship unlikely, if not impossible. Fuller direct data on the Friends is all but totally lacking, and what follows is largely a deduction based on a few bits of contemporary evidence and some argument from analogy.

In these early days of July a group of peers and deputies probably

---

for example, *Oeuvres complètes de . . . Chateaubriand* [28 vols., Paris, 1826–1831], XVIII, 69–126), is dated 30 June 1827 and relates purely to the matter of censorship.

2. The reference is, of course, to the well-publicized by-election of mid-July in Angoulême and the victory of Delalot, the candidate of a united opposition.

3. *Times* (of London), 9 Aug. 1827, p. 4, an article by the special French correspondent. The latter's characterization of the membership of the society is journalistic shorthand, but almost certainly generally correct.

met with Chateaubriand.[4] Just who they were is another matter. Probably Barante and Choiseul were in at the beginning,[5] surely Montalivet and Hyde De Neuville were a bit later.[6] The one peer who had perhaps most often put his talent and prestige on the line for the cause of press freedom, the duc de Broglie, says he was not.[7] Some other prominent men: Agier, a deputy and forceful member of the counter-opposition, Alexis de Jussieu of the *Courrier français,* Bertin de Vaux, founder of the *Journal des Débats,* Narcisse Achille Salvandy, pamphleteer and journalist, and Villemain, who lost his chair at the Sorbonne and was ejected from the Academy for professing ideas not acceptable to the Villèle government – these seem to have been Chateaubriand's chief lieutenants.

Of them Salvandy was probably the most involved and by far the most productive. In 1816 at age twenty-one he had achieved a rare notoriety as author of a pamphlet protesting the continued allied occupation of France; the allies pressed Louis XVIII to punish him, and Louis, far from acceding, awaited the withdrawal of the foreign forces and named Salvandy *maître de requêtes* and *conseiller d'état,* though he had just completed his study of the law. With this sort of recognition his reputation changed from that of foolhardy youth to something substantial, even mildly heroic. With his talent as a writer, he joined the *Journal des Débats,* where he shone. As a devotee of Chateaubriand and the causes of the Friends, he was the source of a gusher of short essays put out in pamphlet form. They were humorous, sarcastic, informative, and in the political sense, hortatory. It is hard to say which of the dozen or more most helped the effort – whether it was his first and second *Lettre de la Girafe au Pacha d'Egypte,*[8] his *Explication de la nouvelle loi sur les collèges élec-*

4. Duvergier de Hauranne, *Gouvernement parlementaire,* IX, 289.

5. These two names appear in the roster given by Delavau, the prefect of police of Paris, in a report to the minister of interior dated 7 September 1827 (AN F/7 6772 Seine). Among participating peers of the "constitutional opposition" other than Barante and Choiseul, Delavau names Daru, Molé, Pontécoulant, and Broglie, all of whom were known for their concern with the freedom of the press and all of whom except Broglie may be correct attributions. But this report, considered in its entirety, shows such a dolorous confusion that I am loath to accept any of it without other evidence. See also notes 14 and 22, below.

6. Montalivet and Hyde de Neuville both wrote pamphlets under the society's by-line.

7. Achille, duc de Broglie, *Souvenirs – 1785–1870 – du feu Duc de Broglie . . .* (4 vols., Paris, 1886), III, 101.

8. Paris, [12 July and 8 Aug.], BN Lb/49.621 and 654A. The "Girafe" of these pamphlets was a real giraffe which had arrived in Paris in the early summer – a present to

toraux,[9] or his eight or more *Lettre[s] à M. le rédacteur du Journal des Débats.*[10] Broglie notes that he carried three quarters of the burden of his organization, that he was in his office at the *Journal des Débats* working in shirt-sleeves from morning till late at night and handing out his scratched-up manuscripts faster than the compositors could set them in type.[11]

Though no other author in the Chateaubriand group matched the production record of the tireless Salvandy, at least three turned out pamphlets which equalled his in readership and influence: Félix Bodin's *La Malle Poste . . .* , Montalivet's *Lettre d'un jeune pair de France aux Français de son âge,* and Villemain's *Lettre d'un électeur de Paris. . . .*[12]

Through all these pamphlets and others, which were probably stimulated if not sponsored by Chateaubriand's organization, run three interwoven strands of thought: censorship of the press disregards one of the basic guarantees of the constitutional charter; to be sure, it is temporary but it could easily be made permanent by a docile legislature; the way to prevent such a disaster is to see to it that the next chamber of deputies will have a majority devoted to freedom of the press and opposed to the notion of censorship. This last strand is then splayed out, with references to the law of 2 May and the opportunities it holds for men with the proper qualifications to get on the jury/electoral lists and how they should go about the business; the likelihood of general elections; and how a union of all oppositions can surely defeat the Villèlist candidates even as at Angoulême. Perhaps the most important words in the last statement were "all oppositions," by which the Friends underscored their endorsement of right- and left-wing oppositions getting together to

Charles from the Pascha of Egypt. The press, whose desire to discuss political matters was being frustrated by the censors, found itself giving a lot of space to the giraffe. Salvandy has the giraffe suggest that if the people of France wish to know what is going on in their country they should read the press of Egypt. He goes on to report to the Pascha the great electoral victory at Angoulême where both wings of the opposition united to defeat a man who had the support of the government.

9. BN Lb/49.677.

10. The fifth of the letters (Lb/49.665, dated 16 August) has much in common with its fellows. It begins with fifty-odd pages of general political news of the sort that the press had had to curtail and swings into praise for a recent pamphlet ascribed to Ludovic Vitet and written for the new left-opposition political group, the Société, Aide-toi, le ciel t'aidera, and for another, written by Hyde de Neuville.

11. Broglie, *Souvenirs,* III, 101.

12. BN Lb/49.633, 645, 649.

make common cause against Villèle. Indeed they seem to have been a good bit more tolerant of left-wing brethren than the leftists of the Aide-toi group were of members of the right.

Though almost invariably attached to the issue of the press, the purely political messages of these and other of the Friends' pamphlets, and the exhortation to those qualified to vote to be sure to get themselves registered and carry through with a vote against the government, were nevertheless unequivocally and forcefully put. So much so that there seems little to distinguish these pamphlets from scores of other ephemeral writings which did not have the censorship as a point of departure, but which were frankly anti-government political tracts and do-it-yourself booklets on how best to use the electoral mechanism.

In all likelihood Chateaubriand and his cluster of admirers in Paris had a minimum of formal organization. The written record, at least that of it which I have ransacked, contains no positive direct evidence concerning any organization at all. One senses the most informal sort of arrangement in which right-wing royalists, some doctrinaires, and even some men from the center-left united in their personal distaste for Villèle, their admiration for Chateaubriand, and their outrage at the imposition of censorship. They met in small groups to discuss lobbying techniques, principally the writing and the circulation of their pamphlets, and the means of financing the printing and distribution costs. It is one's guess that Chateaubriand, a man of great commitment and energy, retained an intimate control over the Friends' by-line. He was, indeed, the society's own censor and, as the London *Times* French correspondent wryly notes, nothing was published without his clearance.[13]

Financing probably offered few problems, for printing costs were modest and many of the group were rich men.[14] As to distribution there is some evidence that the postal service purposely delayed delivery of packets of pamphlets for whose dispatch it had accepted the necessary fees.[15] Whatever the reluctance of the postal authori-

13. *Times* (of London), 9 Aug. 1827, p. 4.

14. Those named in the Delavau report (cited in n.5, above), i.e., Casimir Périer, Benjamin Delessert, and Gros-Davilliers, as "the bankers of this society" were almost certainly not. Their "banking" services were far more likely to have been at the disposition of the Aide-toi group (soon to be discussed). Chateaubriand had his own affluent angels.

15. Barante, *Souvenirs,* III, 416–418. Salvandy wrote to Barante (23 Sept. 1827) asking him how he liked the pamphlets and then remarking how he had had to give up sending

ties they could not and did not impede a wide circulation of the Friends' pamphlets. As far as the written record goes it provides more evidence of a national readership than it does for the pamphlets of the better known Société, Aide-toi, le ciel t'aidera.[16] However this was achieved it was not because the Friends strove for a national organization with corresponding branch offices scattered through the provincial cities. Their effort, such as it was, was clearly concentrated in Paris. When it did reach out into the departments it seems to have done so through the agency of some sympathetic and trusted traveler who would carry with him batches of the pamphlets for distribution among his provincial friends. In such a way was the word carried when not entrusted to the postal service.

The word was impressive. Apprehensive prefects commented upon the splash which names like Chateaubriand and Montalivet, peers of France, made among the citizens of their departments. In his pamphlet Montalivet had mentioned an electoral committee of lawyers and propriétaires helping would-be voters in the Midi to get inscribed on the lists. Apparently similar committees existed also in Lyon, Villefranche (Rhône), Chalon-sur-Saône, and Nancy. With some perturbation the prefect of the Manche reported that a group of lawyers and doctors in St. Lô were following this example, and he feared that other similar committees were being formed in still other towns in his department.[17]

The prefect of the Creuse had a similar message. On 30 August he reported a flurry of written attacks on Villèle and noted that Montalivet's pamphlet had made the greatest impression. "In line with suggestions in this" and other pamphlets, he wrote,

> young lawyers have formed consulting committees in the *chef lieu* of each arrondissement. There the electoral lists are scrutinized and I have been warned that a few days hence I will receive a great number of protests against the inscription of men who in the event of an election would support candidates of

---

them by post because it had held up the delivery of his packages — a piece of business, "the least indelicate and blameworthy among the activities of those who lead us."

16. In the AN cartons F/7 6767 through 6772 there are reports from 13 prefects which indicate that pamphlets of the Friends had arrived and were being circulated in their departments. These are: Hautes-Alpes, 6 Sept.; Ariège, 1 Sept.; Aveyron, 10 Aug.; Charente, 4 Sept.; Côtes-du-Nord, 8 Sept.; Creuse, 30 Aug.; Gironde, 15 Sept.; Hérault, 29 Nov.; Indre-et-Loire, 6 Aug.; Manche, 1 Sept.; Rhône, 26 Oct.; Deux-Sèvres, 7 Sept.; Vienne, 15 Sept.

17. AN F/7 6770 Manche, 1 Sept. 1827.

the government. I hear that [one of] these committees has decided that [its] young men will begin in mid-September to visit liberal voters in the countryside to urge them to gather the documents which will assure their inscription on the electoral lists.[18]

In the Ariège the prefect reported that fifty copies of Chateaubriand's second pamphlet on the censorship had been delivered to an influential citizen and thence on to "royalist" adherents. Since then copies of the pamphlets of Jussieu, Salvandy, and Montalivet had arrived and been similarly circulated – hand to hand.[19] In the Charente, the pamphlets "of Salvandy, Chateaubriand, Cottu, etc. [sic]" were said to have been perverting the spirit of the royalists. The prefect's report hints that the vicomte de Lézardière – a deputy of the Vendée and well known for his distaste for Villèle – had fetched them with him, and goes on to assert that "rich *négociants* of his department had written to Paris for this sort of literature and that book stores in several arrondissements had such materials for sale." He observed that new writings are hatched each day and are being propagated to every corner of the country.[20]

From Gap (Hautes-Alpes) the prefect reported in a message of 6 September that a merchant who had business with M. Ternaux of the famous textile family (who incidentally in the elections to come was twice elected by his opposition supporters) had brought five hundred copies which were readdressed and dispatched by stagecoach "with the request that they be delivered to the voters as speedily as possible." He added, "it appears that packets of this kind are never addressed twice running to the same person for fear that they would be seized. . . ." Along with his dispatch the prefect forwarded sample copies of the pamphlets – three from the Friends and one from the Société, Aide-toi – all of them laden with pressing exhortations to get inscribed on the electoral rolls, instructions how to do it, and predictions of the dire consequences of a general election in which the forces of "the ministry" should prevail.[21]

In one sense the contemporary record of what the Friends undertook and what the organization accomplished is a half-told tale. I have not encountered, for example, a single press notice relating to

18. AN F/7 6768 Creuse, 1 Sept. 1827.
19. AN F/7 6767 Ariège, 1 Sept. 1827.
20. AN F/7 6768 Charente, 4 Sept. 1827.
21. AN F/7 6767 Hautes-Alpes, 6 Sept. 1827.

its work nor a single document in twoscore or more departmental archives. Yet we do have reports from thirteen different prefects which tell of the circulation of the Friends' pamphlets in their departments and of the political activity which these little tracts seem to have engendered. What lends evidentiary weight to this material is not so much the numerical count (which the pages to come will reveal as significant), but the repeated specific identification of the authors of the pamphlets and the organization in whose behalf they were writing. I incline to the belief that this spare record is the surviving archival trace of a significant nationwide campaign.

So much for the Société des amis de la liberté de la presse. The second group to emerge is the better known, though possibly no more influential, Société, Aide-toi, le ciel t'aidera. Although its aims were defined in terms of a strictly legal sort of activity – helping qualified jurymen/electors to get registered on the jury/electoral list – and though it seems to have given meticulous attention to staying within the limits of article 291 of the criminal code, which forbade organizations of more than twenty members unless specifically authorized, there is the sort of dearth of contemporary information about it which is characteristic of the true secret subversive organization – which, of course, it was not.[22]

22. The best source by a contemporary is probably that of Prosper Duvergier de Hauranne (*Gouvernement parlementaire*, IX, 288–309), who was a contributor to the *Globe* and a friend of many of its staff. He is named among the principals of the Aide-toi; he was close to them professionally, politically, and personally.

Guizot, who was among the moving spirits, wrote an article for the first issue of the *Revue française*, of which he was a founder (see above, chap. 1, n.5). In the article he gives a short account of the kind and amount of activity in which the Aide-toi engaged.

An article in the *Journal des Débats* (15 Nov. 1827, pp. 3–4) thanks those who made "the electoral lists less incomplete than the prefects had planned" and who penetrated the secret of the impending dissolution of the chamber.

There are the two reports of Delavau, prefect of police of Paris, to the minister of the interior, of 7 and 19 Sept. 1827 (AN F/7 6772 Seine). They are very troublesome. For my misgivings about the first, see n.5, above. In its treatment of the Aide-toi the report is so far afield from the Duvergier de Hauranne account, and from a good bit of contemporary indirect evidence, that I conclude that Delavau's informant was for the most part wrong. He has Lafayette as the society's president – which is not so – and he gives a great deal of weight to the retooled Carbonari which they are not entitled to and makes no mention at all of the *Globe* group who were almost certainly the founders. The second report contains, inter alia, information about a liberal electoral organization of Paris whose antecedents go back to 1816. It is hard to tell whether he is describing the Aide-toi with special reference to its activities in the capital, which I think to be the case, or some wholly different organization.

Certain things about it are relatively firm. Its founders were the young men associated with the *Globe,* the three-year-old little newspaper which thrice a week published an attractive array of essays devoted chiefly to literature, the arts, philosophy, and historical writing. Their original idea was to put together a group representing all factions of the left-wing opposition which would bury hatchets and make a powerful united effort to see that their fellow-countrymen availed themselves of the benefits of the 2 May law and got themselves inscribed on the electoral lists. How much Chateaubriand's second pamphlet influenced them is hard to say, but the course which they set themselves was squarely in parallel. The early moves to recruit brought in Guizot, at age thirty-seven already famous, but too young to run for office, and a number of other of the junior doctrinaires: Rémusat, Guizard, and Bourgeois. Others in the same age-group whose politics swung somewhat leftward were Duchâtel, Mignet, Joubert, and Odilon Barrot.[23]

We are now probably in early August; prefects were at work composing the first lists to be posted on the fifteenth and the founders of the Aide-toi were having their organizational pains. Guizot, their natural leader, was out of town and in seclusion following the death of his wife. The London *Times* man in Paris reported, "it is doubtful whether they [the liberal writers who wished to form a society for the publication of pamphlets] will be able to come to an agreement. Though united by common sentiments, they have not come to a sufficiently precise understanding as to the principles they would wish to support by an association."[24] What he probably referred to was the bid for participation by some thirty men whose backgrounds were in Carbonarism; they had dropped the damning word from their vocabularies and referred to themselves as *Francs Parleurs.* Whatever the internal strains, the Francs Parleurs got in without dis-

---

On such frail contemporary stuff rests most of the case for the formation of the Aide-toi. Of the modern treatments of the subject, that by Charles Pouthas in chapter 12 of *Guizot pendant la Restauration . . . (1814–1830)* (Paris: Plon-Nourrit, [1923]) is of course the outstanding one. See the Bibliographical Note.

23. See Pouthas, chap. 12.

24. *Times* (of London), 9 Aug. 1827, p. 2. See also *Mémoires posthumes de Odilon Barrot,* 2nd ed. (4 vols., Paris, 1875–1876), I, 79 ff. Barrot thought the young men of the Aide-toi were too self-assured and self-satisfied. "They repelled more than they attracted because of the absoluteness of their doctrines, their unbending attitudes, their intolerance. . . ."

rupting the nascent organization for which Vitet of the *Globe* provided the motto which became its name.

In very short order there were more than a hundred members, a matter which caused immediate concern lest the society run afoul the law which limited the membership of unauthorized organizations (article 291 of the criminal code). Accordingly at a meeting at the house of the banker Paravey, at which Guizot is said to have presided, an executive committee of fewer than twenty was formed and the larger organization abdicated in its favor. Four of the extreme left-wing Francs Parleurs were put on this top committee: Desloges, Joubert, and two unidentified others. The rest were: Guizot, president; Odilon Barrot, Barthe, Damiron, Desclozeaux, Dubois, Duchâtel, Prosper Duvergier de Hauranne, Lerminier, Marchais, Paravey, Rémusat, Renouard, Sautelet, and Vitet. Marchais was the secretary; the premises of the *Globe* was the headquarters. Here was talent in abundance.

In its first publication, Vitet's pamphlet, *Aux Citoyens et aux électeurs,*[25] was articulated the society's overriding practical political goal of having all "friends of liberty" who possessed the qualifications of age, residence, and property get themselves inscribed on the electoral lists. "Above all think to 30 September [the last day in the list-making calendar]," it urged. The ministry is looking at the make-up of the lists as a matter of life and death. If it should see us weaken in our efforts, it will dissolve the chamber, summon the electoral colleges, and on the wave of its victory at the polls, rule for another seven years. As to the business of getting inscribed, in a few days we will print eighty thousand copies of a document, *Manuel de l'électeur,* which will discuss the techniques which you must know.

Along with this message went the injunction for friends of liberty in the departments themselves to organize, but not in groups of more than twenty, and themselves print up hortatory pamphlets. It pointed out that 150 francs could pay the costs of some three thousand copies of a short document.

The Aide-toi's second publication was the well-known *Manuel de l'électeur-juré: Aux Electeurs du département de [l'Ain],* published in mid-August,[26] in a proclaimed 110,000 copies, and destined for

25. BN Lb/49.661.

26. Aide-toi, *Manuel de l'électeur-juré: Aux Electeurs du département de [l'Ain]* (Paris, [1827]) BN Lb/49.670. This pamphlet appeared in 86 slightly different guises.

gratis distribution. After a prognosis of impending elections, which would rest on this year's electoral lists, it urges the engagement in legal battle with the ministry which has oppressed the country these several years. It points again to the provisions of the law of 2 May which ineluctably linked jury service and the right to vote, and hints – in defiance of the legislative history of the law – that this coupling of the two functions was probably designed to make the threat of jury service an inhibition to would-be voters. But note well, it says, you who think to evade the repugnant jury service by denying yourselves the vote may deny yourselves all right, but find to your disgust that the authorities have nevertheless inscribed you on the jury list at some later date. Furthermore, it adds, the existence of the other pool of juror material – the so-called second part of the jury list[27] – lessens the chances of your having to serve.

With these thoughts as an introduction the publication swings into its main theme: What you must have and what you must do to get on this year's electoral list. For nine pages there follow the mosaic of requirements, of the documentation to prove that one has fulfilled them, and instructions as to where and how the documents are to be filed. For all but the trickiest questions of inscription this text would suffice, for it stresses the technical details and the importance of having each one meticulously observed. Indeed, one of the main thrusts of this presentation is the difficulty of the task about to be undertaken, the desirability of getting sound advice from outside advisers, and the necessity for skepticism, if not positive distrust, for the word of any government functionary. Should an applicant's appeal for inscription be denied by the authorities, he should be aware of his rights of appeal, first for a provisional ruling by the prefect in council and subsequently by the courts or the conseil d'état.[28]

Though the text was identical, there was a title page addressed to the electors of each of the 86 departments. The BN has bound up all 86 in a single volume. On p. 1 it speaks of "the six weeks" which remain to get on the electoral lists. This, of course, figures out to about mid-August.

27. The "second part" of the jury list was composed of men who were not electors but whose occupations proclaimed them substantial enough citizens to play a role in the jury.

28. The ordinance of 4 Sept. 1820 required that the prefect act within five days of a formal application for inscription.

Articles 5 and 6 of the law of 5 Feb. 1817 held that the cours royales had final jurisdiction over claims of would-be voters with respect to their civil or political rights and that the conseil d'état had the final say regarding matters of tax payments and political domicile.

Perhaps addressed more to lawyers whose assistance would be queried by aspirant voters with difficult technical problems than to the non-professional citizen was a bibliographical note which cited, inter alia, the treatises of Victor Guichard and Jacques-Julien Dubochet, and of Isambert. Following the reference to these highly relevant works came a second bibliography of twenty pamphlets devoted to the matter of the censorship – many of them the issuances of the Chateaubriand Friends.[29]

Another pamphlet, bearing the Aide-toi device and signed Ludovic Vitet, which probably came out later indicates that the Aide-toi and the Friends had come together and were working in close collaboration. The Vitet publication begins by telling about some of the Friends' pamphlets and goes on to say how important it is that they be disseminated throughout the country. The voters should read them. To help this worthy endeavor he makes a strong appeal for funds to cover the cost of distribution.[30] Duvergier de Hauranne, who should have known, says that "letters" were addressed to the voters of the Cher, Gironde, Rhône, and Seine-Inférieure under the joint editorship of the two groups, which as he says put the public interest above small personal considerations.[31] Obviously getting

29. Aide-toi, *Manuel de l'électeur-juré,* p. 41. The work by Victor Guichard and Jacques-Julien Dubochet was their *Manuel du juré, . . . et commentaire de la loi du 2 mai 1827 . . .* (Paris, 1827). The work of Isambert is cited as "*Guide électoral.*" Presumably this is an erroneous reference to his *Instruction aux citoyens français pour la reconnaissance de leurs droits d'électeurs et de jurés* (Paris, August 1827), "par l'auteur du 'Code électoral' " (BN Le/8.18).

Among other pamphlets cited were Isambert's *Courtes observations adressées aux électeurs-jurés . . .* (Paris, 1827), of which I have found no trace other than this Aide-toi reference; M[oureau de Vaucluse], *Loi sur l'organisation du jury . . . sur les élections* (Paris, 1827); and N. A. Salvandy, *Explication de la nouvelle loi sur les collèges électoraux et les jurys, . . .* ([Paris, c. 20 Aug. 1827]) BN Lb/49.677.

François-André Isambert was a lawyer and student of the law of outstanding reputation. In 1820, on the heels of the passage of the electoral law of the double vote, he published a volume in which he codified for the benefit of the would-be voter the web of legislation which governed the whole electoral process. Its title (shortened) was: *Code électoral, comprenant la charte, les lois des élections, . . .* (BN Le/8.166).

Isambert was a scholar first and foremost, and though his political sympathies almost certainly rested with the opponents of Villèle there are few if any bits of evidence to link him to the active phases of the Aide-toi's campaign of 1827. He probably joined the Aide-toi in 1830.

30. Ludovic Vitet, no title other than the name of the Society (n.p., n.d.) BN Lb/49.666.

31. Duvergier de Hauranne, *Gouvernement parlementaire,* IX, 294–295, 335. Just what these letters were is unknown. One's first thought is that they were the usual printed missive issued in pamphlet form, *Aux Electeurs [of such and such department].* There are such pamphlets in the BN collection: Le/54.208, Cher; Lb/49.676, Gironde (the title

together took some painful yielding on both sides, for there were Chateaubriand adherents who looked upon the left wing of the Aide-toi – represented by the Francs Parleurs – as revolutionary maniacs, and there were Aide-toi supporters for whom no spoon could be long enough to sup with the black reactionaries among the Friends.

Whatever the amount of collaborative writing, the production of the Aide-toi alone was impressive. Between the appearance of the two pamphlets of early August and one put out shortly after the elections in late November, the Aide-toi in Paris got out at least another dozen publications bearing its identifying motto.[32] These carry the classical message of any partiasan political organization intent on winning a national election: first an indictment of the opposing faction and an exhortation for citizens who possessed the qualifications to get registered, as we would say. As the summer wore on and as the government's confidential messages to the prefects about the king's right to call an election whenever he desired began to leak, the Aide-toi pamphlets move on to emphasizing the importance of seeking out appropriate candidates and rallying behind them in unified strength. As the certainty grew that the king was in fact going to exercise his prerogative (the Aide-toi knew of the king's decision to dissolve the chamber seemingly within a day or less), the emphasis moves on to the overriding necessity for the qualified voters to get to the polling place and vote.[33] Except for the

---

here is *Correspondance privée*); Lb/49.665 and 695, Rhône; and Lb/49.694, Seine-Inférieure (entitled *Songez au 30 Septembre*); but only one of them bears the Aide-toi device and none has any reference to the Friends. The content of all four is however straight down the policy line of the two groups.

32. These are, in the BN Lb/49 series: Aide-toi, [no title], 666; . . . *des Obsèques de Manuel,* 681; **Il faut semer . . . ,* 707; **Sur le Projet de dissolution,* 734; **Aux Electeurs,* 745; Aide-toi, [no title], 752; **Manuel de l'électeur,* 753; *Aux Electeurs,* 774; *Dernier Avis aux électeurs,* 777.

In the little bibliographical preamble to Guizot's article in the *Revue française* (see above, chap. 1, n.5) he lists ten Aide-toi publications, four of which are marked above with an asterisk. The other six he mentions are the two I cite in notes 25 and 26 above, plus: *Aux Electeurs du Cher,* Le/54.208 or 209; *Aux Electeurs de la Charente Inférieure,* Lb/49.764; Gallix, *Lettre à un électeur de Lyon . . . ,* Lb/49.662; *Sur la Liste électorale . . . Meuse,* Lb/49.728. Note that the Gallix document above carries no trace of Aide-toi authorship. This suggests that another dozen or more pamphlets which proclaim the Aide-toi general line and bear no trace of its sponsorship may also be of its production.

33. The pamphlet entitled *Sur le Projet de dissolution . . .* (just cited) bears the date 17 October 1827. It begins with the story of the confusion in the government whether or not to go for an election, and ends with the call to organize and vote. It will be recalled that Villèle gave 24 October as the day when the king formally decided to dissolve the chamber (Villèle diary).

incidentals characteristic of the sixth year of Villèle's incumbency there was little that was new or surprising in the broad outlines of the program as developed in these pamphlets. Probably all politically conscious Frenchmen had heard it all before and probably more than once.

A good many historians of both the nineteenth century and our own have written of the campaign of 1827 as if it had begun from scratch and as if the surprising success of opposition candidates derived almost wholly from the men of the Aide-toi. On the face of things such a generalization arouses the well-merited suspicion which I have awarded it.

As already noted there is some contemporary evidence of a general character that describes roughly who the Aide-toi leaders were, what they set out to do, and the enthusiasm with which they spread the word of their program to all parts of the country. Guizot tells of their zeal for publication, their challenges to authority, their indefatigable letter-writings and traveling about;[34] Duvergier de Hauranne, another participant, speaks of meetings taking place everywhere.[35] There is also the very impressive evidence of the pamphlets themselves; they would be hard to surpass as partisan political documents.

But if you are one who likes to have his stories spelled out fully in materials of prime authenticity you will be disappointed in the archival traces of the Société, Aide-toi. Of the large number of prefectoral reports which were responsive to the ministry's request of 5 July 1827, I have found three which mention the Société, Aide-toi by that name.[36] In each case the reference is to the sponsor of a pamphlet, not to an organization. I have found three others in which the title of a pamphlet identifies it as an Aide-toi issuance, but which at the same time lacks all mention of the issuing organization.[37] Finally I have found three reports which ascribe the circulation of pamphlets and other electoral activity to a "comité

34. See his article in the *Revue française,* I, 23.

35. Duvergier de Hauranne, *Gouvernement parlementaire,* IX, 335.

36. These are the reports already referred to in chap. 2 which are contained in the AN cartons F/7 6767–6772: Eure-et-Loir, pref. to min. int., 6 Oct. 1827; Haute-Garonne, pref. to min. int. 4 Sept. 1827; Morbihan, pref. to min. int., 8 Oct. 1827.

37. In the appropriate carton: Landes, pref. to min. int., 29 Sept. 1827; Meurthe, cdr. of gendarmes to pref., 23 Sept. 1827; Meuse, pref. to min. int., 9 Sept. 1827.

directeur" in Paris.[38] If the prefects were aware of the existence of the new group, they did not cite it by name, but went back to the established pejorative. And that is the sum of the incontrovertible evidence regarding the Aide-toi that I have found in the National and Departmental Archives of France.

Evidence of electoral activity in the departments which suggests an extension of the Aide-toi influence from Paris exists in a group of pamphlets each of which bears the Aide-toi label. These, not always printed locally, are addressed to the opposition voters of the Charente-Inférieure, Cher, Hérault, Loiret, Lot, Orne, Seine-Inférieure, Seine-et-Oise, Somme, and Yonne.[39]

There is one other piece of evidence which lengthens the list of departmental organizations with some sort of relationship to the parent group in Paris. This is within one of the best-known Aide-toi pamphlets: *Il faut semer pour recueillir.*[40] Towards its end it notes that there are now publicly organized electoral societies in twenty-one departments and others in the process of formation. Of these departments the Aube, Aude, Calvados, Côte-d'Or, Drôme, Gard, Indre, Indre-et-Loire, Isère, Maine-et-Loire, Puy-de-Dôme, Haut-Rhin, Rhône, Saône-et-Loire, Seine, and Seine-et-Marne are new. The other five are among the nineteen departments already noted. If one assumes that the sixteen new ones are affiliates, though nowhere clearly proclaimed as such, then there were at least thirty-five departments within which the Aide-toi influence was probably direct and demonstrable. This figure is to be contrasted with the findings

38. In the appropriate carton: Côtes-du-Nord, pref. to min. int., 8 Sept. 1827; Manche, pref. to min. int., 1 Sept. 1827; Haute-Saône, pref. to min. int., 29 Sept. 1827. In the Jura and Vosges folders of the AN cartons there are reports from the prefects which connect a local electoral organization to the "Comité Directeur" in Paris.

39. Two of these pamphlets are from the BN Lb/49 series: 693, Loiret; and 734, Charente-Inférieure. The rest are from the BN Le/54 series as follows: 206, Charente-Inférieure; 208 and 209, Cher; 233, Hérault; 260, Lot; 280, Orne; 189 [sic], Seine-Inférieure; 318, Seine-et-Oise; 332, Somme; and 350, Yonne. Guizot says that those for the Cher were prepared in Paris, hence they need not indicate local Aide-toi activity. It so happens that there is a letter in the Guizot correspondence (AN, 42 AP 203) from Duchâtel (9 Sept. 1827) which proves that there was a branch in the Charente-Inférieure, and a pamphlet bearing Duvergier de Hauranne's name from the Cher which pretty much does the same for that department.

Note that these pamphlets are not to be confused with an earlier one; see note 26 above regarding BN Lb/49.670.

40. Lb/49.707, cited in note 32 above.

of other students of the period who say that they have found better evidence – archival for the most part – for a considerably larger number of departments.

If one uses less rigorous criteria than mine – for example, if every time a prefect reports upon the circulation of opposition pamphlets, without designation of title, author, or identifiable sponsor, in his department or reports upon a concerted effort by liberal leaders to get new voters on the lists or to get questionable ones taken off, one assumes that the activity in question was Aide-toi motivated or directed – then the list of departments in which putative Aide-toi influence was being exerted is perhaps twice as long as the one I have set forth.[41] My point is not that there was not a prodigious and effective opposition campaign being waged in almost every department, but that there is not adequate hard evidence to warrant ascribing it all to the Aide-toi.

Without trying to detract from the great accomplishment of the Aide-toi group, there were other forces at work that summer which are owing a share of credit for the outcome of the election. First among these is the Chateaubriand group, which has already been discussed. Its arrangements with the Aide-toi (and they can be discerned only in rough outline), if they accomplished nothing else, lent the Aide-toi strength from a quarter it probably could not have reached on its own.

Next was the opposition press of Paris: the *Constitutionnel* and the *Courrier français* and, to a lesser extent, the *Journal des Débats.* There can be little question that the editors and working journalists of these three newspapers were in close touch with the work of the Friends and the Aide-toi, but it is a difficult thing to document. Whereas it is pretty well established that Bertin de Vaux, the publisher of the *Débats,* and Salvandy, a staff writer, were wholly committed to the electoral program of the Friends, the *Débats* itself carried during the summer and early fall comparatively little news of the struggle to register the opposition vote.[42]

41. For example the prefect of the Vienne wrote on 10 Jan. 1828 that "*comités* of the liberal party [have been] established in all or almost all departments to complain about electoral lists." AN (misfiled in) F/1c/III Vaucluse 4. I would not assume that they were all Aide-toi branches.

42. *Journal des Débats,* 12 July, pp. 3–4. A deadpan notice about how to get inscribed on the list with a verbatim quotation from the law of 2 May 1827 is probably a paraphrase of an official notice issued by Chabrol de Volvic, prefect of the Seine. An article of 22 Aug.

The *Constitutionnel,* with a circulation near twenty thousand (perhaps the largest in France), and the *Courrier français* carried a great number of articles running straight through the period of the censorship, from 24 June to 5 November 1827. There is however within them not a syllable of partisan politics; no mention of the "lovers of liberty of department X or arrondissement Y" and their efforts to inscribe like-minded voters, no mention of the well-known opposition figure who has been persuaded to stand for office. Any hint that the editors believed that there was a general election in the offing had to be wormed out by the diligent reader who asked himself, "if no election why all the fuss about registering?" It had to be this way to satisfy the censors.

But what the censors did not and perhaps dared not forbid was copy designed to inform qualified men what they should do to get on the jury list. If then it was pointed out that appearance on the "first list" of the jury, and eligibility for that repugnant duty, meant that a man was ipso facto on the electoral list, that had to be all right too. The *Constitutionnel* began at that point with a notice to the effect that it was printing a book entitled *Loi sur l'organisation du jury, avec un commentaire des articles de cette loi qui se rapportent aux collèges électoraux,* without mentioning Victor Moureau, the author, by name. Two weeks later it devoted a long piece to the book's content, stressing the author's discussion of the documents necessary for registration of the juryman/voter, his treatment of the recourses open to the applicant who was having trouble with the prefect, and his emphasis on the point that, once registered, the voter could not be cavalierly dropped from the rolls; in other words, the nuisance of getting on the lists ought by law at least to be a one-shot affair.[43]

From there on, two or three times a week the *Constitutionnel* would run an article bearing upon electoral matters. There were for example a number of items urging qualified men to get themselves

(p.2) is the first and indeed the only one with an exhortation to qualified voters to get themselves registered. Its point of departure, like the first, was an announcement by the prefect of the Loiret which told would-be voters that the appearance of their names on the first list (that posted on 15 August) did not mean anything unless they personally had justified their names' presence there by filing a complete set of the necessary documents at the prefecture. This is about all.

43. *Constitutionnel,* 23 June, p. 2; *ibid.,* 10 July, p. 2. For reasons I find inexplicable the author's name is rendered "M.M *** (deV***)."

enrolled,[44] a warning, if they found their names on the initial list, not to relax their efforts to collect and file the documents lest their names not appear on the list that counted: the last one.[45] There were almost a score of articles of the question-answer sort dealing with the legal perplexities of inscription.

Coming from the principal legal experts of the capital, the answers were likely to be authoritative. There is no information about where the questions came from, but it is a fair guess that many came from puzzled lawyers in the departments who were serving opposition electoral committees, of the kind advocated by the Friends and the Aide-toi. Where the answers went was everywhere; the *Constitutionnel* was required reading for most of the politically conscious of France who leaned leftward from Villèle. Even if the reader himself had no registration problem, reading about those of others focused his thoughts for a moment or two exactly where the *Constitutionnel* wanted them directed. Reporting generally about how lists in various departments were coming along probably served this same end.[46]

The *Courrier français* followed much the same course, but with a good bit less insistence. Its question and answer service was less active, but as its legal adviser it had none other than Isambert himself, the leading expert on electoral law.[47] Its exhortations to get on the rolls, its warnings to the undocumented registree who stopped worrying when he found his name whimsically inscribed on one of the pre-final lists, and its notations about the progress of lists in the departments were up to the *Constitutionnel's* standards.[48]

It is perhaps to honor unduly a *fauve* of the far right to include him in this company. But this Jean Raymond Pascal Sarran will have a place here because his was an early exemplar of the circulated newsletter and because even if he made no votes for the ultras of

44. *Ibid.,* 15 July, p. 2; 18 July, p. 2; 2 Aug., p. 3; 2 Sept., p. 3.

45. *Ibid.,* 20 July, p. 2: Chabrol de Volvic's warning to voters of the Seine of the costs to them of failing to put together a complete dossier of the necessary documents; 19 Aug.: same for the prefect of the Loiret; 21 Aug., p. 2: same for the prefect of the Bas-Rhin.

46. See *ibid.,* 12, 14, 16, 18, 19, 21 Aug.; 1, 4, 9, 27 Sept.; 12, 15 Oct.; 1 Nov. The point was probably that this was another bit of allowable news which would contribute to the general interest in electoral matters.

47. *Courrier français,* 30 Aug.; 12 Sept. and 26 Sept. (Isambert's answer); 2, 3 Oct. It gave special notices, not to Isambert's *Instruction,* but rather to the *Manuel du Juré* of Victor Guichard and J.-J. Dubochet.

48. *Courrier français,* 11, 20, 21, 22, and 28 July; 15, 17, 18, 19, 20, 22, 25, 31 Aug.; 1, 24 Sept.; 10, 18. 21 Oct.

the counter-opposition he made a number of prefects very nervous. Son of a tailor of Montpellier, and a man who had had a few unimportant jobs there, he had gone to Paris and set himself up as one of the main props of the monarchy.[49] He had founded in 1821 the *Association constitutionnelle pour la défense des intérêts légitimes,* whose aim was to compensate noble families who had lost their fortunes in the Revolution.[50] Somewhere along the line, he had achieved a civil-list pension with which he was able to support a secret correspondence directed mostly against the Villèle ministry.

"Here is a man," wrote the prefect of the Hérault, "who finds no one royalist enough." The dispatch was written in the context of Sarran's activities during the early days of the censorship of 1827, when he sent out a lithographed announcement of his intention to publish a newsletter. For twenty-five francs the half-year you could have his weekly offering which would publish that denied to the periodic press and more. He would give you the inside story from highly placed sources on the plans and other occult activities of the ministry; he would have news and anecdotes of the court. Probably several hundred such invitations went out, thirty to people of Montpellier alone.

What he actually gave the subscribers was something short of the promise. The substance was largely lurid gossip, and on the face of it, rubbish. But like all effective propaganda, even the most improbable stories had within them a tiny grain of fact upon which Sarran deposited layer after layer of non-nacreous fancy. Prefects reported the circulation of the newsletter in their departments and sent in samples, and the ministry got excited and queried a number of others as to whether or not Sarran had subscribers in their departments.[51] Quite obviously the ministry feared the opposition lurking to its right, and perhaps with good reason it feared that an *exalté* like Sarran could and would galvanize an electoral effort in behalf of ultra candidates. The prefect of the Morbihan told of just such an effort in his hitherto safe department.[52] Given the number of ultras who

49. AN F/7 6769 Hérault, pref. to min. int., 9 July 1827.

50. Duvergier de Hauranne, *Gouvernement parlementaire,* VI, 405.

51. AN F/7 6768 Côte-d'Or: one of the Sarran news-letters is here, dated 6–9 Sept. 1827; F/7 6770 Meuse, pref. to min. int., 9 Sept. 1827; F/7 6771 Hautes-Pyrénées, as above, 3 Sept. 1827: the prefect is answering a ministerial query *re* Sarran; F/7 6772 Deux-Sèvres, as above.

52. AN F/7 6770 Morbihan, as above, 8 Oct. 1827.

were elected on their own or in "monstrous alliance" with the left – it surpassed government estimates by a good bit – the efforts of Sarran almost certainly made their modest contribution to the outcome of the election.

Another contribution, and a quite different one, was made by some of the opposition's great men who traveled about leaving in their wake a surge of political enthusiasm. Dupont de l'Eure and Bignon were active in some of the Normandy departments; Benjamin Constant in Alsace; and Ternaux in the Haute-Vienne. Lafayette *fils* and Dupin *aîné* made appearances in the Massif Central. The man of law Charles Cottu, conseiller at the cour royale of Paris and well-known for his attacks on the government, journeyed to Bordeaux where he met two other opposition leaders, Laffitte and Ternaux, and on into the southerly departments; Gauthier, an opposition deputy of Bordeaux, preceded him to his constituency and was credited with carrying a batch of damaging rumors. Other deputies – not all of them of the opposition – who had firm roots in their departments left Paris with the end of the legislative session in June and went home to cultivate their parishes. Charles Etienne, the well-known writer who had an association with the *Minerve* and who had lost his seat in the chamber in the election of 1824 and sought reelection from the Meuse, was home for the summer and "spared no effort to enlarge the number of liberal voters on the lists and to maintain and widen their estrangement from the government."[53] Later on in the interval between the publication of the ordinance of dissolution and the election there was a great step-up in this kind of activity, but one must regard it as the topping off of an operation begun weeks or months before.

Of all the phenomena in aid of the victory of the two oppositions, the one I feel to have been most important and perhaps least acknowledged by my predecessors was the backlog of practical experience which opposition political figures had garnered in past electoral battles.

By the time the election of November 1827 came around, the 300-franc censeurs had been through the general elections of 1815,

53. See AD Bas-Rhin III M 19, 13 and 14 Aug. 1827; AN F/7 6770 Haute-Loire, pref. to min. int., 15 Aug. 1827; AN F/7 6769 Gironde: memo of min. int. based upon a report from the prefect, and min. int. to pref. of Basses-Pyrénées, 4 Sept. 1827, and *ibid.*, pref. to min. int., 7 June 1827; AN F/7 6770 Meuse, pref. to min. int., 9 Sept. 1827.

1816, and 1824; all regular voters had been through at least one of the partial elections which, after 1816, elected one fifth of the chamber each year in rotation. The regular voters of the I and II series of departments had been through two such partial elections. The so-called departmental voters, those post-1820 who possessed the double vote, had all voted in 1820 and 1824, and those of them who were registered in the departments of the V, I, and II series had all had a second experience in 1821 and 1822.[54] In other words, the years between 1815 and 1824, especially between 1817 and 1824, produced a great amount of electoral business and afforded rich opportunities to learn and practice the electoral arts.

During these years there had been a succession of opposition organizations based in Paris, many of them aimed specifically at the matter of winning elections. There is a dubious trace of such a group for the election of 1816;[55] the evidence for another, or perhaps the same one, for 1817 is better. Vaulabelle, who calls it the "Comité électoral des indépendants," says that it met at Lafayette's house and numbered among its members well-known leftists like Voyer d'Argenson, General Thiard, and Benjamin Constant.[56] There are other fragments which indicate a stirring of this sort.[57]

The record of the opposition effort in the election of 1818 is a bit fuller but only slightly more enlightening. There is evidence of some sort of central electoral apparatus in Paris which enveloped what remained of the Comité of 1817 and moved forward.[58] There are also snippets indicating formal electoral activity in a few departments.[59] At the risk of using a post hoc argument, the outcome of the partial elections of 1817 – a startling success for candidates

54. In 1822 there were two elections, one in May and one in November. This is the only time such a thing happened. There was no regular election in 1823, 1825, or 1826.

55. AN F/7 6772 Seine: the report of Delavau (7 Sept. 1827), cited earlier, remarks that there had been opposition electoral organizations in Paris since the "ordinance of 5 Sept. [1816]" which summoned the 1816 elections.

56. Vaulabelle, *Restaurations,* IV, 312–314.

57. Two pamphlets in the BN Le/54 series, numbers 17 and 18, and two in the Le/8 series, numbers 8 and 9, show an awakened interest in elections and without any wishful interpretation seem closer to advocacy for the opposition than for the ministry.

58. See Vaulabelle, *Restaurations,* IV, 366–368, 453.

59. AN F/7 3686 (8) Rhône contains a report of the commander of gendarmes of the 16th legion (Rhône, Loire, and Ain) which describes a considerable electoral campaign in his area, especially in the Ain. Two fairly sophisticated pamphlets were addressed to opposition voters in the Sarthe and Moselle (BN Le/54.33 and 34).

of the left opposition[60] — does suggest something more contrived than a simple spontaneous awakening of left-leaning voters.

The election of 1819 was perhaps even more of a shocker to the government, for not only were the results more dramatic — Braun's calculations come out 41 opposition wins out of 52, Vaulabelle quotes 42, out of 56[61] — but also the organized political efforts of the left opposition were out in the open for all to see. Almost certainly there was a central electoral committee in Paris which either sponsored the founding of local committees in the departments or got in touch with such groups, if already founded.[62]

I have discovered no evidence which directly links the work of such a group or groups to the *Constitutionnel.* If indeed there was no connection, which is hard to believe, the staff of the *Constitutionnel* using the paper's columns made itself into a thoroughly effective organization. By mid-July of 1819 it had begun to publish bits of pre-electoral news from its many friends and readers in the departments, particularly those of the III series which would be involved in that year's partial elections. Well before the publication of the royal ordinance which set the date for the convocation of the electoral colleges,[63] it ran a laudatory notice regarding the recent appearance of a small book entitled *Guide électoral,* by the leftist publisher, Brissot-Thivars.[64] Twice during August and September

60. If you accept the somewhat conservative estimate of Vaulabelle (*Restaurations,* IV, 368), the left or *indépendants* as he calls them won 23 out of 55 seats. If you accept the findings of J. B. M. Braun (*Nouvelle Biographie des députés*) the left opposition won 35 out of 52. A few of Braun's attributions are wrong and a few more questionable. See the Bibliographical Note.

61. Vaulabelle's arithmetic (*Restaurations,* IV, 456) is somewhat confusing in that his total number of elections adds up to four more seats than there were nominally at issue (56 as opposed to 52). This extra four derived from what in other circumstances would be called by-elections to fill vacancies in the chamber caused by death or resignation.

62. *Ibid.,* 453. Vaulabelle refers to it as the "comité électoral" or, perhaps better, a "comité central électoral des indépendants, devenus libéraux." Duvergier de Hauranne speaks of a "Comité de Paris" as if it were an institution which needed no further explanation (*Gouvernement parlementaire,* V, 222).

63. *Constitutionnel,* 26 July 1819, p. 3. The ordinances appeared in the *Moniteur,* 21 Aug. 1819, p. 1111.

64. The title was something of a misnomer, for whatever guidance it offered the opposition voter was in the form of a series of biographic notes on the political stance of men who had served in the deputies since 1814. To be sure Brissot-Thivars's thorough-going identification of the deputies of the right and extreme right had the effect of flagging them for the enmity of the leftist voter. Just in case he should miss the point, the *Constitutionnel* a bit later gave the names of the men it considered the most dangerous reactionaries (1 Sept. 1819, p. 3).

the *Constitutionnel* published lists of its own favored candidates.[65] Given its wide circulation throughout the country this action along with its drumfire of political comment and exhortation must have made its impress. In the next two elections (1820 and 1821) the state seems to have clamped down on the paper's politicking.

The campaign of 1819 is noteworthy for that odd pragmatic alliance of extremes that kept turning up and which in 1827 aroused the profoundest worries among the followers of Villèle. In 1819 however the surviving record is pretty well confined to a very few departments, most notably the Doubs.[66]

From the point of view of the left's electoral victory, the partial elections of 1819 were the high-water mark in its electoral fortunes. But although the laws of exception and of the double vote arrested the left's progress towards establishing a parliamentary majority in the deputies, they did not dull the left's political ardor. Nor did they occasion a forgetting of the many practical lessons which opposition leaders had learned in the laboratory of annual, though partial, elections. The next five elections (1820, 1821, 1822 May, 1822 November, and 1824) were opportunities to maintain old political friendships, develop new ones, practice old artifices, and learn new. The ending of the left's winning streak probably owed a great deal more to the growing capabilities of its adversary – the bureaucracy, starting with the prefects – than to a slackening of its endeavors.

That there was a continuation of opposition efforts in the black years of 1820 and 1821 seems almost certain. The case for 1820 rests largely with what prefects and gendarme commanders reported from the field rather than with what appeared in the press. The dispatches of these officers contain ample evidence of a mature and active committee in Paris and corresponding groups in at least nine of the departments of the IV series.[67] The work of these organiza-

65. *Ibid.,* 28 Aug. 1819, p. 4; 5 Sept. 1819, p. 4.

66. For the scrappy evidence of this early appearance of the "monstrous alliance" of later days, see Duvergier de Hauranne, *Gouvernement parlementaire,* V, 215, where a presumably leftist group urged that support go to an ultra in a situation where the alternative was a "ministerial" candidate. See also Broglie, *Souvenirs,* II, 66, and the *Moniteur,* 18 Sept. 1819, p. 1224, which pretty clearly states the case for the election in Besançon (Doubs).

67. For information about a committee in Paris, see AN F/7 3689(3) Seine-Inférieure, esp. 14 Sept. 1820; AN F/7 3682(12) Meurthe, 7 Nov. 1820; AN F/7 6694 Aube, 7 and 8 Jan. 1822; *ibid.,* Aude, 8 Jan. 1822; *ibid.,* Charente, 6 Jan. 1822. For information about a relationship between the committee in Paris and similar committees in the departments,

tions seems to have paid off in the relevant arrondissemental colleges which returned some 25 opposition deputies for the 54 vacant seats. They made far less of a showing in the new departmental colleges, in operation for the first time, where there were only 14 opposition wins among the 167 seats at issue. This was not surprising given the make-up of this second electorate.

After what appears to have been a year of semi-hibernation, opposition leaders were back in operation in 1822.[68] There was a central committee in Paris[69] and almost certainly related stirrings in the departments of the I and II series where elections took place in May and November. So too in 1824 (there was no partial election in 1823) when the leftist opposition went down to an obliterating defeat. Almost certainly the reason for this outcome is more easily ascribable to the government's skillful timing and, one fears, a none too scrupulous use of its powers[70] than to a want of effort on the part of its opponents. Indeed, judging largely from the tone of articles in the *Constitutionnel,* and the number of them, it is permissible to discern a livelier opposition campaign than in the immediate

see *ibid.,* Ardennes, 11 Jan. 1822; *ibid.,* Vendée, 6 Jan. 1822. In late 1821/early 1822 the minister queried all prefects about improper or illegal activities in the departments. The date 1822 on the above, and one of the following, dispatches indicates that they were in response to that query. For information about electoral committees in the departments, see AN F/7 3656 Aude, 12, 18, 23 Oct. 1820; AN F/7 3659(7) Bouches-du-Rhône, 10 Nov. 1820; AN F/7 3675(5) Eure, 1 Sept., 1 Oct. 1820; AN F/7 3687 Saône-et-Loire, 21 Aug., 6 Sept., 11 and 23 Oct., 1820; AN F/7 6694 Vosges, 26 Jan. 1822. See also BN pamphlets in the Le/54 series: numbers 71, 72, 73, 79, 80, and 84.

68. The most important bit of evidence of opposition electoral efforts in the partial elections of 1821 (V series) is the appearance of the first edition of the anonymous pamphlet (ascribed to Alphonse Mahul) published by Brissot-Thivars entitled *Tactique électorale à l'usage de l'opposition, . . .* (Lb/48.2166). This little document of 43 pages is witness to some highly sophisticated political leadership on the left. See the Bibliographical Note.

Other evidence is meager. I found nothing in the archival record, only six pamphlets in the BN Le/54 series (numbers 101–106), none of which shows a trace of partisan political activity, and only a few articles in the *Constitutionnel,* which merely pose and answer technical questions about inscription of the would-be voter, e.g., 27 Sept. 1821.

69. The evidence is indirect. Duvergier de Hauranne (*Gouvernement parlementaire,* VIII, 6) tells of two right-wing newspapers (the *Quotidienne* and *Drapeau Blanc*) fulminating against it. See also the *Constitutionnel,* 16 Apr. 1822, p. 1: an open letter to the prefect of the Seine asking for six copies of the electoral lists of Paris which "are essential to us for our own use and to help us serve others. . .". It was signed by Casimir Périer, Laffitte, Delessert, and Gérard. It is a good guess that these men had some important connection with what had been publicly referred to as another "comité directeur." See *Constitutionnel,* 19 Apr. 1822, p. 1.

The pamphlet, noted above (*Tactique électorale*), was republished in a second edition.

70. Vaulabelle (*Restaurations,* VI, chap. 4) tells the story in detail and with no sympathy for the government.

past.[71] This plus one significant pamphlet[72] lead me to give high credence to an impression which Alfred Nettement leaves with his reader. In a few words he tells of the *comité de gauche* in Paris and conveys the thought that similar opposition committees were busy in every arrondissement of the realm.[73] In all events, the thoroughgoing defeat of the left need not in this case be ascribed to an absence of opposition efforts.

Thus from the vantage point of 1824 a backward glance will reveal that the first decade of the Restoration had produced important developments in the realm of elections. The early years of the Bourbon monarchy saw a deep cynicism among many of those privileged to vote, an attitude which had carried over from the absurd electoral ballets of Napoleonic times. Registration was light and attendance at the electoral colleges was desultory. In the general election of 1816 not enough voters turned up at the colleges of four departments to constitute a quorum, with the result that these departments went deputyless for about a year. But soon thereafter – perhaps the electoral law of 1817 had much to do with it – voters began to grasp the importance of elections and the importance of winning them. For those who believed in constitutional monarchy and who disliked the way in which theirs was operating, elections were seen as the legal way to relief. As soon as this was understood, the pulse of political life, as discussed in the preceding pages, began to quicken.

For the opposition organizers the partial elections of 1817, 1818, and 1819 were proof that their ends were obtainable in the successful practice of the electoral arts. In the beginning the sparks came from the famous leftists who clustered in the capital: Lafayette, Dupont de l'Eure, Dupin *aîné*, Constant, Manuel, Cadet-Gassicourt,

71. See *Constitutionnel*, Sept. 1823 through Feb. 1824; esp. 22, 30 Sept.; 17, 19, 21, 25 Oct.; 8, 10, 14, 16, 20, 29, 30 Nov.; 2, 4, 15, 17, 29 Dec.; 1 Jan. 1824 to 25 Feb., three or four articles per week.

72. Gallix, *Lettre à un électeur de Lyon* (Lyon, n.d.; [signed "Valence, 15 Aug. 1827"]) BN Lb/49.662, listed by Guizot as an Aide-toi publication (see n.32 above). The author, writing under Aide-toi sponsorship, looks backward from 1827 and gives a long recital of the activities in 1824 of an opposition electoral committee which sprang up in his city of Valence (Drôme). "The 15 men of commerce and the bar" helped inscribe voters, actively campaigned throughout the arrondissement, got like-minded men to start thinking as a group, got them to unite behind a single candidate, and then provided all the extra services which made it possible for the voters to come to the college to vote.

73. Alfred Nettement, *Histoire de la Restauration* (8 vols., Paris, 1860–1872), VI, 613. He treats this latter point as if it were so obvious a matter that it needed no elaboration.

Mauguin, along with sympathetic and vastly richer men like Jacques Laffitte and Casimir Périer and the owners and publishers of the left-wing press. The sparks kindled a warmth among like-minded men out in the departments who went into action as election time approached, and never wholly cooled off between elections.

When the law of 2 May 1827 brightened hopes for the registration of qualified voters (and new hopes for frustrating the ardors of misguided prefects) and the air became full of rumors about an election in the autumn, opposition spokesmen in Paris once again sent out the message. All over the country it was heard, and the opposition's storehouse of experience had a chance to come back into play. It was heard by men who had had a rich experience with electoral institutions and who were sensitive to the content. They already knew the importance of founding or reviving electoral organizations; they already knew what to do with them and how to go about it. What Paris gave them was the essential stimulus: a feeling of leadership in the capital where it counted and a campaign literature of very high quality which they could pass along or imitate. Without the leadership of Paris the surge would have lacked a sense of direction; without the inventory of practical knowledge in the provinces the surge would have been without force.

The Friends and the Aide-toi had a large role in the election of 1827, one of the most important parts of which was the reviving and stimulating of great latent political forces in the countryside which had been a-building over the decade.

5 / The Campaign of the Oppositions (II)

With the articulate and prestigious leadership in Paris working in concert with experienced hands in the departments, the opposition – both wings of it – moved into the campaign of 1827. It had a number of things going for it.

To begin with, it had the year 1827: the third of Charles's reign and the first in which he had given the electorate an opportunity to express an opinion. In these three years, and in the preceding ten for that matter, he had established himself in the minds of a great many of his subjects as an authoritarian divine-right monarch with commitments to the *ancien regime*. His coronation ceremony at Reims, with its full medieval panoply, carried a powerful symbolic message. But more substantial testimony of his political orientation lay with his keeping Villèle as president of the council and his continuing support for the legislative program born of the rightward thrust of policy, for which he himself had been the prime mover in the declining years of Louis XVIII.

One did not have to be on the leftist fringe of things to be upset by the way that Charles wore his crown. There were those of a far more conservative cast of mind and spirit who now began to fear that the constitutional monarchy which they had come to accept with good heart was in jeopardy. It was not only the measures being put before the legislature and emerging as law – that providing the indemnity for the emigrés, that which recalled the primogeniture of an earlier day, that which levied fearsome penalties against certain acts of sacrilege – but also new turns in the church-state relationship which appeared favorable to ultramontanism and its champions and their works. The king's sympathy with this side of the age-old controversy put him in conflict not only with the Gallicans but with moderate Catholics who were willing to settle comfortably for something within the large area of potential compromise.

If 1827 was Charles's third year, it was Villèle's sixth as a member of the council and his fifth as prime minister. In this span of time almost any kind of leader would have garnered a full quota of enemies and Villèle was not just any kind of leader. First and foremost he was deeply loyal to his sovereign which, of course, yielded him no credit among those who disapproved of Charles. Rather it made him the accessible earthy surrogate for the harsh criticism not appropriate for use against the crown. He had received full bad marks with men to the left of center for his role in the enactment of reactionary legislation and for his apparent sympathy with the ultramontane views of the court. The appointment of two prominent members of the *Congrégation* to important posts in the police apparatus seemed to many as a melancholy proof of just this.[1]

Whereas such a stance would have been applauded by many who would have called themselves ultras, by no means all the ultras were in Villèle's corner. From his early days in national politics (he first came to Paris as a deputy of the *chambre introuvable* in 1815) he had had his differences with extremists (the *impatients*) of his own ultra group, and his role in the dismissal of Chateaubriand in 1824 had won him, as we have seen, the bitter enmity of a great many otherwise important and necessary supporters.

The passage of time did nothing to mend things. In fact, in the first half of 1827 the government's three major assaults on the freedom of the press — the law of "justice and love," the initiative of the deputy, La Boëssière, and the imposition of the censorship — raised tempers within the two oppositions to a new high and provided an ideological basis for a détente and much more between these strange bedfellows. In all this, the enmity which was personalized and sharply focused tended to depict Villèle in true satanic form.

There was another charge, and a grave one, against the government which had little to do with conscience or politics, but which was easily turned to political purpose. It was the evil turn of the national economy. In 1825 after a decade of post-war wild overseas investment, British business had come a cropper. As long as British business prospered so did French, and when the British bubble burst the unhappy effects were felt with almost equal strength across the channel. As Adolphe Thiers wrote in 1826:[2]

> the consequences [in France] are the tightening of capital, the slackening of confidence, the falling off of orders, all those things which add up to the

1. These were Franchet d'Esperey, the director general of police, and Delavau, the prefect of police of the Seine (Paris).

2. Marquant, *Thiers et Cotta*, #69 (30 Aug. 1826), pp. 354–358.

same thing. The English, who had by their considerable purchases given great impetus to our manufactures, suddenly withdrew. Thus all Normandy, Picardy, and Flanders were dropped into dreadful suffering; last winter one even saw the beginnings of trouble among the workers of Rouen. Everywhere there were the cries of unemployment. Though few demonstrable losses can be seen in any branch of commerce, the single evil is to be found in the reign of extreme doubt for the future. The great bankers, hit by the crisis, have been the first to pull in their capital and the first to tighten up credit which they [normally] extend to business and industry. Business has stopped shipping and the manufacturers have shut down production. The dislocations go on down; there is no bankruptcy, but there is annoyance, malaise, and disquiet.

Modern students of the depression paint it in much more somber tones than Thiers. In particular in the matter of bankruptcies David Pinkney points out that in 1826 they "rose by almost two-thirds over the preceding year and the total liabilities involved more than doubled, exceeding one hundred million francs, a record for the decade. In [Paris] alone 663 businesses failed that year [1826], . . . 1827 brought some recovery, but the high level of bankruptcies . . . reflected continuing difficulties."[3]

The dismal science, barely in its infancy, did little to explain and far less to alleviate the woes of French industrialists and men of commerce. A good number of prefects heard the moans of business in 1827 and were probably better aware of the cause than of the possible political effects. In the reports that they wrote during the summer some thirty of them commented on one or another phase of the economic distress that beset their departments. These notes touch upon such matters as the decline in production (for example, off 50 percent from 1823, said the prefect of the Ardennes), general stagnation of commerce and industry in another twenty departments, ruinous prices for grain and wine, and poor harvests as a result of natural calamities.[4] There can be no question that the general

3. Pinkney, *French Revolution of 1830,* p. 59. See also Paul Gonnet, "Esquisse de la crise économique en France de 1827 à 1832", in *Revue d'histoire économique et sociale,* 33 (1955), 249–291, and Bertrand Gille, *La Banque et le crédit en France de 1815 à 1848* (Paris: Presses Universitaires, 1959), esp. pp. 301–329.

4. See the AN cartons F/7 6767–6772 (all communications are pref. to min. int.; all dates are 1827): Ardennes, 9 July; Aude, 20 July; Charente, 15 July; Charente-Inférieure, 3 Aug.; Côtes-du-Nord, 3 Feb.; Eure, 10 July; Eure-et-Loir, 8 July; Gard, 5 Mar.; Haute-Garonne, 2 June; Landes, Oise, 2 Oct.; Puy-de-Dôme, 16 July; Basses-Pyrénées, 10 Oct.; Pyrénées-Orientales, 2 June; Haut-Rhin, 4 July; Saône-et-Loire, 29 Dec.; Somme, 5 July and 9 Oct.; Tarn, 13 July; Haute-Vienne, 31 July; Yonne, 14 July. Prefects in a few departments (Ille-et-Vilaine, Indre-et-Loire, Loire, Loire-Inférieure, for example) reported by contrast a condition of economic well-being.

depression which was probably worse in 1826 was still a real and woeful fact of life in 1827.

Whatever its share of the responsibility, the government was blamed fulsomely by the injured parties. This one gathers better from the prefects who indignantly speak of businessmen's ingratitude to a government which had done all within its power in their behalf than from attacks on national economic policy in the press and pamphlet literature. But whatever the cause and whosesoever the responsibility one thing was sure: the Villèle government made no friends nor did its adherents win any political support from the voters of the business community who were most hurt by the enduring economic disruption. The professional group closest to business — the various members of the legal profession — caught much of the infectious embitterment. Often and often the prefects report them as key members of local opposition electoral groups.

Lastly, in the popular indictment of the Villèle government there were a lot of small things which were not of earth-shaking consequence in themselves but which, taken together, lent themselves to sensationalist journalism. There were the unfortunate incidents attending the Paris funerals of Manuel[5] and the duc de Larochefoucauld, both ranking heroes of the liberal opposition; there was the perhaps equally unfortunate choice of Bonald — the ranking theocrat of the realm, despised even by many an adherent of Villèle — as the chief censor. There was the king's seemingly captious disbanding of the national guard of Paris, an event which was dressed up by champions of the guard and believers in a popular armed force as a first move to dispense with it and to begin to repose the ultimate responsibility for public order and security in the hands of an elite corps directly responsible to the crown.

A good many of the pamphlets issued in the summer and fall of 1827 wrapped up this whole chamber of horrors in a single purple indictment. If you, dear reader, they said, approve of these things your course is easy: just support the ministerial candidate in the election which is just around the corner. If you do not, join with your fellow oppositionists and support a "constitutionnel."[6]

5. See the Aide-toi pamphlet, *Relation historique des obsèques de M. Manuel, . . .* (Paris, [1827]) BN Lb/49.681.

6. In the BN collection the following pamphlets are good examples of this sort of polemical writing: Anon., *Aux Electeurs de Maine et Loire,* Lb/49.674; N. A. Salvandy,

What most of the leftist opposition wanted and talked about out loud, as opposed to what it did not want, is surprisingly mild. The short way to put the matter is to say it wanted just about exactly what, in formal terms, it had. It wanted a constitutional monarchy; it was satisfied with Charles as king (it was not necessarily anti-Bourbon); above all it wanted the constitutional charter and its definition of individual liberties. The nuances of the positive program which were its very heart were left unsaid, as if too obvious, or merely hinted at or otherwise obscured, perhaps in fear of stirring up the internal security apparatus.

These nuances, had they been expressed, would have stressed the limited prerogatives of the crown, the notion of ministerial responsibility to the ruling components of the chamber of deputies, and the panoply of individual rights and liberties which had emanated from the Revolution. Almost the only way in which these essentials were expressed as desiderata was in the peculiar double-talk (perhaps half-talk would be the better expression) of the times. There is for example never a mention of the specific guarantees in historic documents such as the Declaration of the Rights of Man and Citizen, though one senses it is exactly these, and in their broad construction, which are intended by the unangular safe words like "our traditional liberties" or "fundamental freedom."

There can be little doubt that there were deeper dissatisfactions and more radical solutions than those so politely articulated in public. But the evidence for these lies almost wholly within the reporting of the prefects and the police – not the most objective of sources. At the time of the king's trip through some of the northern departments (3–20 September) there was a spate of rumors to the effect that he intended to hole up in St. Omer, with the Pope's blessing suspend the charter, and rule with the support of a loyal garrison army; for revenue he would resurrect the *dîme* and other forms of pre-Revolutionary taxation.[7] Surely this sort of talk did not bespeak a universal confidence in Charles nor loyalty to him and his family.

Explication de la nouvelle loi sur les collèges électoraux ([Paris, c. 20 Aug. 1827]), Lb/49.677; Eugène Plagniol, *Le Tocsin des élections,* Lb/49.754; Aide-toi, *Dernier Avis aux électeurs,* Lb/49.777, and Anon., *Aux Electeurs du Jura,* Le/54.241. There are others in the Lb/49 series (e.g., 675 and 693) and in the Le/54 series (e.g., 208, 250, 264, and 271).

7. See the AN cartons F/7 6767–6772 (all communications are pref. to min. int.; all dates are 1827): Ardennes, 31 Aug.; Loire-Inférieure, 1 Sept.; Haute-Marne, 14 July, are examples.

Nor did other prefectoral messages reporting a rumored crying out of "vive la république," a flashing of the tricolor, or what Christophe de Villeneuve-Bargemont, the prefect of the Bouches-du-Rhône (and one of the most astute in the business), wrote: "the faction [his referent is the 'liberals'] . . . no longer tries to conceal that all its undertakings tend towards a change in the dynasty and the establishment of a republic such as rules over the United States of America."[8]

One would be numb not to sense a layer of resounding radicalism beneath the sort of opposition ideology that found expression in the pamphlets, the press, and speeches made to audiences of dubious discretion. But to confirm it by reading it in print – one cannot. The fact that most of the evidence which does exist derives from the reporting of men who abhorred the radical left and all its works by no means discredits it.

In the foregoing lies the bill of particulars which brought together those opposed to the government of Villèle. As long as the indictment was couched in general terms and unaccompanied by any concrete plan of action, those united in their opposition to the government were on their way but a good deal less than halfway home. What was needed was the message of Chateaubriand's second pamphlet, *Marche et effets de la censure*. With this cry of outrage at the imposition of the censorship, wedded to an instruction as to what should be done, he turned out to be the detonator of a political campaign that reached almost every corner of the realm.

To examine the work of that campaign and to weigh its successes is my aim in the pages ahead.

The elementary steps in any campaign must include three broad lines of endeavor, and the first of these is the registration of the qualified voter. In France of 1827 registration involved a few special wrinkles.

To begin with there was the man who met the requirements but had not yet ever got himself inscribed. Sometimes this was because he had not realized that he was within shooting distance of the fran-

8. Maurice Onslow in a pamphlet, *Aux Electeurs . . . de la Haute-Loire* (Le Puy, [1827]) BN Le/54.252, alleged that the cries "vive la république" were uttered at a local banquet in honor of Lafayette *fils*. He subsequently retracted the allegation (see BN Le/54.254). For the statement of Villeneuve-Bargemont see AD Bouches-du-Rhône M/2(III)–9, pref. to min. int., 20 Nov. 1827. This document is one of the remarkable series of reports which the prefect wrote in response to the minister's request that he be personally kept informed during the list-making weeks. I have not found any of the series in the AN. The ones in Marseille are in draft.

chise; sometimes because he realized this all too well and did nothing for fear of being chosen for jury duty; and yet again because some of his claims — most often in the complicated area of his cens — were disallowed by the authorities. In each of these cases whether or not he got on the list was likely to depend upon his willingness to make the try and upon the amount of outside suasion and expert help that he received.

Once persuaded that voting was a high obligation of citizenship and made to believe something or other comforting about jury service — either that it too was a duty and responsibility which he ought to welcome; or that his chances of being called to jury duty were so slim that no normal man would worry about them; or that, if he planned to buy immunity from the jury by denying himself a place on the electoral rolls and paying with his franchise, he ran a substantial chance of finding himself to his disgust a voteless jury-man, for he might still qualify for jury duty as a member of the second jury list[9] — then came the matter of telling him what documents were necessary for his inscription and how he should round them up.[10] Those relating to date of birth and to claims of political domicile could in some cases offer difficulty but they were relatively far less numerous and easier to deal with than those bearing upon payment of the cens. These often offered a bewildering complexity. One need only glance at the stacks of documents in the "M" series of many a departmental archive to catch the puzzles involved in assigning political credit for the direct taxes paid by multiple-ownership businesses, inter-vivos trusts, and various share-cropping systems not to mention taxes paid on an array of properties in a

9. These contradictory arguments appear singly, be it said, in a good number of pamphlets. The first was made in a high-minded essay of Eusèbe Salverte, *Du Droit et du devoir d'un électeur* (Paris, [1827]) BN Lb/49.755; the second, in *Appel aux électeurs de la Seine-Inférieure* (Paris, [1827]) BN Lb/49.765 — a pamphlet full of highly erroneous arithmetic proving that a qualified juror was likely to be called up once in 30 years; and the last one was made in the Aide-toi's *Manuel de l'électeur-juré* (see above, chap. 4, text and n.26). Other pamphlets in the Lb/49 series which deal with this absorbing matter are 674, 694, 772, and 776.

10. There are a number of pamphlets which deal very explicitly with this business of documenting the would-be voter. One of the early treatments is in the Aide-toi pamphlet cited in the preceding note. For the *Manuel*'s bibliography of more thorough and — in the legal sense — much more technical monographs, see above, chap. 4, text and n.29. During the summer and fall a number of other pamphlets published in the departments carried the same sort of exhortation and lists of instructions. See BN Le/54.218 (Eure), Lb/49.662 (Drôme), Lb/49.669 (Calvados), Lb/49.694 (Seine-Inférieure), Le/54.206 (Gironde).

number of departments. Since the law required that title to the property in question must have rested with the claimant for one year,[11] the determination of the precise time when the arrangement, the purchase, or the sale was made became of crucial importance – and this in itself could and did become a matter of deep controversy.

Another set of puzzles nested around the right of widows who were property holders and wished to delegate the political credit attaching to their tax payments to a son, a grandson, or a son-in-law. The order of precedence just given was that of the law.[12] But suppose a widow had had a son who had died leaving her a grandson of four years; suppose too this woman had a married daughter whose husband (the woman's son-in-law) was of voting age. Did the woman have to delegate the cens to the boy who could not use it, or could she skip the grandson and delegate directly to the son-in-law who could?[13]

The problem of documenting the would-be voter for his first appearance on the lists did not end the matter. Those men who had been inscribed for the first time to vote, say in the election of 1824, dared not assume that they would be automatically reinscribed in 1827. Indeed the prefects might not inscribe anyone on the final list (that of midnight of 30 September) who had not filed a complete and up-to-date documentary claim. There was nothing to prevent the prefect from himself collecting and filing the documents of a man whom he had personal reasons for wanting to enfranchise – the man was sure to support the government's candidate – and nothing to prevent the prefect from inscribing on the early lists almost anyone else within reason. But those of this latter group for whom no new documentation turned up prior to the closing of the lists could not and would not appear on the final and operative lists.[14]

Article 5 of the law of 2 May had been designed to minimize the

11. Art. 4, law of 29 June 1820 (Duvergier, *Lois,* XXIII, 13).

12. Art. 5 of the same law (*ibid.,* p. 15 [14]).

13. A number of prefects had held to the letter of the law and denied the move of the widow in question to help enfranchise her son-in-law. In a critical case a widow of the Creuse took her grievance to court on appeal against the prefect's decision and won. See the pamphlet, *Question électorale: Arrêt de la cour royale de Limoges* (Paris, 1827) BN Lb/49.708.

14. There was a great deal of confusion on this subject, and by no means confined to the voters. Many prefects themselves needed enlightenment and got it from the minister of the interior.

Sometime in early July Chabrol de Volvic, the prefect of the Seine, formally put the

need for repeated document-gathering and reinscription. As we have seen in an earlier chapter the thrust of the formal text amounted to not much more than telling the prefects that they should not drop someone from the lists out of simple caprice and telling the dropped voter that he had an appeal.[15] Whatever its intent it could not be regarded as a heroic remedy. Prefects went right on dropping men who had appeared on prior lists and in the event of a remonstrance could tell the objector to take the matter up with the cour royale or the conseil d'état depending on the nature of the case.[16]

Getting the substance of this message across to men who to their delight had found themselves inscribed on an early list, without having raised a finger, was both uncongenial and difficult. Oftentimes, of course, the passage of time and the change of circumstances introduced brand new and unsuspected problems to the documenting of a man. Those concerned with the campaign to register the vote probably spent as much or more time and effort keeping old registrations valid as achieving brand new ones.

How much of this scurry for documents was undertaken by the would-be voter himself and how much was done by third parties (members of a local opposition electoral committee) is impossible to sort out. There is one well-documented case of the intervention of outsiders.[17] There is no reason to think it was unique nor the way it was handled, typical.

---

voters of his department on notice that unless their documentation was complete and accurate they could not appear on the final (and controlling) electoral list no matter if they had appeared on its predecessors. The *Constitutionnel* (20 July 1827, p.2) ran an article repeating Chabrol's warning and praising him. In such fashion it got a piece of political advice through the censorship. Later on, the prefect of the Loiret issued much the same sort of warning.

15. See above, chap. 1, text and n.51. For the text of the law, see Duvergier, *Lois,* XXVII, 117–124, esp. p. 119.

16. See above, chap. 1, text and n.52. During the early days of the Martignac government the shortcomings of art. 5 of 2 May 1827 were clearly recognized, with the result that a new legislative remedy emerged. It was the law of 2 July 1828, which caused a major turmoil in the business of list-making but did not wholly eradicate the problem (Duvergier, *Lois,* XXVIII, 227–229).

17. A lawyer of Rouen, Aroux, probably the sparkplug of the opposition organization there, undertook to achieve the registration of some twenty of his fellow citizens. He appears to have gathered and presented their documents to the authorities, only to be told that they would not be received as part of a bona fide application for inscription. He then got sworn/stamped depositions from each of the twenty stating that each had formally asked his help and had authorized him to act. The prefect again turned him down. He then took the case to the ministry of the interior who backed up the prefect. AN F/1c/III Seine-Inférieure 5: Aroux to pref., 30 Sept. 1827; pref. to Aroux, 30 Oct. 1827; Franchet d'Esperey, dir. of police/min. int., to Aroux, 20 Oct. 1827.

Along with trying to register men who were entitled to the franchise and who would support the opposition candidate went a parallel effort to try to cause the erasure of the names of men who were known to be supporters of the government and whose claims to the vote were considered defective.[18] Needless to say the struggle in these cases between opposition committeemen and the prefects was probably even more unequal, and what evidence I have found of erasures does not remotely indicate whether or not they were motivated by an outside stimulus or by the prefect's desire to observe the law.[19]

With respect to the opposition's first and positive task – registration – there is happily a lot more information. Sorting it out does offer some problems.

The final electoral lists – those which were published as soon after 1 October 1827 as the printers could handle the manuscript – contained almost exactly 88,000 names. As we have seen, this figure represented a growth of nearly 25 percent or some 18,000 over the number of names on the first lists. There can be no question that the opposition effort to register the vote accounts in large measure for this dramatic increase. Surely one cannot claim that all 18,000 incremental voters were opposition supporters certain to support candidates of the left; some of the 18,000 were there because prefects, perceiving an alarming tide of new and suspect registrants, bestirred themselves to try to even things up. But this in itself was an indirect result of the oppositions' campaign.

As to correlating the oppositions' efforts and their successes in pressing the registration of sympathetic voters, it cannot be done in any systematic sense. As soon as one takes all eighty-six departments and begins arranging them in two lists: one where the effort was great and the growth in registration commensurate and the

18. In a dispatch to the ministry, the prefect of the Vienne wrote (10 Jan. 1828) that "committees of the liberal party were established in almost all departments to complain about [allegedly improper inscriptions on] the lists" AN F/1c/III (misfiled in) Vaucluse 4.

For an instance of an angry citizen trying to achieve the erasure of illegally inscribed voters, see the case of the Vosges below, chap. 6, text and n.35.

19. In the first lists of three departments (Drôme, Côte-d'Or, and Haut-Rhin) there were about 2,100 names. By election time some 250 had been deleted. Of these one was a domicile case, about 20 because the men were dead, and the rest for failure to pay the cens or to provide the prefect with a full array of documents. Who pointed these derelictions out to the prefect can never be known. The three lists are in the ADs as follows: Drôme (6 M 27); Côte-d'Or (2 M 20); and Haut-Rhin ("Voies extraordinaires") #634.266.

other where the effort and growth were both small, he finds he must create two more lists. In one of these he finds departments where the effort was great and the growth small, in the second, the converse of this. The four lists, to be sure, are not numerically identical, but the very existence of the second pair makes the whole procedure statistically ridiculous. Attempts to exorcise the spoiling variables by going deeper into the data fail simply because the other data are not there. One is however left with certain convictions that can perhaps be conveyed if not systematically demonstrated.

This has involved an attempt to make two correlations: (1) that between estimated opposition electoral activity and the registration of voters, and (2) that between such activity and the "getting out" of the vote.

The methodology of the first correlation begins with arranging the eighty-six departments in rank order according to the change in the number of registered voters between the issuance of the first published list (15 August 1827) and the last (midnight of 30 September 1827). The first department is the Creuse whose registered electorate actually shrank 15 percent between these dates, then the Allier with a diminution of 12.7 percent. The next to last department is the Rhône whose electorate grew 97 percent over the registration period, and the last, the Haute-Vienne, with an increase of 250 percent. The median is at a growth of about 10 percent and the average a growth of about 25 percent.

Take the twenty-three departments whose registration grew more than the average: the final twenty-three on the rank-order list. Look now at the evidence of opposition electoral activity in these twenty-three departments. For six of them there is practically no evidence of anything; for the remaining seventeen there is evidence to show varying degrees of activity. As a general proposition it is richest and most convincing of a high degree of effort in five of the six departments which showed the greatest increases (the ones at the bottom of the list). For example, the principal reason behind the dramatic 250 percent augmentation in the Haute-Vienne is pretty well documented. It must have been the vigorous campaign waged by an electoral organization with the anti-Villèlist deputy, Pierre Bourdeau, at its head.[20]

20. AN F/1c/III Haute-Vienne, 20 Aug., 5 and 20 Sept., 3 and 18 Oct. 1827.

Registration as a function of opposition electoral activity (in those departments with the highest and lowest percentage change)

	% Change in Registration	Opposition Activity: High	Medium	Low	No Evidence
Creuse	- 15%		X		
Allier	- 12.7			X	
Lot-et-Garonne	- 9.6				X
Maine-et-Loire	- 9	X			
Finistère	- 4				X
Ardèche	- 3			X	
Haute-Saône	- 3		X		
Cantal	- 2			X	
Hautes-Alpes	- 1			X	
Aveyron	+ 1			X	
Pas-de-Calais	+ 1				X
Vosges	+ 1		X		
Doubs	+ 1.8			X	
Dordogne	+ 2				X
Nord	+ 2.8			X	
Meuse	+ 3	X			
Drôme	+ 3.1		X		
Tarn	+ 3.6			X	
Côtes-du-Nord	+ 4.1			X	
Sarthe	+ 4.4			X	
Var	+ 4.5	X			
Haute-Garonne	+ 4.8	X			
Eure	+ 5.5	X			
.........[a]					
Lozère	+ 25.6			X	
Puy-de-Dôme	+ 27		X		
Tarn-et-Garonne	+ 27.5	X			
Mayenne	+ 29.2		X		
Corrèze	+ 29.8				X
Somme	+ 30	X			
Meurthe	+ 35		X		
Gers	+ 36				X
Ille-et-Vilaine	+ 36			X	
Cher	+ 36.8	X			
Saône-et-Loire	+ 37.5		X		
Aube	+ 39		X		
Oise	+ 46				X
Vendée	+ 46.2				X
Indre-et-Loire	+ 50	X			
Loire-Inférieure	+ 64		X		
Gard	+ 77				X
Seine	+ 79	X			
Seine-Inférieure	+ 79	X			
Seine-et-Oise	+ 82	X			
Isère	+ 92				X
Rhône	+ 97	X			
Haute-Vienne	+250	X			

a. For a comment on the 40 departments in which the increase in registration was between 5.5% and 25.6%, see n. 21, below.

Just as well documented are the less startling, but still considerable, increases, for example in the Rhône (notably in the city of Lyon), in Paris, in the Seine-Inférieure, the Seine-et-Oise. As for the Isère with its 92 percent growth in registration, I incline to the belief that the absence of evidence of electoral activity is perhaps irrelevant. For the Isère was Périer country — the native land of this prominent family well known for its opposition to the Villèle government. Even with nothing tangible to go on, one must believe that some sort of purposeful political activity lay behind the new registrations and the rare accomplishment of Casimir's brother, Augustin. He won elections in no less than three out of the four arrondissemental colleges of the department.

Take now twenty-three matching departments at the head of the rank-order list. These are the departments which showed the least growth in registration; in nine cases there were actually fewer registrants on the final list than on the first. Here one perceives something of a contrast with the first group which, within the frailties of the methodology, may still be significant. In only four of the departments of this group is there an absence of evidence of opposition electoral activity and in five, evidence of high activity. For the balance the evidence suggested to me a low or at best a medium order of political effort.[21]

Now suppose one were to reverse the methodology and look at the departments (there are sixteen of them) where there is the best evidence of an intensive electoral effort on the part of opposition organizations.[22] If he now looks at what happened to the registration figures he will find an augmentation of 8,548 voters up from 21,448, or of almost 40 percent (about 15 percent *above* the national average). To complete the exercise, if one looks next at another sixteen departments where the evidence leads one to suspect a limited

21. In several of the forty departments which lie between the two groups in the table above, one finds modest growths in registration and the best sort of evidence of organized opposition electoral activity. The Charente-Inférieure, whose lists grew by 10 percent, is a case in point. Charles Duchâtel, an Aide-toi adherent whose home was in the department's arrondissement of Jonzac, wrote Guizot telling something of his own campaign activities and stressing in particular the importance of the pamphlets (presumably from the Aide-toi or the Friends in Paris) in awakening a concern to get on the lists (AN, 42 AP 203: 9 Sept. 1827).

22. These departments are the Aube, Aude, Calvados, Charente-Inférieure, Cher, Eure-et-Loir, Hérault, Indre-et-Loire, Maine-et-Loire, Nord, Haut-Rhin, Rhône, Seine, Seine-Inférieure, Var, and Haute-Vienne.

effort or none at all, he will find a very modest growth of 648 voters up from 10,430, or only about 6 percent (some 19 percent *below* the national average).[23]

Although the analysis above fairly creaks with subjective judgments with respect both to my appraisals of the surviving evidence and to my use of such quantifiers as high, medium, and low as applied to campaign activity, I cannot believe that it means nothing. I have emerged from my tussle with the data with the conviction, if not an objective proof, that opposition efforts to inscribe like-minded voters were successful and constituted an important ingredient in the outcome of the election.

Even before the registration period ended and the final lists were posted, opposition political counselors were well into the task of identifying potential candidates to run for office – men of the correct political philosophy, of adequate means and years to meet the legal requirements (a cens of 1000 francs and forty years of age), and of a disposition to accept the unsalaried deputyship, if tendered. Obviously finding such men was not easy, but the prime difficulty lay in discovering such a man who also could claim support across the spectrum of opposition factions. Any serious division in the opposition vote was a guaranteed success for the ministerial candidate. But arriving at a consensus candidate well in advance of election day took a great deal of doing.

The problem was particularly acute in those districts where a good number of voters were united in their disapproval of Villèle and hopelessly divided on every other issue. Pragmatic politicians of both right and left wings of the opposition saw that unless some sort of alliance were patched up, a ministerial candidate would unavoidably win. Although such an arrangement was clearly unpalatable to the Aide-toi group, whose early pamphlets had stressed the importance of a union only of the disparate factions to the left of center, it could not shut its eyes to the lesson of the triumphant

23. In the AN cartons F/7 6767–6772, the 1827 dossiers for the Allier, Basses-Alpes, Corrèze, Dordogne, Gers, Lot-et-Garonne, Lozère, Haute-Marne, Nièvre, Basses-Pyrénées, and Bas-Rhin contain a single document or no documents at all. Oddly for these same departments and 5 others, namely: Ardennes, Bouches-du-Rhône, Cantal, Doubs, and Finistère, there is little if any indication of opposition work in the BN's pamphlets.

Corsica is a 17th department in this category, but because it was so special a case (less than 50 voters, more eligibles than voters, the election not held until Jan. 1828, etc.) I have not included it in my calculations.

by-election in Angoulême. Chateaubriand's Friends saw this lesson clearly and were also mindful of similar arrangements made, as in 1819, in past elections.

During the summer, talk of an alliance – called "monstrous and criminal" by adherents of the ministry[24] – grew. By November the reality materialized in a number of departments and with the grudging support of the Aide-toi. In one of its late publications, issued after the ordinance of 5 November, it undertook to categorize three types of candidates to whom it gave its implicit support: the *libéral* (obviously pretty far left), the *constitutionnel* (left and left-center), and the *contre-opposition* whose members were "more royalist than *constitutionnel* but possessed of honesty and candor . . . ; for 10 years . . . they have felt that the charter alone can defend the monarchy and from love of the throne they have become partisans of liberty. They too opposed the press law of the last session."[25] What turmoil so modest an endorsement of ultras caused in Aide-toi ranks can only be imagined, but in terms of impact it was probably worth the pain and more. Well before election day both oppositions had got together in a score or more departments and suppressed normal animosities in the interest of good political sense.

In some cases, depending on how the forces were split, the arrangement would be made in the favor of the candidate whose majority was clear, in others a straightaway horse trade was made with respect to two seats: ultra voters would support a constitutionnel in one arrondissemental college in exchange for constitutionnel support of an ultra in another or in the departmental college. A pamphlet from Nîmes put the matter squarely in urging the constitutional voters to support two candidates, one of whom was a well established leftist, the other "a member of that other opposition, a phenomenon of our time. . . . Voters of the counter-opposition," its plea runs, "You and we, our party and yours . . . 'constitutional royalism' is our common motto."[26]

With the end of the censorship (5 November 1827), the far right

24. Anon., *Correspondance électorale* (Paris, 1827) BN Lb/49.767. See also the *Quotidienne* (9 Nov. 1827, pp. 1–2) and *Courrier français* (17 Nov. 1824, p. 4) which says that it was the alliance of the two oppositions which stirred the government to use every trick in the bag in its endeavors to win the election.

25. Anon., *Aux Electeurs* (Paris, n.d.) BN Lb/49.774.

26. Anon., *Aux Electeurs constitutionnels* (Nimes, n.d.) BN Le/54.266.

Quotidienne published lists of candidates to whom it gave its endorsement.[27] Of the almost eighty names seventeen also received a similar endorsement from all three leading dailies, well to its left: the *Constitutionnel, Courrier français,* and *Journal des Débats.*[28] There were another eight endorsed by the *Débats* only, and one by the *Courrier* and *Débats* jointly. These lists are eloquent testimony to the fact of the "monstrous alliance," for among the names were half a dozen strangers to the normal preferences of the *Quotidienne* – Auguste Cambon, Lézardière, Preissac, and Alexis de Noailles, for example – while not a single one of them would have been the *Constitutionnel's* chosen cup of tea. And the fact that twenty-one out of the twenty-five won is witness to the efficacy of the arrangement. There were other less well-publicized instances where the alliance did much to account for the number of counter-oppositionists returned to the chamber.[29]

No matter, really, the political persuasion of the opposition candidate nor the political climate of his district, he did not step boldly forth when he sensed an impending election and proclaim his qualifications to serve in the chamber. The customs of the day were quite other. Most candidacies were probably hatched in confidential, almost conspiratorial, conversations among a handful of men which might or might not include the subject. They would decide that M. Simon, say, was the man they wanted to elect, and if they found Simon amenable they would continue to broaden their semi-secret soundings and promotional moves. When so many were in on the secret that it became all but public knowledge someone might confront M. Simon and ask flatly if he were indeed a candidate. At this point Simon would dig his heel in the ground and give some stilted and self-conscious answer as did none other than the marquis de Lafayette:

27. Published in the issues of 9, 12, and 13 Nov. 1827.

28. These men were: Delalot (Charente), Alexis de Noailles (Corrèze), Tixier de la Chapelle (Creuse), Beaumont (Dordogne), Richard (Gard), Auguste Cambon (Haute-Garonne), Gautier (Gironde), Bacot de Romans and Fiévée (Indre-et-Loire), Leclerc de Beaulieu (Mayenne), Hyde de Neuville (Nièvre), Boucher (Orne), Leyval (Puy-de-Dôme), Bertin de Vaux (Seine-et-Oise), Agier (Deux-Sèvres), Lézardière (Vendée), Raudot (Yonne).

29. Peyronnet, the minister of justice, was defeated in one of the arrondissemental colleges of the Gironde. He ran the next week in the departmental college of the Cher. Here the ultra leaders induced the leftist candidates to withdraw and contribute to Peyronnet's final defeat. See Duvergier de Hauranne, *Gouvernement parlementaire,* IX, 350.

I have been asked to respond to two propositions: (1) that I have decided to do nothing, and (2) that if the voters of Meaux were to choose me as their representative, I would not accept the honor. Both propositions are barren of truth. My personal obligations to the voters . . . are such that even if I should believe that I would not be useful and they were of a contrary view, I would accept the honor of their support.[30]

The elder Dupin could hardly have described the mood more to a nicety when he says that he issued no circular about his desire for election, that his candidacy was the spontaneous action of his friends, but that "surely I would not press self-abnegation to the point of hurting my chances." Dupont de l'Eure, another leading figure of the far left, wrote his friend Béranger as late as 3 November 1827,

you ask me if one of my ambitions is to be elected from Paris, and if I intend to put myself forward? I answer you today as in the past: I have no urge for election nor do I ask one. If I am honored by an election from Paris which I have not requested and do not anticipate, those who say the contrary are wrong and judge me poorly. If this year I am not returned from Paris (which seems probable), I will not be at all surprised and I will not complain.[31]

A pamphlet of an earlier election describes campaigning in France as "limited to intriguing in secret. One may wish to be named, but pride and self-respect forbid that this be made known in public. Ask a man in public if at the bottom of his heart he desires . . . to become a member of the chamber . . . , he will answer you that he has never dreamed of such a thing."[32] So it was in 1827.

The result was that no matter the stress put upon the importance that the oppositions line up candidates and do so early, not many took the advice to heart. At least if some did, they did no talking out loud until well into the autumn. Prior to the announcement of the dissolution, the surviving record shows fewer than half a dozen men who came (or were put) forward as opposition candidates. Leftist leaders in the Vienne were busy looking early in October.

30. *Correspondance et manuscrits du général Lafayette* publiés par sa famille (6 vols., Paris, 1837-1838), VI, 246-247.

31. *Mémoires de M. Dupin [aîné]* (4 vols., Paris, 1855-1861), II, 13, and Paul Hacquard and Pascal Forthuny, eds., *Lettres inédites de Béranger à Dupont de l'Eure . . . 1820-1854* (Paris: Zaretsky, 1908), pp. 72-75. (Hereafter cited as *Lettres de Béranger.*)

32. Anon., *Du Gouvernement représentatif et les élections de 1824* (Bordeaux, 1824) BN Le/54.150. Cited by F. B. Artz, *Journal of Modern History,* 1 (1929), 205-218. I have used Mr. Artz's translation.

Durand de Richemont had proclaimed his availability two weeks earlier in the Haute-Vienne (he was not heard of again in the campaign); Preissac and Belissen were selected late in October as the opposition choices in the Tarn-et-Garonne;[33] there were a few others like Etienne who had been beating his own drum, discreetly, in the Meuse for months.

Whatever had gone on during the summer, one knows little; but as October waned and the news of the king's decision to dissolve the chamber and summon the colleges (24 October)[34] leaked, the search for candidates began in earnest. Still little broke through the surface until the *Moniteur* of 7 November published the ordinances which made it all official.

Chronologically the first major overt signal that the opposition was going into phase two – the identification of candidates – had occurred with the publication of the 8 and 9 November issues of the *Constitutionnel, Courrier français,* and *Journal des Débats.* Each of them carried a list of candidates to whom the paper gave its endorsement. The three lists were not exactly identical, for the *Débats,* say, was willing to support a few men whom the *Constitutionnel* could not stomach and vice versa, but of the total of 268 different names, about 200 appeared in all three lists. The editors of the *Constitutionnel* relate how

> we pulled together all the information which had been furnished us in advance and which we had been at pains to stimulate; we consulted all enlightened men, true friends of the *pays* who wished to lend their wisdom. Last night [6 November] a large gathering of zealous defenders of constitutional monarchy met; there were former deputies – *constitutionnels* – and a group of notables . . . who from their relations with the departments were able to contribute valuable information. [At that meeting] each man told what he knew of the disposition of the voters of the country.

In so far as time and circumstance had permitted, the departmental notables had communicated with the electoral districts and confirmed what they had believed to be the true preferences of the voters.[35]

The large number of candidates backed by all three papers indi-

33. AN F/1c/III Vienne 4, pref. to min. int., 5 Oct. 1827; *ibid.,* Haute-Vienne 4, pref. to min. int., 20 Sept. 1827; *ibid.,* Tarn-et-Garonne 2, pref. to min. int., 2 Nov. 1827.

34. As already noted, this datum is from Villèle's diary, 24 Oct. 1827.

35. *Constitutionnel,* 8 Nov. 1827, p. 1. The article carries the dateline of 7 Nov.

cates that the men whose names appeared on the published lists were not limited to those whose political coloration matched up with that of the *Constitutionnel.* Indeed, not only were there the names of men of more conservative stripe, probably representative of the sentiments of the *Courrier français* and the *Débats;* there were in addition a handful of names straight out of the ultra counter-opposition. These – and to name the best known: Agier, La Bourdonnaye, and Hyde de Neuville – also received the endorsement of the *Quotidienne* – a fact which again underlined the entente of the two oppositions. There is no indication of where the lists of names came from other than the *Constitutionnel's* cryptic note; surely there is nothing to indicate that the opposition voters of the districts in which these men would stand had been formally caucused and polled.[36]

From 10 November to the twenty-fourth the three papers continued printing lists of candidates whom they favored, but these had less the character of Parisian selections and more that of local choice. Also by and large they were a cut or two below the first lists in the fame and national standing of the nominees. It is a good guess that most of the 164 who dribbled in during this fortnight were men who had gotten some sort of backing in their districts, maybe that of a full-dress caucus, maybe something much less formal and of much less political value.

As to full-dress caucuses there is good evidence that one or more occurred after the announcement of the election in at least nineteen departments.[37] Paris with its eight arrondissemental colleges and its single departmental college which was to elect four deputies shows the opposition effort to select candidates in advance at its peak. Caucuses took place in each of the capital's electoral arrondissements and among the oppositions' quota of departmental voters.[38]

36. The lists contain no endorsements for the 12 Parisian seats. These were not published for about a week. The reason why is obvious: Parisian political leaders had not yet determined the slate and wanted no shooting from the hip prior to formal nominating procedures.

Anon., *Electeurs indépendants* (Niort, n.d.) BN Le/54.216 is a short pamphlet blasting the presumption of Parisians and the Paris press for taking upon themselves the right to name candidates suitable for the departmental constituencies.

37. Reported in the *Constitutionnel* of 11, 12, 13, 14, 15, 16, and 19 Nov.; in the *Courrier français* of 10, 11, 12, 13, 15, 17, and 24 Nov.; and in the *Journal des Débats* of 13, 14, and 17 Nov. 1827.

38. How Dupont de l'Eure won the nomination of the opposition voters of Paris's first electoral arrondissement is told in two letters which his friend Béranger wrote him. This is the only treatment in detail that I have found. Apparently the younger Cadet-

Other well-planned and well-advertised caucuses took place in the Calvados, Rhône, Seine-Inférieure, and the Seine-et-Oise. The winner of a caucus in the Yonne had perhaps not sought the honor; in all events he let it be known that he would not make the run and that he favored the candidacy of M. Gillet, the very man he had just defeated.[39]

However nominated, whether by caucus or by the more informal route described by the *Constitutionnel,* the approximately 450 candidates whose names appeared in the Paris papers between 8 and 24 November made quite a splash in the elections: 158 of them were elected and 57 ran strong-but-losing races. Out of the total of anti-Villèle deputies elected (about 230), almost 70 percent came from this cast of characters[40] – some of them elected by more than one constituency.

This matter of multiple elections of a single candidate was not wholly by accident. There were those political sophisticates who felt that one way of robbing the government of some of the fruits of its secretiveness (in calling the election at all and then in calling it so speedily after the ordinance of dissolution) was to stretch things out. The best way to do this, they urged, was to go for double, triple, and more elections of the same man, only one of which he could accept.[41] His resignation from the other seat or seats would force the government to summon by-elections at a later date. The time thus purchased could be put to good advantage by opposition leaders. If the same candidate were to receive an election from a rural constituency and at the same time another from one of the Parisian districts, he should of course opt for the former and rely upon the opposition strength of the capital to fill his empty seat with another like-minded man.[42] Indeed, six of the opposition's

---

Gassicourt, who was Dupont's unofficial, if not unauthorized, campaign manager in Paris arranged for a vote-taking at his house. One doubts that all were present at once, for almost 300 participated of whom 227 chose Dupont. Three days later there were two ballotings in the other administrative arrondissement of the first electoral district in which Dupont won out over baron Louis. See *Lettres de Béranger,* the letters of 13 and 16 Nov. 1827 (pp. 79–84, 85–91).

39. AN F/1c/III Yonne 3, pref. to min. int., 16 Nov. 1827.

40. For the figures, see Appendix III(A).

41. The *Journal des Débats* (10 Nov. 1827, pp. 2–3 and again on p. 4) carefully spells out this strategy. See also the pamphlet, [Bellon], *Lettre aux électeurs de tous les départemen[t]s* (Paris, [1827]) BN Lb/49.772.

42. *Lettres de Béranger,* pp. 85–91.

eight winners in Paris's arrondissemental colleges followed exactly this course of action. For the country as a whole there was a total of twenty-six seats that had to be vacated because of multiple opposition wins. In consequence twenty-six by-elections had to be called in the spring of 1828 at which opposition candidates did handsomely. The strategy had paid off.

The number of qualified voters who did not get on the electoral lists cannot be known. The number who did, and then went on to their electoral colleges to vote, can be told with a high degree of precision. Of the 88,000 who were listed as regular censeurs and entitled to vote in the arrondissemental and special colleges almost exactly 75,000 (or 85 percent) voted, and of the 21,500 listed as departmental voters 17,700 (or 82 percent) voted.[43]

For the overwhelming majority of the voters, the casting of the ballot was anything from a mild nuisance to a considerable hardship. At a minimum, everyone had to give up a weekend.[44] Those who lived a day's travel from the polling place lost two days more. For the working landholder, the businessman, and the professional to absent himself from his calling was difficult enough, but when the trouble and expense of the trip and the lodging were added one marvels at the low number of no-shows. For the voter who was well known as a sure vote for the government candidate, there were semi-official ways of lightening the burden; these will be discussed in the next chapter. On the other hand, the voter known for his sympathy with the opposition had to look to his own organization for a similar range of services or bear the expense himself.

The elder Dupin wrote of his experience in November 1827 at the college which met at Charité-sur-Loire in the Nièvre:

43. For the methodology of calculating the number of inscribed voters, see chap. 4. The number of men who actually voted in both types of election in 1827 are to be found in the procès verbaux of each election in the cartons of the AN F/1c/III series. Usually the figures are given in the biographies of the winners as they appear in the Robert, Bourloton, and Cougny, *Dictionnaire des parlementaires*. Presumably the authors got the figures in the first place from the procès verbaux noted above.

44. If the voters arrived in time for the election of the permanent bureau, a procedure which occupied Saturday, 17 November, the arrondissemental elections required two days attendance. If on Sunday's voting no one had achieved an election, the college would reassemble on Monday; then if still deadlocked, on Tuesday. In these extreme circumstances a voter might be away from home four nights. A voter living close to the polling place could skip the Saturday session, go to the Sunday session, and come home in the same day. Probably not many rural voters had it this way.

This small town was at the distant boundary of the arrondissements of Cosne and Clamecy; it had been chosen in preference to the two *chefs lieux* in the hope that the distance and the difficulty of the roads . . . would prevent a number of voters from making the trip. One planned that the pro-ministry voters for whom transportation was provided would be there in force. But the stratagem was frustrated; each [opposition voter] got there as he could, but he got there. The town was literally full to bursting. The house of M. Tremeau-Soulmé where I was put up lodged more than twenty voters. All the rooms were full. Six beds had been made up in a large room like a dormitory; I was in one of these beds. We slept badly; there was a lot of talking; about midnight three delegates from the *Aide-toi* . . . were announced; the lights were turned up, and I sat up to receive them.[45]

It is a good guess that many an opposition voter had the assistance of the local organization. In at least two pamphlets the Aide-toi told of the necessity to make advance reservations in public conveyances for voters who had a considerable trip to make or, in the event that no public transportation was available, to arrange for something else. It told of the need to reserve lodging at inns. It urged that as much of this kind of special service as possible be deputed to young people who were politically keen and active but not yet at an age to vote. These too could be impressed to do the essential farm chores which a landholder could not leave unattended.[46]

To correlate one's estimate of the oppositions' organized effort with their successes in getting out the vote and in winning elections is more rewarding than trying to correlate between the oppositions' labors and the registration of the electorate as was hazarded a few pages back. Consider again two groups of sixteen departments, call them Group A (the group for which there is virtually no evidence of organized opposition electoral effort) and Group B (the group for which there is a good amount of convincing evidence). The departments of Group A had on their final electoral lists 11,078 names of whom 8,828 voted in the arrondissemental colleges (or 79.7 percent, some 5 percent below the national average). The departments of Group B had a larger electorate – 29,896 voters – of whom almost 26,000 voted (or 87 percent, 2 percent above the national average). The 7-plus percentage points which separate the accomplishments of the two groups would seem to be statistically significant.

Comparing the two groups in terms of how many opposition candi-

45. *Mémoires de M. Dupin [aîné]*, II, 12–13.

46. See Aide-toi, *Manuel de l'électeur* (Paris, n.d., but published after 5 Nov. 1827) BN Lb/49.753, for a discussion of this subject matter. See also Gallix, *Lettre à un électeur de Lyon* (cited in chap. 4 above, notes 32 and 72).

dates they returned, one finds roughly the same statistical magnitudes. The differences are slight, but probably they too are statistically indicative of a cause-effect relationship between the efforts and the successes of the oppositions.[47]

A similar correlation of effort and success in three cities where the fact of opposition activity is well attested – Paris, Lyon, and Rouen – shows the first two a bit above the national average for percent of voters voting, i.e., 89.5 and 88.5 percent respectively, and the third, Rouen, at the national average of 85 percent. In Lille, where two opposition candidates ran good but losing races, there was a turnout of 87.8 percent, in Marseille where Thomas, a left-wing lawyer, ran hard against the conservative Strafforello, the turnout was 82 percent. Only in Bordeaux, where opposition efforts were late in starting but which nevertheless returned two deputies, was the turnout well below the national average: 76 percent.

Upon such substantial evidence rests the conclusion that the electoral success of the two oppositions was no accident. It was earned. The men responsible for the campaign, whether they were the prominent leaders of the Friends and the Aide-toi in Paris or the less famous veterans of past elections in the countryside, proved themselves adept in the political arts. In every facet of the conduct of a winning election – registering voters opposed to the government of Villèle, finding politically correct and electable candidates and persuading them to make the run, and getting out the vote in support of these men – the opposition commanders and workhorses must receive good marks. Their accomplishment is the more noteworthy when one takes into account the handicap which censorship of the periodical press imposed upon them and the formidable strength of their collective adversary, the national government. The next chapter tells how that government used its resources.

47. Percentage of opposition candidates elected

	Number of departments	
	Group A	Group B
Zero %	2	1
1 - 20%	2	1
21 - 40	2	0
41 - 60	4	6
61 - 80	5	5
81 - 100	1	3

6 / The Government in the Election

Any discussion of the role of the government in Restoration elections should stress at the start two self-evident truths: namely, that the government was a passionate partisan and that it disposed a vast reservoir of political power which at election time it used pragmatically and enthusiastically. In these terms members of the cabinet most concerned with domestic affairs – in 1827 these were of course Villèle, not merely as president of the council of ministers but also as minister of finance, Corbière, the minister of the interior, and Peyronnet, the minister of justice – and their numerous subordinates, comprising the bulk of the national civil bureaucracy, would (and did) add a new line to their job descriptions.

In addition to their conventional duties, they now took on the specialized tasks of registering like-minded citizens, finding and promoting like-minded candidates, and seeing to it that the mix of voters and candidates was such as to result in a like-minded majority in the chamber of deputies. In the absence of any true political party based on private sectors of the society, this group of government officers, in their purely political identities, constituted something akin to those statist official parties of our century. It would be stupid to overstress this point if for no other reason than that this "official party" of 1827 deferred sufficiently to higher authority – the charter, law, and common decency – to suffer that which no true totalitarian party has permitted, i.e., a resounding defeat at the polls. In a way this political organization garnered the worst of two worlds: it played the political game to the point of outraging a large number of citizens, at the same time it did not play it hard enough to win.

As has been remarked earlier, the passage of the law of 2 May 1827 alerted the Villèle government to possible trouble ahead. Early on it must have recognized that any national election which took place between 1 October 1827 and, say, about 15 August 1828 would have to rest upon the electorate which was to be registered between 15 August and 30 September 1827. If going to the country during this time-interval was to result in the victory of a majority of pro-government candidates, clearly the electoral lists should, insofar as possible, be tailored to this end.

The first step which the government took was the issuance of some printed circular messages to the prefects, explaining in detail the content of the 2 May law and what the prefects should know and do to put it into effect.[1] Following soon after came the first of a series of intimate instructions signed for the most part by or for Corbière and classified "confidential" – and for reason.[2] It is this and its successors which put the leaders of the central government in Paris beyond any shadow of doubt right in the middle of what soon turned out to be a desperate political campaign. The message of the first confidential circular is unmistakable; a brief paraphrase would read like this: *M. le préfet;* see to it that no man who is eligible for the franchise and whose vote is likely to be cast for a pro-government candidate is left off your electoral list; give us the names of men whom you think would make politically satisfactory candidates, and take what measures you may to achieve their election.

The tone of all the messages of the series is decorous, formal, and correct. It does not make for racy reading; its elaborate circumlocutions are frequently just plain tedious; obviously the writers knew the dangers of the terrain they were traversing. Well aware that the

1. Chronologically the first of these messages was the royal ordinance of 27 June 1827 (Duvergier, *Lois,* XXVII, 300) which gave certain precisions to the May law. The next was an issuance by the minister of the interior (29 June 1827) which spelled out more of the details of inscription of voters and their erasure from the lists (*ibid.,* pp. 301–302). With this circular are some 20 pages of model forms which a prefect should follow in his complicated bookkeeping. These are not printed in Duvergier. I have seen a complete set in AD Ille-et-Vilaine 3 M 1/3. On 30 June the minister of justice sent out an instruction which explained the May law considered as a measure regulating the jury. Fifteen pages in length, it covers some of the ground of the previous circular (incomplete text in Duvergier, *Lois,* XXVII, 303; there is a full text in the AD Côte-d'Or, 2 M 53). On 19 July 1827 the minister of the interior sent out more instructions relating to the model forms of the 29 June circular. The copy I have seen is in AD Ille-et-Vilaine 3 M 1/3. I have a feeling that all these printed circulars must be available in a central place, but I have not found it.

2. I have found none of these documents in the AN. The score that I have found have been in the ADs, though no single AD has a complete set.

One may be almost certain that the documents in question were circular instructions probably sent in nearly identical form to all 86 prefects. A few are unique longhand communications, most are lithographs of longhand. In the latter, the last line on the first sheet carries the legend "A M. le préfet du département . . ." in the hand of the writer of the text and, for example, "de la Marne" in another hand.

In my references to specific messages which follow I will use a short title, as "min. int., confid. circ., 14 Sept. 1827." For the full references, see the Bibliographical Note.

"confidential" slug might not give them the privacy they desired, they often formulated the thought in a way that would not be too painful to find in the press, should a leak occur.[3] There are, for example, numerous injunctions to obedience of the letter of the law over which broods an obvious pragmatism. Perhaps the clamors following the election of 1824 had hit the mark and the government wished to avoid a repetition if possible. Hence prefects were admonished that when they inscribed a voter on their own authority (*d'office*) they must be scrupulously careful that they also had collected and had in their file all the documents to prove that he in fact fulfilled the prerequisites of the franchise. Again they are reminded, "you owe to your adversaries full justice, but you do not owe them anything in the way of unofficial favors."[4]

The opposition is seldom referred to in incendiary language; never "jacobin," for example. The strongest terms – "revolutionaries" used in the context of the "monstrous alliance" and "les ennemis de l'ordre public" – appear only once; milder but direct phrasing, as "opposition de gauche ou de droite" occur on a few occasions, but most often it is referred to as the "factions" – a thoroughly neutral word.[5] The government side is composed of "royalistes disposés à appuyer le gouvernement," or men inclined "en faveur des véritables intérêts du pays, qui sont le maintien du bon ordre, l'affermissement de nos institutions, et l'appui du gouvernement." Its candidates are identified by such phrases as "dans la ligne d'opinion suivie par le gouvernement."[6] They are never referred to as "our candidates," as many a prefect termed them.

A few of the messages are short and crisp, most are a few hundred words in length, and the most formidable (that of 22 October) runs to more than two thousand words. Generally speaking they fall into two main categories: requests for information on the one hand, and instructions and exhortations on the other.

The reason behind the levies for information is obvious. From

3. The Villèle diary (4 Sept. 1827) gives a sort of positive confirmation to what a reader of these circular messages would sense. The entry's first sentence is, "Travaillé avec les commis de l'intérieur: adressé une circulaire aux préfets sur les listes électorales"; and the third clearly related to it, "On n'envoye pas les circulaires confidentielles aux préfets du Tarn, de la Haute Loire, et de l'Indre de crainte d'indiscrétion."

4. Min. int., confid. circ., 14 Sept. 1827.

5. Min. int., confid. circ., 4 Sept., 14 Sept., and 22 Oct. 1827.

6. Min. int., confid. circ., 4 Sept. and 14 Sept. 1827.

early in the summer one must guess that the triumvirate in Paris saw the possibility of a general election and wished to be prepared to make the wise decision whether or not to go for it. What the triumvirs needed to start with was information as to how the electoral lists were shaping up. No sooner had the first published list been posted than Corbière was telling the prefects that he wanted them to keep him informed of their progress in list-making, to forward news of any unusual developments which they felt that he should know about, and especially to pass on any insights they might have about the make-up of the lists as this might relate both to the jury and to electoral prospects.[7] Two weeks later the minister concluded a message: "Already my confidential dispatch of 18 August requested your first impressions of hoped-for results; I now hasten to ask you for greater precision. This is to alert you to give particular attention to the study of the elements which must comprise your list."[8] And ten days later the minister was back with the ultimate demand, namely that the prefects go over their lists and make a count of the voters "likely to support the government, those likely to support the candidates of the opposition of the right, and those the candidates of the opposition of the left."[9] With the lists still two weeks from completion some prefects complied only later to make what they hoped were more authoritative estimates on the outcome of a possible election, for that in essence is exactly what the minister wanted to know.[10]

7. Min. int., confid. circ., 18 Aug. 1827. The minister really meant it. Eleven days later, not having received from the prefect of the Eure a copy of his first list, the minister wrote again telling him he was about two weeks delinquent, to send the list along, and to send also the first revision due momentarily. The prefect continued to be sloppy and received another reminder dated 19 October saying that he was still owing copies of the fourth revision. AD Eure 4 M 104.

8. Min. int., confid. circ., 4 Sept. 1827.

9. Min. int., confid. circ., 14 Sept. 1827.

10. Compliance with this request was seemingly spotty. As I have noted in chapter 2, some prefects probably combined their answer to this question with their dispatches written in response to the circular of the director of police relating to information about the "esprit public." Or it may be that all prefects made the written estimates, many of which may have been destroyed or misfiled. In all events, the cartons of the AN F/1c/III series contain only a few answers. See in this series Tarn-et-Garonne 2, pref. to min. int., 28 Aug. and 6 Oct.; Var 4, pref. to min. int., 12 and 14 Sept.; Vendée 3, pref. to min. int., 4 Oct.; Vienne 4, pref. to min. int., 22 Oct.; Haute-Vienne 4, pref. to min. int., 6 Oct. 1827, in which the prefects essay a numerical count of the way their voters would probably vote.

In these estimates the prefects gave an indifferent performance. For the Tarn-et-Garonne the result was only half as bad as they predicted: instead of losing all 4 seats the government

By mid-September the government was already soliciting in cautious, not to say oblique, terms news of possible candidates. The paragraphs run,

> thus . . . the many thoughts I have asked of you . . . would be otherwise incomplete, if you did not indicate the candidates, who in the event of elections, might be put up by each *nuance d'opinion,* their chances of election, and their personal [political] leanings, for it could be that some of them in their striving for election put on an outward appearance which is [quite] different from their true selves.
>
> Always include . . . incumbent deputies; tell me how they feel about running again and their probable chances of winning over presumed opponents.[11]

Although there is no specific mention of pro-government candidates, they are clearly bracketed into the generalized appeal. No prefect could afford to miss this message and those who responded did not.

A month later, and getting down to brass tacks, the ministry queried the prefects about their recommendations for presidents of the electoral colleges, just in case it should please his majesty to call for elections. In many more cases than not, the man who received the presidency was by that fact the government's chosen candidate. He would hold a prestigious office and, more important, would hold it by virtue of the king's personal choice: the presidencies were announced in a royal ordinance. On the other hand the linking of a candidate's name to the presidency was upon occasion the very thing that could bring on his defeat. In these cases obviously some one not in the partisan political swim should be chosen. In the dispatch at issue prefects were asked to put up three nominees for the presidency of each arrondissemental, special, and departmental college, and to bear in mind the highly important consideration as to whether or not the nomination for president would help or damage the chances of a favored candidate. Naturally all of the nominees should be from among those in the "ligne d'opinion suivie par le gouvernement" and should where appropriate include incumbent deputies. The pre-

---

lost only 2; for the Var the prefect called it correctly, 5 government wins for the 5 seats; for the Vendée the brand new prefect, Suleau, was over-optimistic to the extent of estimating a win for all 5 seats while the government actually lost 3 of the 5; for the Vienne the prefect's estimate of 5 wins out of 5 was correct; and for the Haute-Vienne the prefect's estimate of losses for all 4 seats was over-pessimistic – the government lost only 2 of the 4. It won the 2 departmental college seats.

11. Min. int., confid. circ., 14 Sept. 1827.

fects were asked to finish the task "in the three or four days which follow the arrival of this letter."[12]

Relatively early on the minister was troubled by the possibility of the two oppositions within a given department entering unholy alliance for the electoral defeat of government supporters, and he wanted information on the horrid subject. His phrasing of the matter is revealing of the government's distaste. "I do not suppose that you have to fear in any of your colleges alliances of the oppositions. I am persuaded that your efforts plus the proper indignation of right-thinking men will suffice to prevent or neutralize such arrangements." For in these cases the royalists are sacrificing their cause for their ambition, "and the revolutionaries are acting only in the hope of later promoting division and faithlessness in royalist ranks. As I have said I would not suppose that you might have to see such business, but in any case give me the benefit of your conjecture."[13]

Once the decision was firm to call the election, the government sent out a circular which told the prefects to use all haste in getting their returns to Paris;[14] and once the election was over and done with the government went back again for information about putative wrongdoings on the part of the bureaucracy which would lead to accusations during the organization sessions of the new chamber. The government wanted to be prepared in advance.[15]

Throughout the correspondence the minister repeatedly memorialized the prefects, and through them the bulk of the civil bureaucracy, on the seriousness of the pre-electoral tasks and how the government expected each to perform with zeal and devotion. At the end of the long dispatch of mid-September, Villèle, signing for Corbière, says he wants to know if they did. Or as he put it,

> You will then have to report (and each year henceforward at this time) those officers who are not disposed to fulfill this important duty. Do not fear to tell me the whole truth: it is a debt you owe to the task entrusted to you and to you yourself so that you will not be blamed for errors which were not yours, but which your own zeal could not prevent. What you write me — whether it be a matter [indicating that a] transfer [should be in order] or something more severe — will be for my eyes only. I will take up with my

12. Min. int., confid. circ., 14 Oct. 1827.

13. Min. int., confid. circ., 14 Sept. 1827.

14. Min. int., confid. circ., 12–15 Nov. 1827. The lateness of the date is somewhat surprising. Many of these outgoing messages, however, probably went by the telegraph.

15. Min. int., confid. circ., 26 Dec. 1827.

colleagues information affecting officers of their ministries, but you may be certain that nothing you report will be exposed to the indiscretion of their office staffs.[16]

With election day about a week away Villèle again addressed the prefects, this time in his role of minister of finance. His concern now was to have reports on the behavior of the employees of the *fisc* whose work on the tax records was of great importance in list-making. Curtly he asked about the conduct of these officers and ended, "I hope that you will have nothing but praise to report, but if things are otherwise please be so kind as to inform me of the derelictions."[17]

As an earnest of the government's continuing interest in the political complexion of the electorate one last levy for information went forth. This one was in the nature of a true postmortem. Let us find out, the sense of its message ran, what went on in the recent election while the memory is fresh; let us find out both as a matter of curiosity, but more as a preparation for other elections to come.

I desire [*M. le préfet*] that you turn to at once to annotate man by man and according to your latest intelligence your electoral lists from the point of view how each man voted. You will confine yourself to only two political outlooks, that of the right and that of the left, which you will designate (on the list with the appropriate initial letter) a D [droite] or a G [gauche].

Doubtless you cannot fit all your voters into these two categories for in each college there will be a larger or smaller number without a firmly held position . . . these you will designate with an F [flottant] for "floating."[18]

This was not the first time that the prefects had been called upon for such a census. They found the task difficult and its conclusions of dubious value; their performance seems to have been spotty to say the least. In all likelihood the fall of Corbière, along with the rest of the Villèle government, at the end of 1827 was reason enough for most prefects to dare to forget about the business. I have found a few traces of prefectoral efforts[19] but nothing to show that compliance

16. Min. int., confid. circ., 14 Sept. 1827.

17. Min. finance, confid. circ. to prefs., 9 Nov. 1827.

18. Min. int., confid. circ., 5 Dec. 1827.

19. The prefect of the Marne took the request seriously enough to pass it on to his subprefects, all of whom seem to have taken it seriously enough to do some work on it. However, only the tallies of the subprefects of Epernay and Vitry (a fragment) survive. You may see these and other letters by other subprefects in AD Marne 7 M 7.

was general enough to warrant a wrapping up of conclusions in the ministry of the interior.

The second category of circular message sent out from the ministry of the interior embraces a host of instructions and exhortations and prompted a more enlightening response from the recipients than had those circulars which requested catalogues of information. Two pervasive themes, both of which have already been mentioned, run through this correspondence. They are the themes of secrecy and of the urgency that the civil bureaucracy, starting with the prefects, put forth its utmost effort to secure the election for the partisans of the ministry.

As for secrecy, nearly all of the outgoing messages from Paris and the bulk of the prefectoral answers bear the confidential classification. Whatever the technical meaning of the word "confidentielle," its presence on these documents would seem to indicate that the government had begun early to prepare for a possible election and did not want anyone outside the government to know it. It may be that the government sensed a vulnerability in its moral position. In all events it wanted to win the election, should one be called, and it well understood the pragmatic value of tactical surprise.

Sophisticates like Villèle and Corbière could not have believed that something known to most of the prefects constituted a secret; obviously they knew that there would be leaks. But by the same token they reasoned that an element of uncertainty could be fed into the minds of those who cracked into the secret by way of a cover story. Hence, over and over again, the circular messages carry the injunction: now do not get ahead of the game; do not you or anyone else go jumping to conclusions, for it is within the king's most cherished prerogative to dissolve the chamber and summon the electoral colleges any time he pleases and on short notice. All of us wish to be ever in a condition of perfect readiness, just in case his majesty makes up his mind. There is no more to it than just this.[20] Of course there was, and of course those taken in by this artless cover story were certainly not the sharp opposition politicians who clustered about Chateaubriand's Friends, the Société, Aide-toi, and the local notables of the left and far right.

As for the importance attached to an all-out electoral effort throughout the bureaucracy, it was well understood. Prefects got the

20. Min. int., confid. circ., 4, 14, 27 Sept., and 14 Oct. 1827.

word from Paris and passed it on, often with emphasis added. The comte de Frottier de Bagneux, prefect of the Maine-et-Loire, sent out his own circular in early November: "Placed at the top of the administration of this department," it went,

> I am . . . charged with the important matter of the elections . . . and am to instruct [you fellow functionaries] as to the wishes of the government and the line which the government wishes all to follow. I am required to report upon the . . . conduct which each [officer] will display and [at the same time] am also no less rigorously enjoined to identify those [officers] whose lukewarmness, apathy, and lack of zeal hinder them in their duty. . . . I doubt not that you will respond with all the effort expected of you.[21]

Coster, prefect of the Haute-Vienne, who confronted a formidable opposition campaign and had a very serious problem on his hands, wrote a more direct and less flowery cognate. Addressed to his subordinates, it began,

> His majesty desires the reelection of most of the members of the last chamber. All officers of the administration owe the king their full cooperation. If they are voters they are to support the king's nominees – the presidents of the colleges – and to urge all other voters over whom they have any influence to do likewise. If they are not voters they are to persevere discreetly to this same end. To do the contrary or even to sit idly by is to refuse the government the cooperation which is owed it: it is to separate one's self from the government and to renounce one's position. Present these reflections to your subordinates. . . .[22]

The word went down the chain of command and laterally in many directions. It is a fair guess that there was no one on the government payroll or in an unsalaried honorific position that did not get the message. The prefect of the Charente-Inférieure harried his subprefects for prompt action on their electoral list; in the Bouches-du-Rhône the subprefects were active campaign agents; so were they in the Yonne. In the Eure and the Seine-et-Oise one of the subprefects made a point of reporting the lack of "zeal" among laggard bureaucrats. The prefect of the Lot's own weekly house organ, which went to all the mayors of his department, devoted three issues

21. AD Maine-et-Loire 8 M 6, from the *cabinet de prefét,* 7 Nov. 1827: probably a draft outgoing to his subordinates.

22. This particular prefectoral circular fell into enemy hands and was reprinted and widely circulated in the department. The opposition candidate (and winner) Bourdeau, learning of the prefect's displeasure, wrote the latter owning that it was he who had arranged for the printing; if the prefect wished to make something of it, Bourdeau would like nothing better than to join battle and in public. AN F/1c/III Haute-Vienne 4. The text of the circular is printed in *Lettres de Béranger,* p. 87.

as to how important it was to support the pro-government candidates, how important to disregard the poisonous weeds being sowed by the now uncensored opposition press, and how one might celebrate the joyous outcome of the election in which all four arrondissemental winners were government adherents.[23]

Officers of the fisc, the *percepteurs* of the direct taxes, were of course among the most important men of the campaign. After all, it was their bookkeeping and their figures which were the essential ingredient in the computation of the cens. They were required to serve the concerns not only of their own prefects, but also of distant prefects who wished to inscribe a right-minded voter whose taxable real property was scattered over several departments.[24]

Likewise officers of the courts, *procureurs,* and even judges of the lower tribunals, seem to have been expected to participate in the campaign;[25] so too were the security forces. The *procureur du roi* in Figéac (Lot) sent out a printed flyer to the auxiliary police of the commune in which he announced that "the Revolution has taken the occasion of the election to make a last effort," and he exhorted the policemen to give their full attention to those who would "damage the sacred property inherent in the exercise of political rights."[26] The prefect of the Drôme called upon the gendarmerie to assist in delivering the electoral lists to the communes of the department and overseeing their posting. The commanding general of the 21st division of the army had apparently informed his troops that those who had the vote should return the king's confidence in the army by voting for candidates who would support the government. He wrote the prefect a note asking him to report how his soldiers voted![27] And so on.

23. AN F/1c/III Charente-Inférieure 7, pref. to min. int., 3 July 1827; AD Bouches-du-Rhône M/2(III)-9; AN F/1c/III Yonne 3, pref. to min. int., 25 Aug. 1827; AD Eure 4 M 104; AD Seine-et-Oise II M 11(2); AN F/1c/III Lot 4; see esp. the printed *Mémorial administratif,* nos. 98–100.

24. AD Drôme M 31, pref. to dir. contribs. directes, 20 July 1827, and AN F/1c/III Charente-Inférieure 7, pref. to min. int., 3 July 1827.

25. AN F/1c/III Tarn-et-Garonne 2, pref. to min. int., 21 Nov. 1827. The prefect reports the dereliction of two judges of the civil tribunal of Montauban.

26. AN F/1c/III Lot 5.

27. AD Drôme M 31, pref. to the cdr. of gendarmes of his dept., 9 Aug. 1827, and AD Creuse 3 M 36, commanding general to pref. of the Creuse, 7 Nov. 1827.

The commanding general of the 8th division of the army with its HQ in Marseille wrote the prefect that he could rely upon the writer's full cooperation in the direction of matters affecting the electoral college "to the end of achieving the results expected by the government of the king" (AD Bouches-du-Rhône M/2(III)-9, 9 Nov. 1827).

The large general undertakings which the officers of the government were required to perform were in essence almost exactly those of which the political leaders of the opposition were seised. The differences were in important incidentals, not in basic substance. In a word, they too had to register the electorate, endeavoring to get as many friendly votes on the lists as they could, and no more unfriendly ones than observance of the letter of the law would dictate. They had to participate, indeed play a key role in the identification of suitable candidates, some of whom would be named presidents of colleges, some not. They had to campaign for the election of these candidates, using whatever wiles and leverages they could muster, and they had to get their supporting voters to the polls in the expectation that they would vote as pledged.

List-making or registration of the electorate looked at in the constitutional sense was a public, not a political, service. Supposedly, to read about it in the law, it was an exercise in which the appropriate officers of the state took official cognizance of those who fulfilled the conditions of the franchise and who had proved their qualifications by depositing with the authorities their collection of validating official documents. But for the prefects and their subordinates the task had, as we have seen, a political twist, partly because the apathy of a sizable proportion of the possible electorate offered an opportunity for the administration to inscribe *d'office* those men it knew would vote for government candidates, and also because the minister of the interior told them of this opportunity and urged its exploitation in no uncertain terms.

"*M. le préfet,* word from your colleagues and other similar news leads me to make this most important recommendation," begins Corbière's confidential circular of 14 July.

Many are saying that the very men whose principles offer the best guarantee of a proper . . . electoral list, . . . gripped by a repugnance for jury service, are neglecting to get themselves inscribed. It is for the prefects to frustrate this negligence by stimulating their zeal and [if necessary] to inscribe them *d'office.* The absence of these men's names from the list would result in a great loss for the cause of justice, doubly so if they were also omitted from the first part of the jury list [i.e., of those jurors who were also electors].

You are aware what care these inscriptions – done without the participation of the registree – require. Do what is necessary and see to it that the administrative information you use be correct and beyond criticism. You personally should follow and verify the work of your staff in this respect.

In less formal language: Do not let jury-dodging pro-government voters stay off the electoral lists; inscribe them on your own authority, and in putting together the dossier of their documents, personally see to it that no mistakes are made. The message goes on to instruct the prefects how to make up the first published list, that of 15 August. "Reinscribe voters who were on your predecessor lists [often those prepared for the election of 1824] unless you are sure that they no longer qualify. As to new registrants, all of them will be obliged to produce their own documents; none can require you to inscribe them *d'office* and you will not take the responsibility of so doing *except for sufficient reason* [emphasis added]. . . ."

These points are given further elaboration in other messages from Paris. That of 4 September begins with a highly significant note taking account of the "ardor with which *comités directeurs* [opposition electoral organizations] have prompted the inscription of all the voters whom they believe will serve their schemes." It continues to tell the prefects that it is up to them in their turn to inscribe d'office all "peaceful and well-intentioned voters whose negligence could deliver the electoral colleges – when they shall be summoned – to the influence of the 'factions' [read, 'opposition']." And that of 14 September goes on: "it is probable that you will have inscribed *d'office* some of [our adversaries from among] your department's great *notables*. In this case it would be correct to keep them just as you would royalist voters. . . . Thus in avoiding embarrassing erasures, especially when they would be numerous and ascribed to your partiality, you enhance your operations without spoiling the quality of your lists."

What the minister suggested was, after all, nothing new. If ministers of the past had not suggested it, prefects in the past had done it and seem to have done so pretty much as a standard operating procedure.[28] So were they doing in the early fall of 1827. The

28. The *Constitutionnel* (1 Oct. 1820, p.2), quoting from the *Journal du Cher*, asserts that the custom of the prefects was to issue a first list which they had confected d'office and then in subsequent lists to drop would-be voters whose documents were not in order.

In a draft circular which went out in advance of the election of 1824, the ministry tells the prefects: "So as not to be too much harmed by registree negligence; the administration may . . . *procure d'office* the [voter's essential] documentation. . . . It is a service which the administration renders not an obligation which it fulfills. Time and means would be inadequate to take care of all omissions and in consequence voters have nothing to claim

thought was that in meeting their first deadline (15 August) the prefects should draw heavily upon predecessor lists, dropping men whom they knew to have died or moved out of the department or lost their fortunes. They probably also dropped men whose cens had been close to the margin the last time around and who were known adherents of the opposition. At this stage of the game no one had as yet begun his scurry for documents and no great harm had been done.

From that moment on, however, things changed. Those voters known to be government supporters and reluctant to be vulnerable to jury service and who therefore would do nothing to round up their documents discovered that they were going to be voters willy-nilly, for the prefect had himself collected the documents. Those other voters known to be in opposition may have learned then and there that they could not vote unless they did something about their documents. Perhaps they had to gather the whole collection again from scratch, perhaps find out which of those already on file had been unacceptable to the authorities. If they did not learn of the matter until the publication of one of the late lists, they might not have time to set things right before the final deadline.

"My first list," wrote the prefect of the Tarn, "is composed almost wholly *d'office*. Such is the repugnance for jury duty that no one comes forward. . . . I have collected the appropriate documents from the mayors and the collectors of direct taxes." A week later his colleague of the Tarn-et-Garonne reports, "I am busy at the moment in verifying the claims of royalist [pro-government] voters who were dropped (along with many others) from the lists [by a predecessor]. All who can be legally reinstated will be so before the end of the month." The prefect of the Eure, as some of his brethren had done, gave notice that his first list was provisional and that no one on it could be sure of being on the final list unless his documents were on file. This went for all, including the voters of the arrondissement of Bernay, who less than six months before had procured their full complement of documents so as to vote in a by-election. A group of them, among whose largely illegible signatures appear those of the notable oppositionists, the duc de Broglie and Dupont de l'Eure, realized full well that they were probably not to

or expect of the administration. They know that it is their own responsibility to 'justify their rights' [read, 'get themselves on the lists']." AN F/1c/II 52, dated 24 Dec. 1823.

be among the chosen who would be inscribed d'office and protested the burden of once again collecting their documents.[29]

The prefect of the Var reported that he was gathering documents for the account of royalist voters, but letting the *électeurs libéraux* fetch their own.[30] The prefect of the Vaucluse, a meticulous man, was sorely troubled by what he felt to be an inequity in following ministerial instructions to the letter. His problem involved opposition voters whom he had carried on his first list, only to drop for want of documentation – at the last minute. Several people had come to him about the matter and he was going back to the minister for advice.[31] The prefect of the Vienne looked back at the list-making days and told of the deplorable insouciance of the voters of his first electoral arrondissement; few had raised a finger to get on the list. Of the 357 whom he had inscribed on his own authority, 141 had had no documents, and of these he had kept 110 and rejected 31 who were of the political stripe to which, according to the minister's advice, no favor was owed.[32]

"I have observed your instructions scrupulously," wrote the prefect of the Haute-Vienne. "I have treated the government's adversaries with justice without doing them favors. [On the other hand] I have put all my energy into collecting the documents of the voters upon whom the ministry can count." Much the same message came in to Paris from the prefect of the Yonne.[33]

The business of inscribing d'office a voter whose taxable property was scattered over several departments gave the prefect a lot of extra work. To the extent that he took the minister seriously and made a point of gathering the necessary documents of the men whom he was inscribing on his own authority, he had to communicate with brother prefects asking the latter to dig out tax receipts and, upon occasion, birth certificates. The records for the Vaucluse show the prefect sending off more than a hundred messages during the late

29. AN F/1c/III Tarn 4, pref. to min. int., 30 Aug. 1827; *ibid.,* Tarn-et-Garonne 2, pref. to min. int., 8 Sept. 1827; AD Eure 4 M 104, 26 Aug. 1827.

30. AN F/1c/III Var 4, pref. to min. int., 9 Sept. 1827.

31. *Ibid.,* Vaucluse 4, pref. to min. int., 8 Sept. 1827. I say meticulous of this worthy man because, of all the prefects whose records I have perused, he is the only one who kept a careful record of his outgoing messages.

32. *Ibid.,* Vienne 4, pref. to min. int., 12 Oct. 1827.

33. *Ibid.,* Haute-Vienne 4, pref. to min. int., 20 Sept. 1827; *ibid.,* Yonne 3, pref. to min. int., 12 Sept. 1827.

summer bearing on this subject to, for example, the prefects of the Ardèche, Gard, Bouches-du-Rhône, and Seine. In the Somme the prefect coped with perhaps an even greater number of cases dispersed over an even wider spectrum of departments; so too in the Calvados and Cantal.[34] In this particular phase of the electoral business there was no want of prefectoral zeal and devotion to duty.

It was not for nothing that the minister urged prefects to exercise the utmost caution in those inscriptions d'office where they themselves undertook to procure the voter's documents. The case of the prefect of the Vosges offers an ex post facto justification of the minister's warning. Meulan, the prefect, was not only careless; he was downright negligent, and the worst was that he got caught red-handed. In extenuation, he had a special problem.

The Vosges was a department which had five administrative arrondissements and fewer than four hundred voters. In the elections prior to 1824, this meant that voters of the department, in accordance with the electoral law of 1820, assembled and voted in a single special college. Incidentally the vote in the 1820 election went predominantly to opposition candidates. But in 1824 the number of voters grew beyond the four hundred mark, and accordingly the department lost its special college status and voted in three arrondissemental colleges and one departmental. Full-dress legislation had been required to effect the change in the structure of the colleges. Under the new arrangement the government's fortunes at the polls improved markedly. Now came 1827. The prefect soon saw the bind he was in, for his electorate had again dropped to below four hundred, requiring the reinstitution of the special college, but this seemingly could not be achieved without the same sort of legislation which would repeal the law which had been passed three years earlier. He seems to have decided that the best way out was to inscribe d'office enough voters to take him up and over the magic number 400 and then proceed as in 1824.

He acted without taking account of an angry lawyer, M. Mougeot of Epinal, whose political sympathies lay not with the government. Mougeot began taxing him in mid-September pointing out some

34. AD Vaucluse Z 11; AD Somme #107,555 (includes Aisne, Aube, Eure, Ille-et-Vilaine, Jura, Landes, Loir-et-Cher, Marne, Moselle, Pas-de-Calais, Saône-et-Loire, and Yonne); AD Calvados 10 M 13–14; AD Cantal 33 M 14. In this category are some 200 letters going to and coming from 13 departments.

twenty voters whose names should not be on the list. If the prefect had erased all twenty, his list would have been below four hundred. In justifiable quandary he went to his boss, the minister, for advice. The archival record in Paris shows no response, nor any response to a dispatch from Epinal a fortnight later saying that the "liberal faction" was challenging fifty voters as not being fully qualified. Of these the prefect acknowledged weaknesses in the claims of twenty-one and he cut them, but by now his cushion of legality was down to a few marginal voters above the four hundred minimum. Not daring to go below it he allowed the election to take place on his terms.

The outcome was a dual disappointment: the government lost four of the five seats and the outraged opposition leaders of the department carried their case to the chamber of deputies. The latter appointed a committee to look into the affair which found the prefect in such grievous error that it recommended the nullification of the whole election. And so it came to pass that because the prefect had tried to inscribe a group of voters – more than one hundred as it turned out! – whose documents could not validate their right to vote, the prefect and the government got a big black eye and in the most public way possible. Furthermore in the new election the government lost five out of five. No wonder the minister who might have foreseen disasters of a lesser magnitude warned of the perils of the inscription d'office.[35]

The circular messages of instruction beginning in mid-September and running into early November are full of the detail relating to the rectification tables. In the long dispatch of 27 September the minister writes at length about the men entitled to get on the lists after the 1 October closure, for beyond that date there would be a final revision or rectification table. They would be those who had successfully appealed an earlier prefectoral decision and those whose ducks had been in order, but who had been temporarily left off the list pending the prefect's final decision.

35. AN F/1c/III Vosges 6, numerous dispatches, pref. to min. int., Sept. - Nov. 1827. There are other cases, not as spectacular as that of the Vosges. See for example the complaints of some petitioners of the Lot (*ibid.,* Lot 4, one undated, one 18 Nov. 1827).

See also AD Seine-et-Oise II M 11(2): a letter from the mayor of Boissy to his subprefect which points out that the final lists have several errors of the sort which a close attention to business would have made impossible. There are, for example, two dead men, one who has changed his political domicile, and one who does not pay the cens.

There was another circular dealing with the limitations on the rights of third parties: in order to intercede on behalf of would-be voters they had to have valid powers of attorney; and, to object to putative improper inscriptions, they themselves had to be registered voters.[36] Still another circular dealt with the posting of the final lists,[37] and a last one introduced a new note on the qualifications of those who could there appear. It modified prior instructions (and the law too, as this student has striven to understand it) in that it permitted the prefect to inscribe "those who have acquired their rights after 30 September."[38] It was a fair guess, and one that the *Constitutionnel* made, that the men who made the grade at the last minute were not necessarily those known for their support of the opposition cause.[39]

In the identification and promoting of candidates whose political views were acceptable to the ministry, the prefects played an important role. The problem of the government candidate frequently involved that of the presidency of the college; it also involved a half dozen or more variables which were likely to be peculiar to the men themselves, the electoral district, and even the voters at issue. In some cases the problem was really non-existent: a highly valued incumbent appeared set to run again and would be helped by being named to preside at the election.[40] In other cases, where the incumbent was withdrawing from public life, the prefect had either to try to dissuade him or to find another man who would be acceptable to the local notables. Thomas Strafforello, one of the leading merchants of Marseille, had sat in the chamber since 1820 where his loyalty to the conservative side and his business sense had made him a highly valuable deputy. He was sick of it and let it be known

36. Min. int., confid. circ., 9 Oct. 1827.

37. Min. int., confid. circ., 5 Nov. 1827. This document indicates that final lists need not be posted more than two or three days before the convocation of the colleges.

38. The text of this perplexing sentence reads, "Celle ci vous autorise au cas où il se présentat, après la publication du tableau de rectification, des droits admissibles dans ce tableau, c'est à dire acquis depuis le 30 Septembre ou conservés par une réclamation antérieure à les inscrire supplémentairement. C'est une modification à la dépeche du 22 Octobre. . . . "

39. *Constitutionnel,* 19 Nov. 1827, p. 2.

40. Bausset, deputy of Aix (Bouches-du-Rhône), would have been such a man. He was correct as to politics, wanted to run again, and received the prefect's endorsement for the presidency of his college. AD Bouches-du-Rhône M/2(III)-9, pref. to min. int., 21 Oct. 1827. This long dispatch offers an intimate view of a prefect wrestling with the problem of the candidate/president.

he would not run should an election occur in 1827. His prefect, Villeneuve-Bargemont, finally persuaded him to do so, realizing that if elected he would soon resign.[41] He was and he did.

In the Tarn-et-Garonne the prefect was having difficulty finding a man who could defeat the opposition deputy Preissac and, realizing that no one could do this without some appeal to leftist voters, put forward the name of Caumont. He wrote the minister saying that the urgency of beating Preissac required giving the presidency to Caumont even though all on "our side would not be wholly satisfied."[42] In other rare cases, prefects and the crown actually agreed to name as presidents men who were in the opposition. And in the Charente Jacques Hennessy of the left opposition was almost certainly named in the hope that he would defeat Martell, a man of much more extreme views.

Villeneuve-Bargemont had the obverse of this problem in the Bouches-du-Rhône. One of his favored candidates was Jean Pardessus, a deputy, one of the vice-presidents of the chamber, and a legal scholar of some renown, whom he felt was certain to be defeated in the departmental college. Hence he was reluctant to nominate him for the presidency and have him risk the public humiliation of not being elected.[43]

Added to the prefect's headaches in finding willing candidates was that of acknowledging and yielding to the force of localism. Unless a man were a truly national figure, he would have difficulties in his search for political support far outside his own electoral district.[44] One of the reasons that the departmental voters of the Cher rejected the candidacy of the comte de Peyronnet, minister of justice, was that he was a foreigner from Bordeaux. The very rare election of an out-of-department government candidate went to Auguste Ravez, whose tenure of the presidency of chamber of deputies had

41. AD Bouches-du-Rhône M/2(III)–9.

42. AN F/1c/III Tarn-et-Garonne 2, pref. to min. int., 26 Oct. 1827.

43. As of n.40 above. Shortly before the publication of the ordinances, Pardessus wrote a personal letter to his friend, Villeneuve-Bargemont, telling him that for "obvious reasons" he had not wished to come to Marseille to campaign in September and that he could not come now. Would the prefect therefore represent his willingness to serve another term and convey his thanks to his friendly supporters.

44. One may be sure that electoral organizations of the opposition had their own difficulties in this respect. However, they receive only passing notice in the pamphlet literature. Furthermore, at least 26 opposition constituencies elected deputies not native to the department.

endured the best part of a decade and probably constituted the main reason that the departmental college of the Nord was willing to stomach an outsider from the Gironde. Incidentally he was the only government candidate to achieve a double election in 1827.

Local preferences and animosities obtained at several echelons below the level of the old province or department. One of the reasons that the prefect of the Tarn was keen on the candidacy of Joseph de Lastours was that, although born and brought up in Castres, he was nevertheless acceptable to the voters native to the neighboring town of Lavaur. Another without his special Lavaur connections could not count upon their support and might therefore be defeated.[45] Likewise, Villeneuve-Bargemont was delighted with the candidacy of Lagoy of Arles, who was one of those rare Arlesiens acceptable to the self-conscious voters of neighboring Tarascon.[46] No question but that one of the conditions which a potential winner had to meet was that he not antagonize these extraordinarily intense localisms.

Once the king had issued the ordinance naming his choices for the presidency of the electoral colleges, nothing but another ordinance could change the nomination. If prefects had second thoughts they therefore kept them to themselves for the most part.

As a general proposition a man served as presiding officer at an electoral college because it would help his own candidacy or help the larger cause, or because it was an honorable service requested by the crown. Some men received compensation; but my guess is that the number was small.[47] There is the case of the prefect of the Aube writing late in December that in his opinion the man who served as president of the departmental college, Delahuproye, an official of the cour royale in Paris, had been put to expenses heavier than should be asked of a man of his modest means. The prefect asked

45. AN F/1c/III Tarn 4, pref. to min. int., 7 Oct. 1827. Note that this letter, which deals with candidacies and presidencies, was written a week before the minister's circular asking for nominations for presidencies.

46. AD Bouches-du-Rhône M/2(III)–9, pref. to min. int., 21 Oct. 1827.

47. Frederick Artz in his "*Electoral System in France during the Bourbon Restoration,*" cites AN F/1c/II 52 as his authority for saying that the presidents received fees of 1500–3000 francs, "though sums as high as 47,000 francs were sometimes paid" (p. 209). I think that the document which Mr. Artz cites contains the sums issued to prefects out of the minister's secret fund. More about this fund and its use later in this chapter. Some of the monies involved may have gone to the presidents for their official entertainment, but the bulk was put to quite different purposes. I did not find the 47,000 franc figure in this document.

that he be reimbursed to the sum of eighteen hundred francs. The record indicates that he did not get it.[48] On the other hand, a potential last-minute substitute – the original nominee had become too ill to function – said he could not accept unless his expenses were underwritten. In this instance the ministry acted speedily and authorized the prefect to issue him one thousand francs.[49]

It goes without saying that the prefects and their subordinates, so thoroughly enmeshed in election politics, were ardent campaigners for their chosen instruments. But electoral campaigns for ministerial candidates, no less than for those of the opposition, were strangely low-key affairs in which politicking was generally done on a man-to-man basis with the modern sort of open gathering and its speech-making virtually unknown. Administrators toured their parishes, talking with influential citizens and endeavoring to enlist the latter themselves to talk up the given candidate in their own immediate circle of friends.[50]

As for the promotion of official candidates via the political pamphlet, the *Journal des Débats* claimed that this was done in secrecy and on a large scale. It spoke of a deluge of pamphlets presumably issued by the candidates and by their official sponsors, which, contrary to law, bore no identification of author, publisher, or even printer. It asserted that many were set in the type face of the *imprimerie nationale* and easily recognizable as such.[51] The *Constitutionnel* reported that numbers of pamphlets supporting the government cause were being slyly addressed "Aux Electeurs indépendants," a rubric which in common usage meant voters of the opposition.[52]

A count of pamphlets of the sort noted above in the two Paris

48. AN F/1c/III Aube 7, pref. to min. int., 12(?) Dec. 1827.

49. *Ibid.,* Ardennes 4, pref. to min. int., 14 Nov., and min. int. to pref., 16 Nov. 1827. In the prefect's letter he asks that the minister act favorably as he already has in *another case.* Exactly what these really quite large "expenses" were, one cannot be sure. Often the president had some sort of reception the evening before the first day's balloting for the deputyship. It is probable that these sums were to pay for such entertainment. Rich men who were presidents might carry this sort of charge themselves.

50. AN F/1c/III Tarn 4, Tarn-et-Garonne 2, Var 4, Vendée 3, Vienne 4 and Haute-Vienne 4 contain the richest documentation on the busyness of prefects and other administrative officers in matters electoral.

51. *Journal des Débats,* 11 Nov. 1827, p. 3.

52. *Constitutionnel,* 17 Nov. 1827, p. 3. The article in question was borrowed from a report in the *Ami de la Charte* of Nantes.

newspapers shows that if these stories are true the bulk of the pamphlets which they mention have been lost. Of the 175 in the Bibliothèque Nationale Le/54 series for the campaign of 1827, less than 25 are obviously pro-government in tone and message. This sort of evidence is suspect on its face, but it has a certain value in reinforcing the notion that the government, after all, had handier ways of passing the word than through the printed pamphlet.

On the other hand the government was clearly stung by the tone and volume of opposition writings during the censorship and by the polemics of the periodic press after the censorship was lifted. In the circular of 3 September prefects were urged to follow the reporting of the *Moniteur* to get the true story of the king's trip to the northerly departments. In that of 8 November they were informed that the rampaging opposition press was being answered in the *Moniteur* and the *Gazette de France*. Quick, ran the exhortation, have these articles reproduced and disseminated; send in to your own local newspapers your answers to the opposition-press stories.

When higher authority decided to move the day of the convocation of the colleges from 15 to 17 November, the minister of course composed a message to the prefects to that effect. Seemingly as he drafted he bethought himself of the king's day — the feast of St. Charles — which was coming up on 4 November. As a matter of custom this was a day of national celebration, when among other things high officials of the administration held receptions for the famous and well-born where the king's health was toasted. Obviously this year the day could serve another and, be it said, related purpose. "Between now and the election," wrote the minister,

> you will have celebrated the [feast of] St. Charles, always dear to the king's faithful subjects and which this year . . . can be made an opportunity to help in the coming elections.
>
> You will be able to assure yourself of the views of the principal public functionaries and the men of substance whom you habitually entertain on the king's day. You will neglect not this happy occasion . . . to increase the prestige of the administration, nor to extend its relationships and strengthen the confidence in which it is held by its friends.[53]

Generally speaking, caucuses of pro-government voters seem more

53. Min. int., confid. circ., 29 Oct. 1827. Note that 15 November as the opening day for the electoral colleges had been set in the confid. circ. of 22 Oct. 1827.

infrequent than those of the opposition. It may be that they were not as necessary, for the officialness of candidature once bestowed was likely to put a stop to most of the turmoil about who was going to make the run. Furthermore there was a lethargy among the pro-government voters as noticeable to the prefects as was its opposite among adherents of the opposition.

The prefect of the Yonne, perhaps fearful that the loss of two out of five seats might be ascribed to his want of "zeal," wrote in after the election to tell how zealous he really had been. He told of having arranged a meeting of royalist voters from all of his arrondissements in order to explain the advantages of working together.[54] The only other meeting of the sort I have encountered in specific terms took place under very different conditions. One, which is nicely documented for the departmental college of the Seine-et-Oise, was held in the royal *écurie* at Versailles in the late afternoon of 24 November. There adherents of the ministry heard a gloss on a last circular from Villèle[55] exhorting them to an all-out effort to elect three devoted ministerial candidates.[56]

It is likely that this caucus of the pro-government faithful had its counterparts at many other departmental colleges and that, as a consequence, there was more closing of ranks behind a given candidate than would have otherwise been the case. Incidentally, the little meeting in the stable at Versailles helped the government cause not a whit. It lost three out of three.

Getting out the vote capped the range of duties expected of the prefect and the civil bureaucracy. Nothing should be allowed to interfere with a pro-government voter's getting to the polls and casting his ballot for a pro-government candidate.

There was an apparent established tradition which permitted military men and civil employees of the state to absent themselves from

54. AN F/1c/III Yonne 3, pref. to min. int., 19 Nov. 1827.

55. Min. int., confid. circ., 20 Nov. 1827.

56. AD Seine-et-Oise II M 11(2) 1827. Among the documents of this bundle is one which shows that Villèle had an extra reason to hope for the best in the departmental election in the Seine-et-Oise. The arrondissemental college in Pontoise of that department had just returned the baron Alexandre de Lameth, a man personally obnoxious to the king for having forsaken the noblesse with which he had been seated at the Estates General to join the third estate. Villèle had earlier conveyed the king's sentiments to the subprefect in Pontoise, and in indicating that he realized that the election of a pro-government candidate was too much to expect, he trusted that the opposition winner would not be Alexandre de Lameth. This is one instance I have found of the king's concern about the outcome of a specific election.

their official duties if their voting residence was distant from their normal station. Someone, the would-be voters themselves or interested third parties, went through channels to get the authorization.[57] An army officer of the Eure stationed in far-away Seu d'Urgel near Andorra gaily went outside channels writing directly to his prefect to ask his assistance; a sailor of the same department seeking a similar dispensation wrote directly to the minister of the navy.[58] The prefect of the Hérault reported that credit for a government victory in his departmental college should be given to some soldiers who had traveled two hundred leagues [sic] to cast their votes.[59]

Some government voters, like their opposition counterparts, lived at a distance from the polling place and might have refused to make the trip unless offered transportation and lodging. To underwrite this sort of expense was the principal end of a considerable secret fund entrusted to the minister of the interior. In his long circular telling the prefects that the king had decided to call the election, the minister remarks that it would be a good thing if transport were assured the distant voter and that he was extending a credit to cover this sort of expense and any other which the prefects thought necessary.[60] The sum varied in size in conformity with some rule of thumb. The prefect of the Seine, who would probably have a minimum of transport expenses but a lot of voters to deal with, got ten thousand francs; the prefects of the Basses- and Hautes-Alpes, who had few voters of any sort to worry about, got one thousand each; other prefects received sums which swung between these extremes. The total outlay was somewhat in excess of 264,000 francs.[61]

57. AN F/1c/III Allier 3. In this document the prefect of the Allier wrote direct to the minister of finance to request the latter to authorize four of his officers in dispersed departments to take leave so as to be able to vote in the Allier. The date here was 6 Feb. 1824.

58. AD Eure 4 M 104, a captain of artillery to pref., 11 Nov. 1827. The sailor's request is reflected in min. navy to pref., 2 Nov. 1827.

59. AN F/7 6740 Hérault, pref. to min. int., 29 Nov. 1827.

60. Min. int., confid. circ., 22 Oct. 1827. Subsequent circulars of this series, notably those of 29 Oct. and 8 Nov., elaborated somewhat on these stark instructions. The matter of lodging was added to transport as a legitimate charge against the credit, but prefects were warned to have a just regard for the *amour propre* of their clients – which I judge is the polite way of telling them not to suggest anything so crude as swapping favors with monetary value for a vote.

61. AN F/1c/II 52. The document, which carries the sums issued to each of the prefects does not in itself identify what uses these monies are to serve. This can be and indeed is established, as can be the significance of the document itself, in other documents in the

Some prefects exceeded their allowance and wrote in for a sum to cover the overdraft;[62] many underspent and returned the unexpended balance.[63] Precisely what the bulk of the monies bought will never be known, for the prefects were well aware just how secret a secret fund was. There are however some revealing leaks in the record. We have, for example, the case of the voter of the Aveyron who quite frankly billed his mayor for his expenses in traveling to the electoral college,[64] and that of a voter of the Vendée who, when presented with a bill, gave the innkeeper his card of admission to the college and told her to use it to collect what was owing at the prefecture. Then there are prefect Suleau, a short-timer in the Vendée, who estimated in advance of the election that the four thousand francs allotted him was not going to meet the expenses he anticipated for transport, lodging, and the usual banquets given by the presidents of his electoral colleges, and the prefect of Corsica, who had been given no monies whatever from the secret fund and found out what he had missed when he came to Paris in January of the new year. He speedily put in for fifteen hundred francs to cover his out-of-pocket expenses. For example, heavy snow made it necessary to move the small group of Bastia voters by sea to Ajaccio where the college met. This service alone had cost him 627 francs.[65]

But most of the men who spent the money did not do much specifying. The normal practice of prefects seemed to be to divide

---

AN F/1c/III cartons and in copies of the confid. circs. of 22 or 29 Oct. in the ADs of the Bouches-du-Rhône, the Loire-Atlantique, and the Marne. In upwards of a dozen cases the exact amount noted in the F/1c/II 52 document is repeated in the more personal documents of the other series and identified as expendable, or actually spent, for the wide range of permissible activities.

62. AN F/1c/III Aude 3, pref. to min. int., 31 Mar. 1828, asks for 442 francs "pour remboursement de l'excédant de dépenses autorisées en Octobre dernier." He got it.

63. *Ibid.*, Cantal 4, pref. to min. int., 5 Dec. 1827, notifies the minister of an unexpended 390 francs. See also *ibid.*, Gard 5, pref. to min. int., 4 Dec. 1827.

64. AN F/1c/III (erroneously filed in) Meuse 6; M. Valette to mayor of Sicheley, 20 Nov. 1827. The letter is quoted in my *Electoral Procedure*, p. 90.

65. Un Electeur, *Détails sur ce que s'est passé . . . pendant la réunion du collège . . . de Bourbon-Vendée* (Paris, n.d.) BN Le/54.338; AN F/1c/III Vendée 3, pref. to min. int., 9 Nov. 1827; *ibid.*, Corse 5, pref. to baron Capelle, 20 Jan. 1828. The minister might be pardoned if he did not reimburse, for the bulk of the voters so carefully fetched from Bastia elected two opposition candidates, one of whom was two years shy of the age of eligibility. This was the young and able Antoine François Vatimesnil who made his mark in the July Monarchy.

the total among their subprefects and then if they got any detailed accounting from them not to pass it on to Paris.[66] Some prefects charged the account for last-minute printing expenses (the post-1 October rectification tables, for example) not submitted with the larger bill for printing up the electoral lists,[67] and some drew on it for "gratifications" to the clerks who had worked back-breaking overtime for a matter of weeks. Prefect Floriac of the Aisne gave his clerks 340 francs, the gendarmes 120, and paid some confidential informers 540.

One possible expenditure, often suggested, was that for the outright purchase of a vote for money. Obviously one cannot be certain that it did not happen; in fact it is almost certain that it did. But there are three things which argue against it as widely practiced. The first is that the electorate was affluent by definition: a man who paid three hundred francs or more in direct taxes had a fairly substantial stake. The second is that belonging to the electorate was in itself a status symbol, though not coveted by jury-fearers, and not the sort of thing a man would light-heartedly cast in the mud. The vote had its built-in inhibitor to venality. Lastly, if one is going to buy a lot of rich men, he will need a lot of money, far more than was available in the secret fund. To the extent that the fund was used to influence a vote it must have been largely because it helped pay the voter's extraordinary expenses of travel and keep, and filled him with good food and drink, not because it paid him in cash.

With the clearing of the fog of the electoral battle came accusations that the government and the officers of its administration had been guilty of grievous wrongdoing. Angry citizens of the opposition made them the subject of petitions to the crown, the peers, the ministers of justice and the interior, and to the chamber of deputies. Such petitions appear to have covered the whole panoply of alleged malpractice with the possible exception of the clandestine use of public funds (a quarter of a million francs worth) for the promotion of the government's political fortunes. This, which might have been a difficult charge to handle, may not even have been made; if it was made there is little if any trace.

66. See, for example, *ibid.*, Ain 5, pref. to min. int., 31 Dec. 1827; Aisne 7, pref. to min. int., 5 Mar. 1828; Calvados 5; Jura 4; Loire-Inférieure 3; Lot-et-Garonne 4.

67. In 1827 this larger bill ran to about a half million francs. There is a summarizing document in AN F/1c/II 53 and a great many showing the costs to individual departments in the cartons of the F/1c/III series.

The problem of the petitions themselves fell upon Martignac, the new minister of the interior and soon to be president of the council. On 30 April 1828 he established a commission of six prominent citizens (three from the council of state and three from the bench of Paris) to conduct the investigation. For almost a half year the commission labored; they gave their report in October. It shows a process of continuous refinement of the charges: from the original large number, the commission first focused on the alleged wrongdoing of twenty-two prefects, of which it exculpated twelve and found two guilty of minor improprieties. Of the remaining eight, the committee found four guilty of "less grave offenses." It cited the remaining four for the perpetration of the "gravest offenses," i.e., acts which resulted in the unwarranted disenfranchisement of certain voters.[68]

On the whole the findings of the enquiry seem on the mild side to one who has read a deal of the prefectoral correspondence, not to say some of the high-decibel utterances of the uncensored press. Most surprising to this witness is the absence of any mention of the particular derelictions of the prefect of the Vosges who, as we know, registered upwards of a hundred unqualified voters and permitted an election which the chamber of deputies itself annulled in its entirety. On the other hand, I suffer for prefect Roussy of the Deux-Sèvres who was among the last four and who was moved from the lovely little city of Niort and the good salary which went with the post to the austerity of Gap in the Hautes-Alpes and the considerably lower stipend of a smaller department. Few prefects have left behind a clearer record of the zeal and devotion that the ministry so often spoke of, and few had a clearer view of the unfavorable result which one should expect from the election. I do not believe that the commission's judgment was swayed against Roussy because he lost two (perhaps three) out of three, but I do think that the unhappy Roussy thought so.

Whatever other action was taken, beyond the rustication of the prefect of the Deux-Sèvres, is hard to say. Surely there was no wave of retribution against the other erring prefects, many of whom also presided over losing elections. In fact, Guizot, writing several months after the election, observed, "the old administration still

68. AN F/1c/II 52: "Rapport sur les travaux du comité d'enquête chargé d'examiner les pétitions relatives aux élections de 1827" [October 1828].

administers: same principles, same spirit, same behavior, same talk. What is strange about this? These are the same men – this prefect, this subprefect, this mayor, this captain of gendarmes – who tried [in vain] to see what constitutional oppositionists would lose the election . . . [these men] are still there, still masters of their conquerors."[69]

Of course they did not stay there forever, but most of them probably did for another two and a half years. When they did move on, after the July Revolution, it was surely not because of their overzeal in the election. Rather it was because irrespective of their efforts the Villèle government lost that contest at the polls: Why and by how much is the subject of the pages to come.

69. François P. G. Guizot, "De la Session de 1828," in his *Mélanges politiques et historiques* (Paris, 1869), pp. 467–496; reprinted from the September 1828 issue of *La Revue française* (No. 5, pp. 301–322).

7 / The Outcome of the Election of November 1827

The principal reasons why the Villèle government went down in the November elections are set out in the preceding chapters. To touch briefly on their high-spots:

The rightward thrust of policy alarmed more of the electorate than it pleased. It alarmed those who had made their peace with the Restoration and with Louis XVIII's philosophy of governance, and it outraged those farther to the left who were anti-Bourbon and anti-clerical, if not frankly anti-monarchist. Of those others who were ideologically attuned to the policy, a good number were at daggers drawn with Villèle, its official spokesman. Leaders of this group inside and out of the chamber of deputies were in the forefront of what was generally called the counter-opposition. They vigorously opposed the prime minister and all his works.

The economic depression, now in its second year and destined to continue, was a burden for the entire nation, but an especially heavy one for men of the business community. Their willingness to blame the government more than was perhaps justified became reason enough for many to vote against ministerial candidates. Surely this is one reason why such candidates fared so poorly, notably with urban constituencies — or more properly put: why so many opposition candidates won in the cities.[1]

The popular malaise about the condition of the polity and economy created an atmosphere generally antagonistic to the seemingly eternal government of Villèle, but was by no stretch the only reason for the triumph of the oppositions. Their political campaign had been well led, and well organized. It reached virtually all corners of the metropole and, at a guess, the majority of the electorate. Towards the end when it might have faltered it was greatly reinvigorated by a dual last-minute blessing, ironically enough conferred by the

1. Arrondissemental colleges only: Paris eight opposition wins in eight constituencies (i.e., 8/8); Lyon 2/2; Lille 0/2; Bordeaux 2/2; Rouen 2/2; Toulouse 0/2; Dijon 1/1; Marseille 1/1; Clermont-Ferrand 1/1; Strasbourg 1/1; Montpellier 1/1; Nîmes 1/1; Metz 0/1; Nantes 1/1. Total opposition wins for these city constituencies: 21/26.

king himself. On 5 November, with the royal ordinance which dissolved the chamber and convoked the electoral colleges, Charles issued two other ordinances. One of them lifted the censorship of the periodical press, the other announced the creation of seventy-six new peers, none of whom presumably would associate himself with legislative causes of the opposition.

We have already seen with what fervor the left-wing press of Paris and the *Quotidienne* exploited their new-found freedom. In the ten days or so before the arrondissemental colleges met and the three weeks before the last session of the slowest departmental college they made up for lost time. The publication of the names of a multitude of opposition candidates with the papers' endorsements – this and new exhortations to the voters throughout the kingdom had the effect of lifting the campaign to a new high.

As for the packing of the peers, nothing could have offered a higher incentive to the oppositions, especially the leftward one, to gain control of the deputies. Since 1824, with the lower house in thrall to Villèle, the liberal upper house had acted as the last bulwark of the "traditional liberties." Time and again it had slowed or stopped the rightward course even as it had in the case of the law of "justice and love." But now no more of this; from here on if there was to be an institution to play the curbing role it would have to be the deputies. A new imperative had entered opposition politics.

The election took place in two stages. In the first, which began on 17 November and ended three or four days later, the arrondissemental and special colleges met.[2] The count went strongly against the government. As one of the most deeply concerned, the comte de Villèle watched the returns as they trickled in to Paris and revealed some of his agony in his diary. The entries run:

> 17 Nov. Worried about the elections all day. Total defeat in all the Paris colleges – presages nothing good for the elections in general. [Villèle meant by this that the Parisian voters were challenging the temporary bureaux in the arrondissemental colleges and would probably elect quite different permanent ones.[3]]
>
> 18 Nov. – Passed a very bad day. News of the elections is very bad. Of the outcome known in 54 colleges, 28 have upset the temporary bureaux.

2. The arithmetic for these elections: of 265 seats in contest, 247 filled by elections in 247 arrondissemental colleges and 16 in the special colleges; total, 263 filled. Two seats in Corsica, a special college, not filled until the delayed election took place in January 1828.

3. For a discussion of the role of the "bureaux," see chap. 3 above, pp. 76–78.

19 Nov. – Bad news about the elections continues . . . detestable everywhere. Much upset all day. Saw the king who received me well, but he [too] is disturbed . . . the dauphine is more so.

20 Nov. – Continuation of bad news about the elections. We have had today 90 disappointing results [as against] 24 royalist [wins].

21 Nov. – News from Toulouse [Villèle's own electoral district. The family chateau was at Mourville just outside the city.]; all the [temporary] bureaux have been confirmed. In *conseil* with the king during which we received news of 20 good elections, including my own.

22 Nov. – By post received news of more good and bad elections. At day's end we stood with 116 elections of liberals and 88 royalists [i.e., 204 of the 263 arrondissemental and special elections].

23 Nov. – Received news of new elections which carries the number of liberals to 125 – less 26 seats involved in multiple elections [and the number of] royalists of all nuances to 116 [i.e., 241 of the 263 total].

24 Nov. – Received news of all [arrondissemental and special] elections except four. The final figure stands at 132 liberals – of which 26 must be subtracted for multiple elections – and at 127 royalists.

The second stage in the elections began on 24 November when the departmental colleges met in the chefs lieux of seventy-nine departments.[4] This time the news which began badly became more heartening to Villèle, but as the diary indicates the overall picture was somber indeed. He wrote:

25 Nov. – At the château the king was very sad. A sad time at the *conseil,* a bad day. In the evening still worse with the news of the rejection of all our candidates at Versailles. [These would have been the first returns from a departmental college, that of the Seine-et-Oise.]

26 Nov. – Better news about the elections this morning and during the day.

27 Nov. – Election news favorable during the day. [But] Cornet d'Incourt [the director general of direct taxes, one of Villèle's ablest supporters in the chamber, and a personal friend] has lost.

28 Nov. – Good news of the elections continues. During the day had 211 royalists as against 135 liberals. In *conseil* with the king who was suffering greatly.

29 Nov. – Ended the day with 100 more royalists than liberals.[5] Saw the king; we talked of Peyronnet and Corbière. He judges their separation from the council [of ministers] inevitable and spoke to me of taking the [portfolio of the] interior.

30 Nov. – Received the rest of the election [returns]. . . . Saw the king,

4. In the seven departments where the special colleges met (see p. 74), there were, of course, no departmental elections.

5. Villèle's use of the words "royalists" and "liberals" was I fear heavily tinctured by his wish. No one knew better than he that there were at least three strains of royalists, only one of which would have supported him. As for the liberals he mentions, he used the word loosely (and pejoratively) to include most of those who opposed him from the left.

who has spoken with his family about my taking the [portfolio of the] interior which did not please them any more than the nomination of Martignac.

Went to see Corbière who could not receive me, so deeply affected was he.

One begins to lose confidence in the staying power of the ministry. From many sides I am being pressed to accept the interior.

1 Dec. – Passed a sad day.

Saw my colleagues who are all of a mind to offer their resignations to the king. . . . Saw the king in the evening and he seemed little disposed to consent to our resignation.

5 Dec. – Met with the council *chez moi* where it was decided to offer the king our resignation. . . .

Villèle's entries of 23 and 24 November refer to multiple elections, twenty-six of them. Actually there was a twenty-seventh, that of his friend and supporter Ravez, whom he omitted. The fact of these multiple elections meant that at the very moment that the balloting was over in the slowest of the colleges and the election completed, it was not completed. Automatically there were twenty-seven vacancies in the new chamber: twenty-five for winners from the leftist opposition, one for a winner of the counter-opposition, and Ravez. These would have to be filled through by-elections which would be summoned in the next few months. Furthermore, it happened that before these bys could replenish the chamber more vacancies occurred: two, when the king elevated Villèle and Corbière to the peerage;[6] one, when death took a newly-elected member; four when that number of deputies resigned even before the new chamber convened; and eight because the chamber refused to accept the credentials of eight deputies and annulled their elections. Thus before the lower house could do its first piece of substantive business, it had lost forty-two of its brethren.[7] Replacements for most of them were elected in by-elections called for April and May, but during the summer and fall the attrition continued. By year's end fifteen more deputies resigned or died and fifteen more by-elections were called to make good the losses.

6. He elevated Peyronnet at the same time, but the latter had failed to win a seat in the chamber, though he ran in two constituencies; hence two vacancies rather than three.

7. One of the 42, Nicod de Ronchaux of the Jura died in mid-December 1827 and his replacement was named early enough (5 February 1828) that he could be present at the beginning of the new legislative session. On the other hand, the 5 deputies of the Vosges whose elections were annulled were not replaced until August 1828.

In Appendix IV I have tabulated the details of losses in the membership of the chamber and the outcome of the resultant by-elections for 1828, and for 1829 and 1830 as well.

Thus for someone trying to be realistic as to how the elections of November 1827 came out there is something of a methodological problem. What should be the cut-off point? Villèle's chosen 30 November 1827? 1 February 1828? 1 July? or later in 1828?

I have decided to stop the clock at the end of November 1827 and to discuss the anatomy of the new chamber as of that moment. There are disadvantages, the most obvious of which is the multiple counting of the nineteen deputies who were elected to fill forty-six seats: the worst comes from counting Royer-Collard seven times. Happily however the results of the twenty-seven related by-elections make this disadvantage more illusory than real, for in the by-elections leftist opposition candidates won them all. In other words, not taking account of the multiple elections does not significantly skew my conclusions on the political complexion of the chamber.

On the other hand there is a twofold advantage in taking the November date. We see the chamber as the electorate formed it the first time around. Also, we see it as Villèle must have seen it when he and his colleagues decided to resign and as Charles did when he decided to form a new government.

What they saw was no opposition landslide. Nor was it by any stretch a vote of confidence. In my calculations I have counted 195 deputies who in most foreseeable cases would have rallied to Villèle's support. I have counted 199 whose sympathies lay leftward of him (i.e., the left center, the few doctrinaires, and the far left) and who would have opposed him. I have counted 31 of the counter-opposition who were opposed to him from their position on the far right. There were 5 deputies whose political allegiance I could not identify.[8] In sum, on a vote of confidence Villèle seemingly could not win.

There are perils in citing precise numbers as I have in the text and in the Appendix, for the information does not exist to permit a confident identification of the political coloration of perhaps 10 percent of the deputies. This acknowledgment of frailty must not be taken as a license to recompute the election returns to make Villèle the winner. Obviously he was not, and the possible error in my figures is most likely in underestimating the success of the oppositions. I will return to this subject. But first to describe briefly the main

8. See Appendix III(B) for my calculations.

political components of the new chamber and a number of the sub-factions. I will move from right to left.

On the extreme right were the ultra-royalists of the counter-opposition. Villèle referred to them as "pointus" in his diary and clearly recognized both their royalism and their bitter animosity to him. I have identified thirty-one of them in the table. This number may be low (de Bertier de Sauvigny estimates some sixty to eighty).[9] But numbers aside for the moment, members of this group shared a veneration for the Bourbons and a violent disapproval of the kind of constraint which the constitutional charter imposed upon divine-right rulership. No matter how impossible they knew their wish to be in realistic terms, they liked to think and talk as if the years of revolution and Napoleonic usurpation should be extinguished from memory and as if the good institutions of old regime authoritarianism should be reinstated.

Among these men one perceives perhaps three sub-factions; maybe there were more — in a way each man came close to being a faction in himself. But for simplicity's sake consider three. The first was made up of some quite practical reactionaries who, realizing that they could not get far under their own steam, gladly welcomed an *alliance de convenance* with the left opposition. They fell in with the program of Chateaubriand's Friends and with that of the Société, Aide-toi. They accepted left-wing support for many of their candidates and in turn supported leftist candidates in electoral districts where their own strength was slight. Fifteen men of this stripe won election, running as counter-opposition candidates with the public support of the very newspapers (the *Constitutionnel,* the *Courrier français,* and the *Journal des Débats*) which were simultaneously beating the drum for far-out leftists like Mauguin, Constant, Dupont de l'Eure, and the Lafayettes. Like similar royalists of an earlier day and others in Louis Philippe's day, they were willing to compromise a certain amount of principle in the urge to realize the single paramount practical objective of modern politics: get elected.

Prominent in this faction were François Agier of the Deux-Sèvres, Hyde de Neuville, and Delalot — three men whose political behavior offers many a problem — the baron Claude Bacot de Romans, and Bertin de Vaux, editor of the *Débats* and principal Villèle-hater.

9. De Bertier de Sauvigny, *La Restauration,* p. 392.

A second sub-faction was led by one of the best known of the ultras, the comte François Régis de La Bourdonnaye. Its was a less complicated and ambivalent counter-opposition. One result was that its adherents made the run without support from the left, whether because they would not have it or because the left would not give it, I cannot say. Probably for both reasons. I have counted a half dozen of the group, which included Chabron de Solilhac of the Haute-Loire, Léviste de Montbrian of the Ain, and Berbis of the Côte-d'Or.

The last sub-faction was a tiny group of unredeemed theocrats, men who took their spiritual leadership from Bonald, a peer since 1823. They parted company with their brethren largely, if not entirely, on the issue of the role of the ultramontane church in the political affairs of France. Needless to say their number was small and their exhortations for a higher degree of clerical control of lay matters made its greatest (and most counter-productive) impression among the very considerable group of professing Catholics who hated Jesuits and even distrusted the secular clergy.

Such was the so-called counter-opposition, no numerical powerhouse and riven in factionalism. But in its antipathy to Villèle there was a unanimity and a determination not exceeded at the other extreme of the political scale. The election of this group of "royalists" was one of those things, and an important one, that made Villèle's continuance an impossibility.

Moving leftward from these ultras is that group of royalists who were the bulwark of Villèle's strength in the chamber. To distinguish them from others, contemporary critics usually called them the "ministerials." To a man they were royalists, intensely loyal to Charles and the Bourbon family, and reconciled to the constitutional charter and the type of monarchy it defined. Many had begun the Restoration with grave misgivings about the charter and Louis XVIII's sympathy for a British type of government but had accommodated to it in both head and heart.

Where they departed most dramatically from their brethren to the left was on the importance of the royal prerogative. They were all for it, they moved continuously to extend it, and nothing got their backs up more speedily than moves to reduce it. The matter of ministerial responsibility was a solid constitutional issue, upon which they harbored strong views. Ministries should be responsible, yes, but essentially responsible to the crown, not to the parliamentary majority, which after all rested on the earthy stuff of the electorate. Who can say how many of them would defend the king's power to appoint any one of his choice as his first minister, irrespective of this man's acceptability to the chamber of deputies? The answer is: a good many, as was proven with the appointment of Jules de Polignac and the support which many of this group accorded him.

As already noted, thirty-six of the leaders of this group, men of the skill, ability, and determination of Humbert Sesmaisons (long an officer of the royal household), Charles-André Maquillé, a humbler-born young notable of Angers, and Joseph Forbin des Issarts, an émigré in his youth and a devoted adherent to the Bourbons and Villèle – to name three – received their peerages in a royal ordinance of 5 November. But there still remained a good number of trusted and potent leaders among the 195 ministerial deputies – men like Louis Sainte-Marie of the Nièvre, an émigré who had fought in the army of the princes and had unflaggingly supported Villèle, and Charles Salaberry, another émigré and one of the Villèle wheelhorses, who had begun his parliamentary career over on the extreme right among the early ultras.

This was the group which had constituted the overwhelming majority of the chamber in the days following the election of 1824. Villèle's break with Chateaubriand in June of 1824 had ripped off its right wing, and his reactionary legislative program culminating in his abortive efforts to curb the press had alienated others. Now the election had dropped it to less than one half of its peak strength. If Villèle meant this group when he referred to "royalists" in his diary, there could not possibly have been one hundred more of them than of "liberals" – that is, if by "liberals" he meant all his opponents lying to his left.

This latter group, which in the table I have numbered at 199 and have not otherwise defined, consisted of perhaps four roughly discernible sub-groups.

The first of these was the large left center, the loyal opposition, whose front lines began just across the aisle from the ministerials above. The political views of these men, probably well over a hundred in number, coincided with those of the right center in many of the essentials. Like those already discussed they too were loyal to the king and charter and to the constitutional monarchy it defined. When they spoke of the charter they were likely to stress its guarantees of individual rights; what had most galled them about the Villèle government was its willingness to put a loose construction on the matter of rights and to encroach upon them. They considered censorship of the press in patent violation of the charter; they believed that ministries should be responsible in the first instance to the chamber of deputies. As for the royal prerogative, they could and did live with it cheerfully as exercised by Louis XVIII, but they wanted the matter to stop right where he had left it. Always fearful of Charles's paying heed to evil counselors of the extreme right, they were likely to dig in and resist any measure which they felt would be likely to expand the power of the crown at the expense of the elected representatives of the nation.

With Villèle as president of the council of ministers, telling the difference between the right and left centers was a fairly easy matter. Almost by definition what he was for, the left center would be likely to oppose on grounds of bare personal animus. But with Villèle gone and the quite different Martignac in his place, the fence between left and right center was a single strand affair and that down a good bit of the way. Martignac's conciliatory legislative program and his inclination to a liberal stance invited enough of the left center to come through the fence to give him a working majority. One should probably not call it a coalition and thereby invoke the classical imagery of the word. One is bound to say, however, that if Martignac had taken a harder line, if he had moved — as most oppositionists estimated Villèle would — against the press or the law on elections, he would not only have lost his left-center support *en bloc,* but perhaps some of his right-center adherents as well.

Prominent members of this group who were proud to be known as constitutional royalists — indeed one of them once publicly asked that they be so termed — were, for example, the Périer brothers (Casimir, Augustin, Alexandre, and later Camille), the Dupin brothers (André, known as *aîné,* and Charles), baron Louis, famous years back in national finance, the lawyer Kératry, Turckheim of Alsace, the elder Duvergier de Hauranne (Jean Marie, father of Prosper), Pelet de la Lozère, and the man of law, Schonen.

On their leftward fringe were such well-known figures as Etienne, the fiery journalist; Jacques Laffitte, the poor boy of the Basses-

Pyrénées who rose to become one of France's most affluent bankers; Cunin-Gridaine, the businessman from the Ardennes; the lawyer Girod de l'Ain; and Gérard, one of Napoleon's outstanding generals. Although there is little hard evidence to sustain the allegation, it is probable that among these men there was pretty general disapproval of the reign of Charles and a secret advocacy of Louis Philippe d'Orléans whom they would gladly take in exchange and whose sons were acceptable as successors.

Somewhere near this group, in a special little pigeonhole of their own, were the doctrinaires led by the true prophet of the "doctrine," Pierre Paul Royer-Collard, who had enunciated their sophisticated political and social philosophy. There were perhaps no more than three or four others: Louis Tirlet, a career soldier and member of Royer-Collard's delegation from the Marne, and Firman Didot, son of the founder of the publishing house. François Guizot, still a bit too young to stand for office (he became forty in October 1827) but sage enough already to be one of the country's outstanding historians and publicists, was already in Royer-Collard's corner as were Beugnot and Victor de Broglie – upstairs in the peers.

Last in the leftward swing were the men of the real far left. Comparatively few in number, probably between a dozen and a score, their leading figures were the Lafayettes, *père* and *fils,* the magistrate Dupont de l'Eure; François Mauguin, the lawyer; and Benjamin Constant, the man of many extraordinary talents.

Censorship being what it was, and the secret police as busy as bees, frank statements of the political credos of this group were relatively difficult to utter in print and fairly dangerous. The result is a paucity of reliable information on the precise dimensions of their beliefs, aims, and plans. Be it said that they were precious close to republicanism, often with a strong Bonapartist tinge. This latter sentiment is most characteristic of the old soldiers, who showed something more than a nostalgic reverence for Napoleon and the great days of France's national glory. But here again the evidence does not exist to sustain a precise formulation of their positive program. Of the negatives all was clear: "Let us be rid of the Bourbons and the whole wretched apparatus of the Restoration – and that as speedily as possible."

In the foregoing, the absence of crisp lines of definition between some of the major groupings and most of the factions within them is obvious. This sort of situation is a characteristic of a polity which operated without benefit of the formal political parties of a later era.. It accounts also for part of my concern about the accuracy of my analysis of the outcome of the election. But not all. The balance of my worry derives from the great difficulty of deciding into which political filing boxes I should drop perhaps twoscore of the deputies. Let me illustrate.

The *Dictionnaire des Parlementaires* of Robert and his colleagues, and the contemporary sources upon which their individual biographical notes rest, leave many problems of political identity unsolved.[10] They do not, nor can they, do much with the obscure men, those who seldom came to sessions of the chamber, who never spoke up in debate, and whose votes, like those of all their fellows, on any and all measures were unrecorded. The passage of time has not made the diagnosis of their political stance any easier. Consider Pierre Albert Bouchet, who was a rich propriétaire of the Ain and the mayor of one of its communes and defeated the president of his arrondissemental college. It is known that the president, Léviste de Montbrian, who won in the subsequent departmentals, was far to the right. This could lead to the inference that Bouchet's politics was left of center. How far is not told and anyway Bouchet resigned from the chamber in 1829, never to reappear on the political scene. There are other Bouchets to cope with. With respect to only four others I own myself defeated.[11]

Then there were men far more prominent than Bouchet who offer even more perplexing problems. Consider the comte de Preissac of the Tarn-et-Garonne. There can be no doubt of his opposition to Villèle, nor of officialdom's opposition to him. Though a loyal adherent of the crown and a first citizen of his department, he was passed over for the presidency of his electoral college, probably because the prefect of his department thought him an unstable man "too easily moved by the dangerous party."[12] But the reason why the prefect distrusted Preissac – whether because of his putative sympathy with the extreme right or center left – is hard to say. Salaberry's *Souvenirs* puts him with Fussy and Lézardière, "who

10. See the Bibliographical Note for a listing of the contemporary sources which I used in trying to determine the political orientation of each of the 430 deputies.

11. Duvergier de Hauranne (*Gouvernement parlementaire,* IX, 351) owns himself stumped with respect to 24. He does not say who they were.

12. AN F/1c/III Tarn-et-Garonne 2, pref. to min. int., 25 Nov. 1827.

had formed part of the extreme right-wing counter-opposition to Villèle."[13] A contemporary biographer calls him a Villèle man. On the other hand he had the support of the left, received the endorsement of all three leftist Paris newspapers, and in March 1830 voted with the 221 in the teeth of his king and Polignac. I have counted him among the left-center opposition, but without much conviction.

Or consider the less important figure, Jean Raudot of the Yonne. During the years 1824 to 1827 he was among the Villèle majority, but he could not have been too ardent in his support since when the new election was announced he was endorsed by the three leftist Paris newspapers and the *Quotidienne.* When he was elected, the prefect was at some pains to assure the minister that Raudot's heart was really in the right place even though he had opposed the ministry in the last session, and that his victory was really one for the angels.[14] Again, without much conviction, I went along with the hesitant prefect and classed him as a ministerial.[15]

Among the deputies most difficult to place are some of those known as adherents of the counter-opposition. Some of them like Agier, Hyde de Neuville, and Delalot not only defected rightwards from among Villèle's one-time right-wing supporters but also seem to have taken on some of the coloration of their new allies of the left center. One is led to this conclusion by several things capped by their vote on the controversial Address of March 1830. These three, and two others of the 31 counter-oppositionists of my table, were with the 221 thus casting a vote against their sovereign and his first minister, the prince de Polignac.[16] Four more were absent or refrained from voting on the measure.[17] All others of my 31 who were still in the chamber voted against the Address as one would expect a former far-right-winger to do.[18]

13. Quoted from Nicholas Richardson, *The French Prefectoral Corps, 1814–1830* (Cambridge: University Press, 1966), p. 74. Incidentally, I think Salaberry is wrong on both of these men.

14. AN F/1c/III Yonne 3: pref. to min. int., 26 Nov. 1827.

15. Among Raudot's contemporaries there were apparently continuing bewilderments and doubts. When it came to how he had voted on the Address of March 1830, the editors of the *Temps* say he voted against it, while the compilers of the two other surveys of the vote say he was for it and among the 221 (*re* these surveys, see Appendix VI).

16. Léviste de Montbrian and Sainte Hermine.

17. Bacot de Romans, Beaumont, Bellemare, and La Bourdonnaye-Blossac.

18. There were only 15 of them left. Two had died, two had resigned, one had gone to the peers, one had had his election annulled, and one had received a double election and opted out of one of the two seats.

These being the difficulties of identifying the political stance of the 430 men chosen for office in those elections of 1827, it is little wonder that there is no unanimity of conclusions among the many of us who have tried to crack the problem.

Among historians of our own century Sébastien Charléty[19] cites some 250 seats for the oppositions and some 200 for the pro-Villèle group. Guillaume de Bertier de Sauvigny says, "In the end and at first glance, the new chamber was to number only 150 to 180 Villèlist royalists, as opposed to about the same number of liberals plus 60 to 80 royalists of the counter-opposition." In the same paragraph he assigns about 205 wins to the two oppositions.[20] Recently, Patrick [and] Bernard Higonnet awarded only 160 seats to the anti-Villèlists.[21]

Among the nineteenth-century writers, three of whom wrote of an event they had witnessed, Prosper Duvergier de Hauranne counts 249 deputies of all nuances of the opposition, 157 deputies for the Villèle government, and 24 unknowns, and F. P. Lubis gives the Villèlist group no more than 120 to 150 seats (which would of course allocate to the oppositions the far-too-high numbers of 280 to 310 seats). Achille de Vaulabelle avoids a use of precise numbers and is content to say that the opposition (sic) ended up with a majority of about 60 seats – a calculation not wholly incompatible with Duvergier's.[22]

19. The fact that Charléty's figures add up to a total which is 20 seats in excess of the chamber's membership makes detailed comment difficult. His allocation of winners within two categories of college (he does not separate out the special colleges) is, however, consistent with his incorrect figure for the total (Sébastien Charléty, *La Restauration,* vol. IV of Ernest Lavisse, *Histoire de France contemporaine* (Paris, [1921]), p. 262).

20. The figures cited by de Bertier de Sauvigny (*La Restauration,* p. 392) differ from Charléty's only with respect to the departmental colleges, thus:

		Charléty	de Bertier de Sauvigny
Arrondissemental colleges:	Wins for the oppositions	195	195
	Wins for the ministry	83	83
Departmental colleges:	Wins for the oppositions	55	about [sic] 50
	Wins for the government	117	110
		450	438

Note that the total of wins in each column is larger than the membership of the chamber: Charléty's 450 by a matter of 20; de Bertier de Sauvigny's 438 by (about) 8.

21. Patrick [and] Bernard Higonnet, "La Composition de la chambre des députés de 1827 à 1831," *Revue historique,* 239 (1968), 351–378, esp. p. 356. This figure for the total anti-Villèle membership of the chamber is so far short as to be wholly inadmissible.

22. Duvergier de Hauranne, *Gouvernement parlementaire,* IX, 351; Lubis, *Restauration,* VI, 202; Vaulabelle, *Restaurations,* 2nd ed., VI, 511.

Some of the contemporary reporting in the Paris press reveals the difficulties (with which I am personally familiar) which beset even knowledgeable editors on the spot. The *Constitutionnel* (27 Nov. 1827) undertook to give a round-up of the returns on the arrondissemental and special college elections. It came up with 262 names which is short by the two as-yet-unelected Corsican deputies and one forgotten victor of the Vosges. Its designation of the political affiliation of the winner is just plain wrong in perhaps 10 percent of the cases and all but invariably in favor of the opposition with which the paper was so passionately involved. In its issue of 1 Dec. 1827 the *Constitutionnel* gave its final figure without any breakdown according to type of college. Of the 384 deputies in its count (44 short of the total) 237 were cited as opposition and only 147 as pro-Villèle devotees.

The *Courrier français* counts 226 for the opposition and 195 for the ministry.[23]

The foregoing illustrates the difficulties (and hazards) of trying to call the outcome of the election in terms of precise numbers of men elected, but having made the try, what may now be said of the vote? One should be able to tally it within the 10 percent margin of error I acknowledge with respect to my estimate of the political coloration of the members of the new chamber.

Before looking at the table in Appendix III (C) the reader should recall that voters who went to the arrondissemental colleges wrote a single name on a single piece of paper — one candidate, one ballot, one vote. On the other hand, the voters who went to the special and departmental colleges voted in many cases by the process of scrutin de liste. They wrote more than one name on a single piece of paper (in the special college of the Basses-Pyrénées they wrote five names; in the departmental college of the Seine they wrote four). Thus if one totals up the votes cast for individual candidates (permit me to call such votes "ballots" [sic] hereafter and in the table) in these colleges there will be more of them than voters — something more than twice as many.

From the point of view of percentages, candidates of the two oppositions (both winners and also-rans) polled about 55 percent of the vote in the arrondissemental colleges; received about 46 per-

23. *Courrier français,* 1 Dec. 1827, p. 2. This total is, of course, slightly askew; it should have been 428 pending the returns from Corsica.

cent in the special colleges and about 40 percent in the departmentals.

Whatever the shock which the raw numbers of votes and, more importantly, of deputies opposing Villèle conveyed to the king and his ministers, there was a greater one in store. This came when they had time to peruse the returns man by man. Their losses in familiar and friendly faces were formidable. The overwhelming number of the 253 deputies who did not return to the chamber had been among the supporters of Villèle. Of these we know of at least 69 who made the run with government backing and were defeated. Among them were Peyronnet, Dudon, Cornet d'Incourt, Saint Chamans, Ruinart de Brimont, Pavy, and Borel de Bretizel, devoted adherents to the Villèle government. Thirty-six others did not make the run because, as I have indicated, they were elevated to the peerage by the ordinance of 5 November. In all likelihood the bulk of the remaining 148 either formally bowed out of political life or made little or no effort to achieve a reelection.

By the same token, the absence of these familiar and friendly faces may have been less of a disappointment than the appearance of an almost equal number of familiar and unfriendly ones. These were the important *revenants,* deputies who had served in the leftist oppositions of chambers elected between 1816 and 1824. There were more than 50 of them who had been cut down in the great purge of 1824; now they were back. Some I have already noted in the context of their leadership roles among the constitutionnels and groups farther to the left. As far as Villèle would have been concerned they constituted a veritable *Who's Who* of political undesirables: Lecarlier d'Ardon, Pavée de Vandeuvre, Adam de la Pomme raye, Audry de Puyraveau, Eschassériaux, Voysin de Gartemps, General Gérard, Bignon, Voyer d'Argenson, baron Louis, Laffitte, Humblot-Conté, the Lafayettes, Ternaux, Delessert, and Bertin de Vaux.[24]

Besides the revenants there were 165 men with no prior experience whatever in the chamber. A few more than one half of them took their places in the oppositions – most of them to the left of center, the rest among the one-time Villèle adherents.

24. In the by-elections between November 1827 and March 1830, 11 more of these former deputies who had sat out the post-1824 period returned to the chamber. Ten of them were of the anti-Villèle constitutional left.

As to the structure of the new chamber according to age, it was significantly younger than the one it superseded but still not all that young. The age requirement for eligibility (40) pretty effectively estopped any congress of youth. The median age dropped three years from 56 to 53, and the number of men in their forties had grown significantly.[25] However, comparing the new chamber's age groups to those of the previous one as they, in turn, were immediately after the election of 1824 shows a dozen more men in their forties, two dozen fewer in their fifties, and withal, the median at 53.

The new chamber possessed a smaller number of men with titles of nobility than the old. My count shows 150[26] as against 175. Of equal interest is that perhaps about one quarter of the 150 were politically aligned with the oppositions: three or four were aligned with the counter-opposition and had been party to the "monstrous alliance"; two, the Lafayettes, were of the far left; the balance were to sit with the left center.

Much more notable were the changes which the election wrought in the make-up of the chamber, considered from the point of view of the occupations of its members. The number of men holding salaried government positions dropped from 197 to 165, and those who derived their livelihoods, probably exclusively, from their ownership of land (the propriétaires) dropped from 180 to 148. At the same time the number of men in business and the professions rose from 49 to 107.[27]

With the losses and gains there was a perceptible change in the collective character of the chamber. As one takes note of the diminution of the ranks of the salaried *fonctionnaires* and landed gentry and the doubling of the number of businessmen and professionals, one has a visceral feeling that Charles Dupin was on the right track when he gave his demographic study that interesting political twist.[28]

25. See Appendix III(D).

26. The Higonnets in the article cited above counted 195 nobles "of whom more than two-thirds have titles" (p. 354). They do not explain how they identify the remaining one-third. Did they perhaps rely upon the *particule* in the family name?

Making the subtraction (430–195) they count the remainder of the chamber (235) as bourgeois. This is probably a minimum figure, for the matter of the particule in a name is not a certain indicator of noble lineage.

27. See Appendix III(E) for my analysis of the chamber of deputies, by occupations.

28. For Dupin and his *Forces productives,* see above, chap. 2, text and notes 11 and 14, and chap. 3, note 1.

I rely on the four maps to convey the outcome of the election in geographical terms. Their specific messages I leave to the viewer, but would remind him in advance of two important matters. The first is that averaging out the electoral performance of the various groupings to the left of the government in the general and partial elections between 1815 and 1824 inclusive, one perceives with a glance at Maps #1 and #2 that the left-wing opposition posted a remarkably feeble showing.[29] In order to let them show up at all graphically I had to drop my whole scale of values and depict on Map #1 a low order of left-opposition performances (20 percent-and-above wins). In other circumstances one might designate the low showings as opposition defeats or as high-order government wins. And having skewed things thus for the opposition in Map #1, I have had to confine the top categories of government successes (those in which government candidates won above 80 percent of the seats) in Map #2. Only through the employment of such a double standard could I devise a graphic which would be graphic.

The second message is that he who studies Maps #1 and #2 and then turns to Maps #3 and #4 will perceive a good number of dramatic changes in political coloration. It is important that he understand that the political matrices with which we are dealing are small (total voting electorate of 75,000; some colleges with fewer than 100 voters; very few colleges with more than 500 voters), and that trifling things (the switch of a handful of votes; a bit of artful arm-twisting by a nationally known opposition leader or an able prefect; the nullification of a few votes by the president and bureau of a college; and so on) not only change an election's outcome in a single constituency, but may (in the two-deputy departments) alter the department's political status, on the map, by 50 or 100 percentage points.

The four maps are conceived as two pairs. The first pair, Maps #1 and #2, illustrate after a fashion the successes of the leftist opposition and those of the government in the general and partial elections between 1815 and 1824 inclusive; the second pair, Maps #3 and #4, the successes of the oppositions (both left and the counter-opposition) and of the government in the election of 1827.

29. I have relied very heavily upon J. B. M. Braun, *Nouvelle Biographie des députés . . . 1814 à 1829,* for the data on the outcome of these elections. See Appendix V about the maps.

MAP 1 The 42 departments in which left and left center candidates won 20 percent or more of the seats in the elections between 1815 and 1824, inclusive.

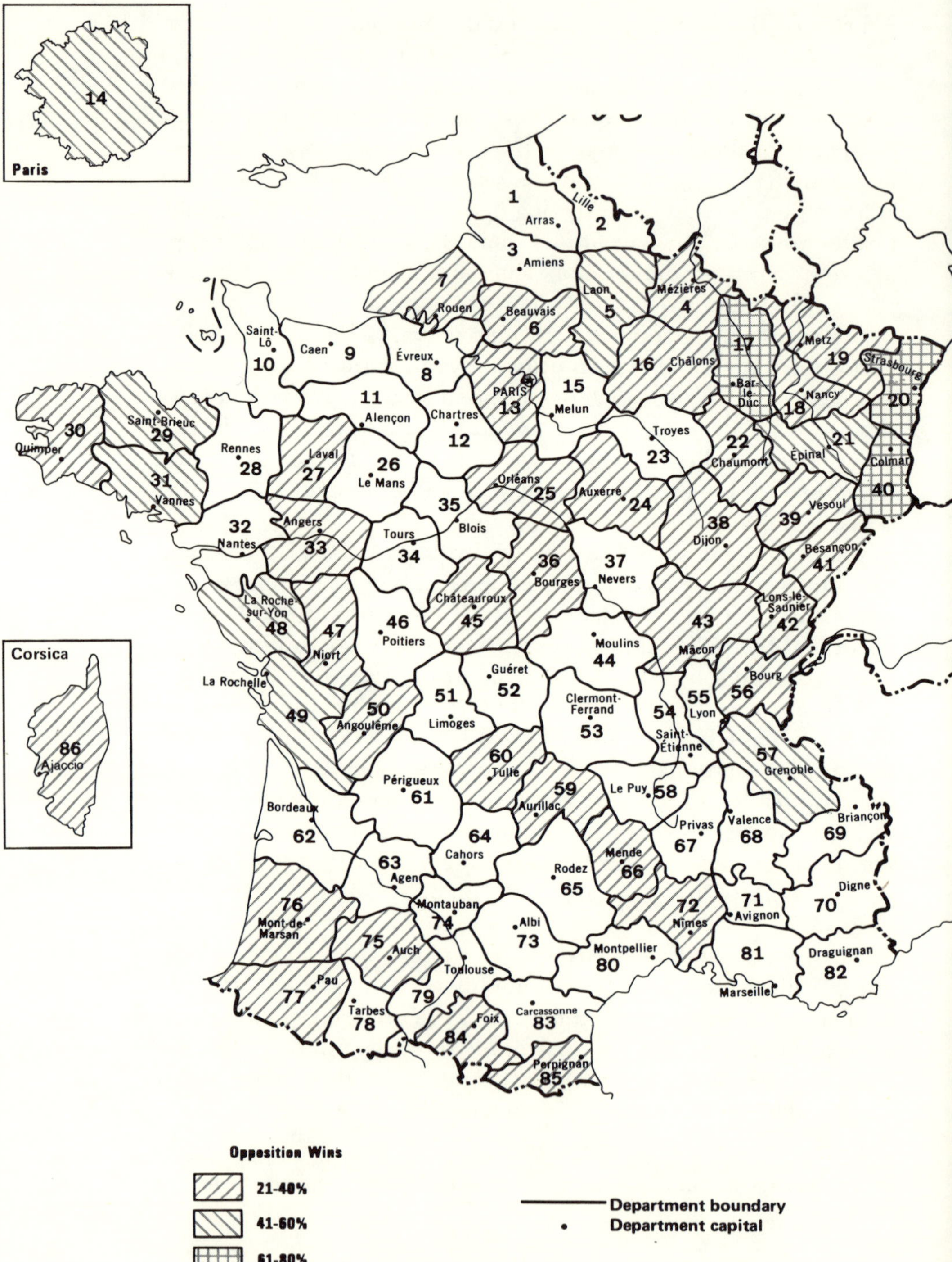

MAP 1 Continued

1. Pas-de-Calais
2. Nord
3. Somme
4. Ardennes
5. Aisne
6. Oise
7. Seine-Inférieure
8. Eure
9. Calvados
10. Manche
11. Orne
12. Eure-et-Loir
13. Seine-et-Oise
14. Seine
15. Seine-et-Marne
16. Marne
17. Meuse
18. Meurthe
19. Moselle
20. Bas-Rhin
21. Vosges
22. Haute-Marne
23. Aube
24. Yonne
25. Loiret
26. Sarthe
27. Mayenne
28. Ille-et-Vilaine
29. Côtes-du-Nord
30. Finistère
31. Morbihan
32. Loire-Inférieure
33. Maine-et-Loire
34. Indre-et-Loire
35. Loir-et-Cher
36. Cher
37. Nièvre
38. Côte-d'Or
39. Haute-Saône
40. Haut-Rhin
41. Doubs
42. Jura
43. Saône-et-Loire
44. Allier
45. Indre
46. Vienne
47. Deux-Sèvres
48. Vendée
49. Charente-Inférieure
50. Charente
51. Haute-Vienne
52. Creuse
53. Puy-de-Dôme
54. Loire
55. Rhône
56. Ain
57. Isère
58. Haute-Loire
59. Cantal
60. Corrèze
61. Dordogne
62. Gironde
63. Lot-et-Garonne
64. Lot
65. Aveyron
66. Lozère
67. Ardèche
68. Drôme
69. Hautes-Alpes
70. Basses-Alpes
71. Vaucluse
72. Gard
73. Tarn
74. Tarn-et-Garonne
75. Gers
76. Landes
77. Basses-Pyrénées
78. Hautes-Pyrénées
79. Haute-Garonne
80. Hérault
81. Bouches-du-Rhône
82. Var
83. Aude
84. Ariège
85. Pyrénées-Orientales
86. Corsica

MAP 2 The 44 departments in which candidates favorable to the government won 81 percent or more of the seats in the elections between 1815 and 1824, inclusive.

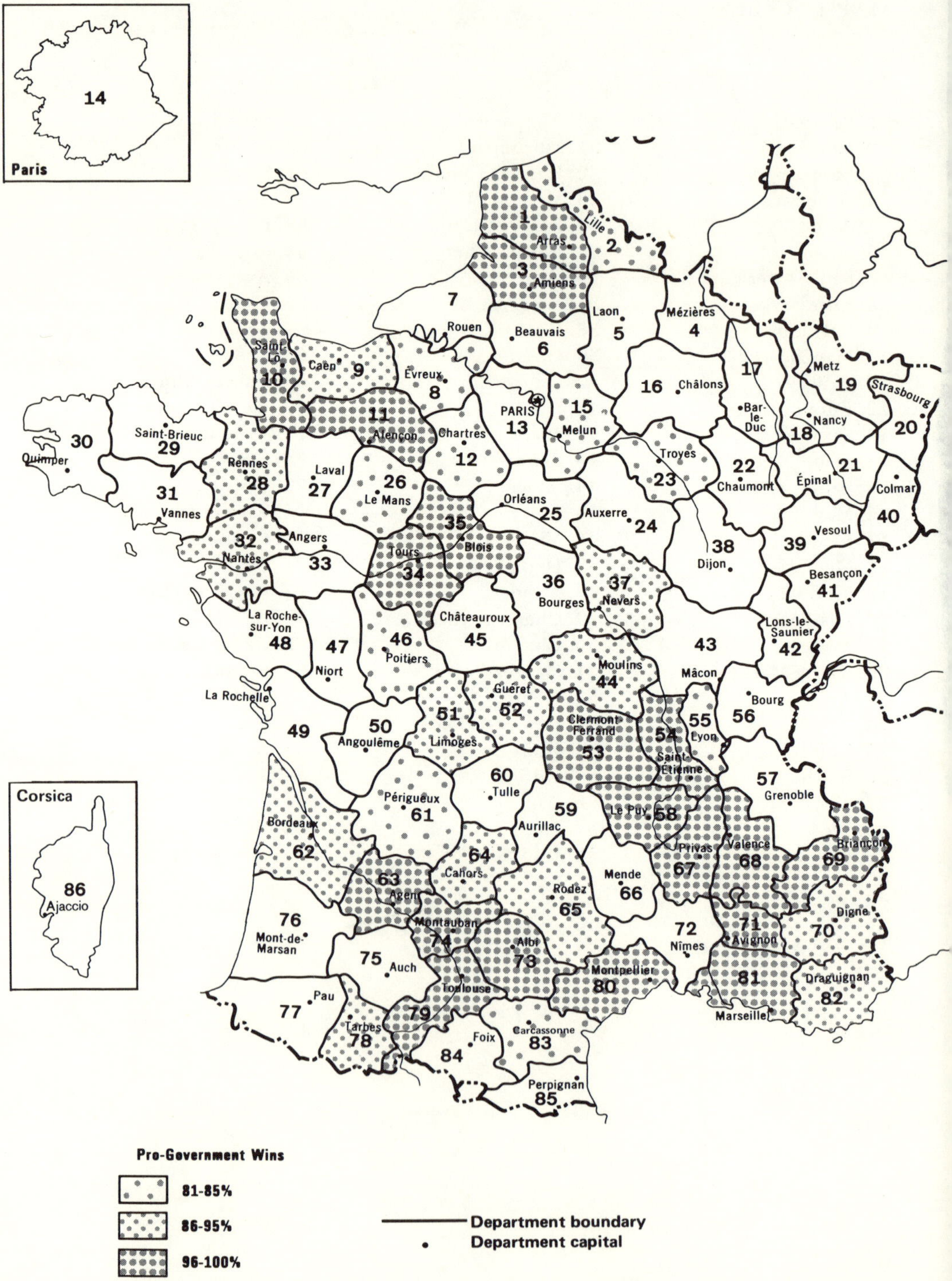

MAP 2 Continued

1. Pas-de-Calais
2. Nord
3. Somme
4. Ardennes
5. Aisne
6. Oise
7. Seine-Inférieure
8. Eure
9. Calvados
10. Manche
11. Orne
12. Eure-et-Loir
13. Seine-et-Oise
14. Seine
15. Seine-et-Marne
16. Marne
17. Meuse
18. Meurthe
19. Moselle
20. Bas-Rhin
21. Vosges
22. Haute-Marne
23. Aube
24. Yonne
25. Loiret
26. Sarthe
27. Mayenne
28. Ille-et-Vilaine
29. Côtes-du-Nord
30. Finistère
31. Morbihan
32. Loire-Inférieure
33. Maine-et-Loire
34. Indre-et-Loire
35. Loir-et-Cher
36. Cher
37. Nièvre
38. Côte-d'Or
39. Haute-Saône
40. Haut-Rhin
41. Doubs
42. Jura
43. Saône-et-Loire
44. Allier
45. Indre
46. Vienne
47. Deux-Sèvres
48. Vendée
49. Charente-Inférieure
50. Charente
51. Haute-Vienne
52. Creuse
53. Puy-de-Dôme
54. Loire
55. Rhône
56. Ain
57. Isère
58. Haute-Loire
59. Cantal
60. Corrèze
61. Dordogne
62. Gironde
63. Lot-et-Garonne
64. Lot
65. Aveyron
66. Lozère
67. Ardèche
68. Drôme
69. Hautes-Alpes
70. Basses-Alpes
71. Vaucluse
72. Gard
73. Tarn
74. Tarn-et-Garonne
75. Gers
76. Landes
77. Basses-Pyrénées
78. Hautes-Pyrénées
79. Haute-Garonne
80. Hérault
81. Bouches-du-Rhône
82. Var
83. Aude
84. Ariège
85. Pyrénées-Orientales
86. Corsica

MAP 3 The 42 departments of Map #1 in the election of 1827.

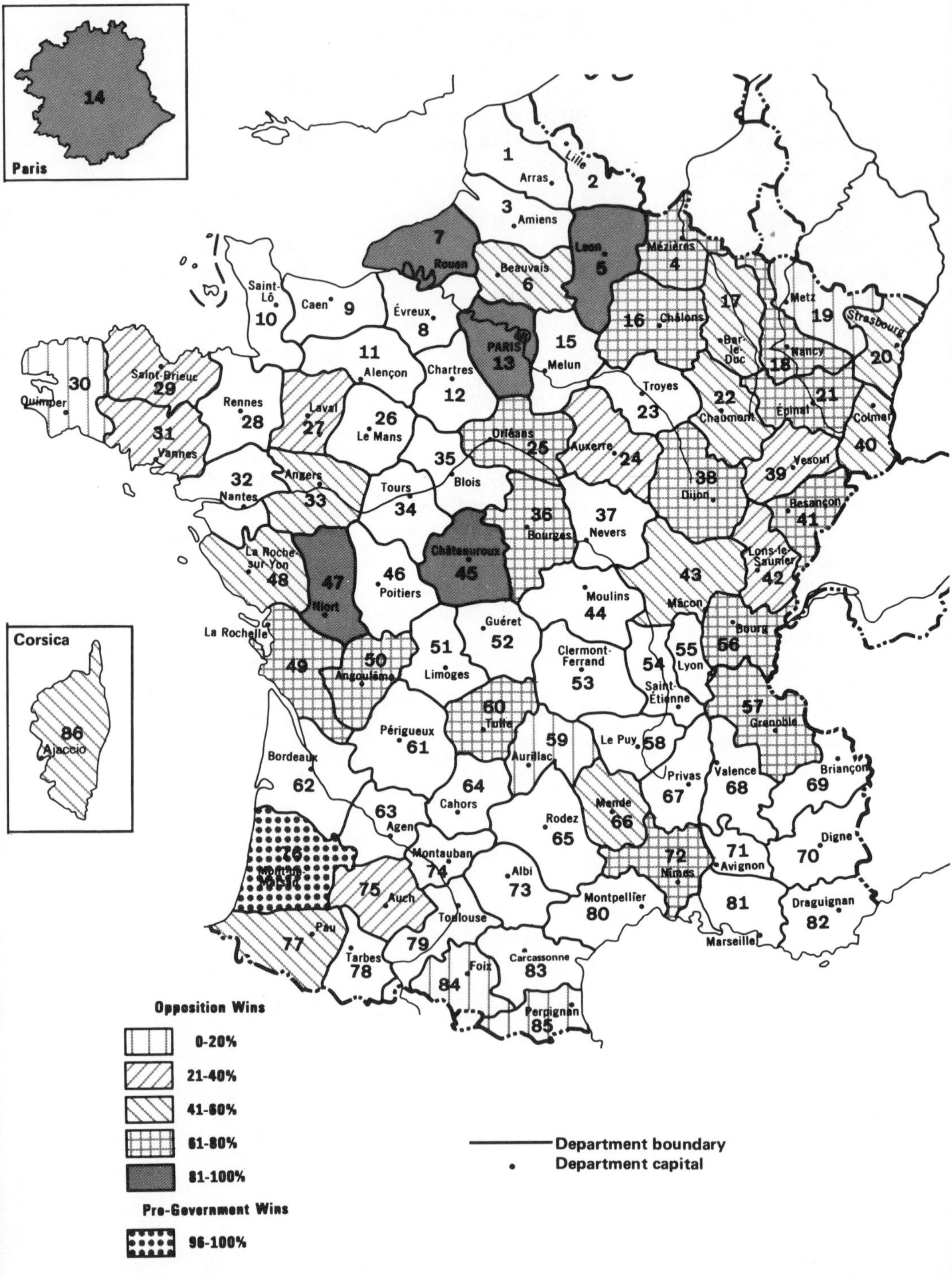

MAP 3 Continued

1. Pas-de-Calais
2. Nord
3. Somme
4. Ardennes
5. Aisne
6. Oise
7. Seine-Inférieure
8. Eure
9. Calvados
10. Manche
11. Orne
12. Eure-et-Loir
13. Seine-et-Oise
14. Seine
15. Seine-et-Marne
16. Marne
17. Meuse
18. Meurthe
19. Moselle
20. Bas-Rhin
21. Vosges
22. Haute-Marne
23. Aube
24. Yonne
25. Loiret
26. Sarthe
27. Mayenne
28. Ille-et-Vilaine
29. Côtes-du-Nord
30. Finistère
31. Morbihan
32. Loire-Inférieure
33. Maine-et-Loire
34. Indre-et-Loire
35. Loir-et-Cher
36. Cher
37. Nièvre
38. Côte-d'Or
39. Haute-Saône
40. Haut-Rhin
41. Doubs
42. Jura
43. Saône-et-Loire
44. Allier
45. Indre
46. Vienne
47. Deux-Sèvres
48. Vendée
49. Charente-Inférieure
50. Charente
51. Haute-Vienne
52. Creuse
53. Puy-de-Dôme
54. Loire
55. Rhône
56. Ain
57. Isère
58. Haute-Loire
59. Cantal
60. Corrèze
61. Dordogne
62. Gironde
63. Lot-et-Garonne
64. Lot
65. Aveyron
66. Lozère
67. Ardèche
68. Drôme
69. Hautes-Alpes
70. Basses-Alpes
71. Vaucluse
72. Gard
73. Tarn
74. Tarn-et-Garonne
75. Gers
76. Landes
77. Basses-Pyrénées
78. Hautes-Pyrénées
79. Haute-Garonne
80. Hérault
81. Bouches-du-Rhône
82. Var
83. Aude
84. Ariège
85. Pyrénées-Orientales
86. Corsica

MAP 4 The 44 departments of Map #2 in the election of 1827.

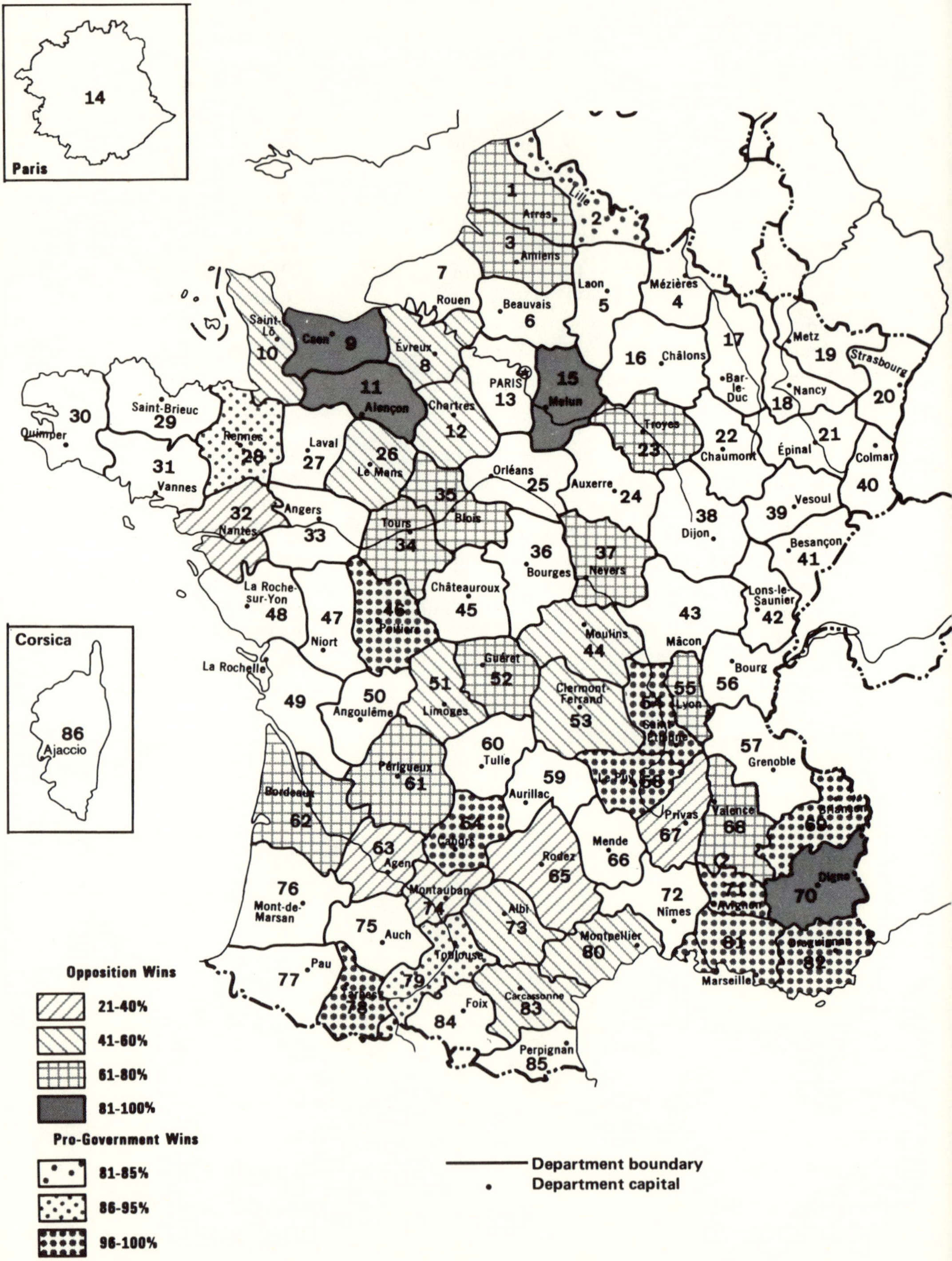

MAP 4 Continued

1. Pas-de-Calais
2. Nord
3. Somme
4. Ardennes
5. Aisne
6. Oise
7. Seine-Inférieure
8. Eure
9. Calvados
10. Manche
11. Orne
12. Eure-et-Loir
13. Seine-et-Oise
14. Seine
15. Seine-et-Marne
16. Marne
17. Meuse
18. Meurthe
19. Moselle
20. Bas-Rhin
21. Vosges
22. Haute-Marne
23. Aube
24. Yonne
25. Loiret
26. Sarthe
27. Mayenne
28. Ille-et-Vilaine
29. Côtes-du-Nord
30. Finistère
31. Morbihan
32. Loire-Inférieure
33. Maine-et-Loire
34. Indre-et-Loire
35. Loir-et-Cher
36. Cher
37. Nièvre
38. Côte-d'Or
39. Haute-Saône
40. Haut-Rhin
41. Doubs
42. Jura
43. Saône-et-Loire
44. Allier
45. Indre
46. Vienne
47. Deux-Sèvres
48. Vendée
49. Charente-Inférieure
50. Charente
51. Haute-Vienne
52. Creuse
53. Puy-de-Dôme
54. Loire
55. Rhône
56. Ain
57. Isère
58. Haute-Loire
59. Cantal
60. Corrèze
61. Dordogne
62. Gironde
63. Lot-et-Garonne
64. Lot
65. Aveyron
66. Lozère
67. Ardèche
68. Drôme
69. Hautes-Alpes
70. Basses-Alpes
71. Vaucluse
72. Gard
73. Tarn
74. Tarn-et-Garonne
75. Gers
76. Landes
77. Basses-Pyrénées
78. Hautes-Pyrénées
79. Haute-Garonne
80. Hérault
81. Bouches-du-Rhône
82. Var
83. Aude
84. Ariège
85. Pyrénées-Orientales
86. Corsica

Note again the difference in scale of accomplishment which obtains between Maps #1 and #2. If opposition candidates won as few as 20 percent of the seats in a department, the fact is registered on Map #1. Government candidates had to score 81 percent or more wins to be registered on Map #2.

Map #3 shows how, in 1827, candidates of both oppositions[30] fared in the forty-two departments of Map #1. One is perhaps permitted the generalization that modest beginnings in the pre-1827 elections paid off in 1827. In only eight of the forty-two departments did opposition candidates suffer a reversal of form, i.e., win less than 20 percent of the seats.

Among the departments of Map #1 were about twenty where Villèle should have been braced for little or no comfort and where he ought to have anticipated the defeat of a good many of the pro-government candidates. To the extent that he and the staff in the ministry of the interior studied the form-sheet of past performance and read the prefectoral reporting, they should have been disappointed only by the magnitude of their defeat in these departments, not by the fact that they did not triumph.[31]

Map #4 shows how government candidates of 1827 fared in the forty-four departments of Map #2 where, during earlier elections, they had fared very well indeed. Map #4 is perhaps the essence of Villèle's misery – a collection of twenty-seven unpleasant surprises in twenty-seven departments, most of which had probably been considered safe for candidates of the government.

Overall as things turned out, the government's alleged estimate

30. Departments whose opposition delegations included deputies of the counter-opposition were:
*Ain 1, Ardèche 1, Aveyron 1, Calvados 1, *Charente 1, *Cher 1, *Corrèze 2, *Côte-d'Or 1, *Côtes-du-Nord 2, Dordogne 1, Gers 1, Indre-et-Loire 1, Loire-Inférieure 1, Lot-et-Garonne 1, Maine-et-Loire 1, Mayenne 2, Morbihan 1, Moselle 1, Nièvre 1, Orne 2, Pas-de-Calais 1, Puy-de-Dôme 1, *Saône-et-Loire 1, *Deux-Sèvres 2, Somme 1, *Tarn-et-Garonne 1.

The asterisk denotes those departments in which there was a probable political alliance between ultra adherents and those of the constitutionnels.

31. Study of the form-sheet would have indicated that the following departments were unsafe for government candidates: *Aisne,* Aube, Aude, *Côte-d'Or,* Eure, Indre, Isère, Maine-et-Loire, Marne, *Meuse, Bas-Rhin, Haut-Rhin,* Rhône, Saône-et-Loire, *Seine, Seine-Inférieure,* Seine-et-Oise, *Vendée,* Vienne, and *Vosges.* The form-sheet and other indicators might have added: Ardennes, Charente-Inférieure, and Deux-Sèvres.

The list of unsafe departments given by Braun (*Nouvelle Biographie,* p. viii) contains these last three and nine of those above, i.e., those in italics.

of twenty or so unsafe departments[32] should have been raised by a factor of three: it did badly in sixty-one departments, not twenty.

In Appendix III(B) I have given the breakdown according to the type of college involved. Let me repeat what must have been the government's greatest blow: the outcome of the voting in the departmental colleges. Clearly the friends of the government were not prepared for what happened. They counted upon the departmental colleges to more than compensate for the dismal results of the arrondissemental and special elections. Of course, this did not happen. Left-center and left candidates won 47 of the 165 seats in contest and candidates of the counter-opposition won 21. It is likely that the government counted on losing some of these seats, say some 20, but surely not 68.

The greatest importance of the general election of 1827 was not necessarily that it brought to an end the remarkable reign of Joseph de Villèle and his durable government. No gainsaying that this was of moment, but of greater importance by far was what it did for Martignac, then Polignac, and ultimately for Charles himself. It made possible the appointment of Martignac, first as minister of the interior and later as president of the council of ministers; it made possible under his aegis a retreat from the rightward thrust of policy and two years of moderate constitutional monarchy; and it made virtually impossible a return to the concept of governance dear to the hearts of the prince de Polignac, and his sovereign master.

32. The Paris correspondent of the *Times* of London (8 Nov. 1827, p. 2) under a 2 November dateline wrote that the chiefs of the ministerial party were sure of 62 departments and that "the liberal opposition, which consists now of from 15 to 18 members, will gain from 60 to 70 votes [seats] and that the Royalist party [sic] will merge in the Ministerial." If this report is more than the idle gossip available to a fairly sharp newsman it may reflect an optimism based upon a study of past performance. Of course it may also reflect the attitude that political leaders would be most likely to display, once they had decided to go to the country: with an irrevocable decision already taken, one would not expect a cloud of premonitory pessimism.

8 / Envoi

There can be little doubt that Charles caught the significance of the election. He perceived in fairly short order that the line-up of political strengths in the new chamber made a continuation of the Villèle ministry a virtual impossibility. On 6 December he told Villèle that he would accept his resignation (which, in fact, he did not do for weeks) and replace his ministry with one composed of moderate royalists.[1] This positive stance of the king was not of long duration.

Whether or not the marquis de Talaru – a peer since 1815 and a defender of the royal prerogative, a maréchal-de-camp, and for a time ambassador to Spain – would rank as a moderate royalist, at least he was Charles's earliest choice to lead a new government. The king asked Villèle to see him and sound him out,[2] a commission Villèle could not acquit during the next three days, for Talaru was out of town. When he returned and the two finally met, Talaru began with diffidence and ended flatly refusing until Villèle persuaded him to sleep on his decision.[3] Next day he made his refusal definite; apparently he told the king as much the day after that. But meanwhile the king, probably under the influence of "madame," had come around to the notion of staying with Villèle, but letting Corbière and Peyronnet go. He would have Chabrol at the interior and Martignac at justice.[4]

Between 11 December and Christmas the king, in a torment of indecision, was beset by conflicting advice from his son, Polignac, Chabrol, and others. During this time Villèle himself listened to Frayssinous tell how he and Chabrol should be authorized to form a government.[5] He also heard from some unspecified "liberals,"

1. Villèle diary, 6 Dec. 1827. Villèle had offered his resignation the previous day. He had also offered, as an alternative, to form a new government without any hold-overs from his old one and presumably without Polignac (*ibid.,* 3 and 5 Dec. 1827).

2. *Ibid.,* 6 Dec. 1827.

3. *Ibid.,* 9 Dec. 1827.

4. *Ibid.,* 10 and 11 Dec. 1827.

5. *Ibid.,* 15 Dec. 1827.

as he termed them without other identification, who put forward a slate which symbolized the alliance of the constitutional left and the counter-opposition – the names of Royer-Collard, Daru, and St. Cyr were being linked with those of Hyde de Neuville, Beaumont, Delalot, and Bertin de Vaux.[6] Meanwhile La Bourdonnaye was suggesting to Villèle that the two of them join together while Laffitte was trying to sell Villèle on the idea of some sort of leftist group. Villèle does not note in his diary how much of this talk he conveyed to his king.

On 24 December Charles seemed discouraged and chagrined and told Villèle that he would not make a change in the ministry until 5 January of the new year. Villèle felt that the likely choice lay between three rival coalitions: one headed by Talaru, one by Polignac, and one by La Ferronnays.[7]

From the vantage point of the Villèle diary it looks as if two days after Christmas the king began to come down in favor of none of the above, but rather for a Martignac government.[8] Still he wanted to hold Chabrol, Damas, and Frayssinous over from the old ministry. By New Year's Eve apparently there were difficulties with Martignac and he had decided to form the new government not around him, but around Chabrol. And then, of course, he went back to Martignac and stayed put (5 January 1828).[9]

Given the political complexion of the chamber the choice of Martignac was a sound one. He and his ministry could count on the support of a good many of the old Villèlist "ministerials" as long as he did not swing too far to the left, and he could count on most of the old left center if he called a halt to the rightward trend of policy. He could even garner some friendly votes from the far left. The pointus of the old counter-opposition and the right-most wing of the former Villèle group would not be amiably inclined, but in themselves were not strong enough to upset him.

Martignac's colleagues within the council of ministers included two holdovers from the Villèle days soon to depart (they were Frays-

6. *Ibid.*, 17 Dec. 1827.

7. *Ibid.*, 24 Dec. 1827.

8. *Ibid.*, 27 Dec. 1827.

9. The date of the official demise of the Villèle government was 3 January 1828. Villèle wrote in his diary for Monday 31 Dec. a sentence characteristic perhaps but not wholly clear, followed by one which is poignantly clear which is: "Le roi voulait encore remettre. Je lui supplie de nous délivrer jeudi." The third of January was a Thursday.

sinous, ecclesiastical affairs, and Chabrol, navy) and five others whose political views were little known except as they seemed to incline away from the right.[10] Only St. Cricq, who received the newly-established ministry of commerce and manufacturing, had been definitely and recently associated with the views of what I have been calling the constitutional left. In short, insofar as one may characterize the ministry's general outlook it was to be to the left of Villèle's political penchant and a good long way to the left of the king's. Could it be that the king was coming around to the particular concept of ministerial responsibility which had long been espoused by the constitutional left? To the hopeful among this group it looked as if this very miracle had come to pass, for the Martignac government seemed to be one which would be responsible to the leftward orientation of the new chamber and to which the latter would accord its support.

Charles's choice of this ministry in no way portended a permanent change of heart. The hesitant support which he gave it, and his supplanting of it at the first good opportunity less than two years later suggest that he viewed it as a necessary but wholly unattractive expedient.[11]

These inner reservations to one side, Charles did take some initiatives that cheered the constitutional left: he separated the supervision of education from the ministry of ecclesiastical affairs; he authorized the dropping of two principal police officials, Franchet d'Esperey and Delavau, long associated – and unfavorably – with the Villèle government, and named the famous leader of the doctrinaires, Royer-Collard, as president of the chamber of deputies. He seems to have interposed no objection to Martignac's initiating two bills, one of which considerably softened the old government's stance vis-à-vis the press; the other went forward from the law of 2 May 1827, adding precision to parts of it and making the manipulation of electoral lists still more difficult.[12]

These pieces of legislation, of course, came relatively late in the parliamentary year and well after the turbulent weeks of February in which the chamber of deputies organized itself. Among these

10. St. Cricq; La Ferronnays, foreign affairs; general Decaux, war; Roy, finance; Portalis, justice.

11. See de Bertier de Sauvigny, *La Restauration,* p. 420.

12. The law of 2 July 1828 (Duvergier, *Lois,* XXVIII, 227-240).

sessions, which occupied more than half the month, those dedicated to the validation of the credentials of the newly elected deputies produced pages and pages of print in the *Moniteur*. Charges and countercharges of improper electoral activities of both the old Villèlist government and the left opposition were levied and discussed at great length. Much of the verbal ammunition at the disposal of the enemies of Villèle had been collected at the behest of the Société, Aide-toi in one of its post-November pamphlets.[13]

What went on in the chamber in these February days strengthened the resolve of the anti-Villèle leftist leaders to maintain the momentum they had achieved in their work of the campaign. One reads little of Chateaubriand's Friends, but much of the Aide-toi. Far from sitting back, it went on to increasing activity and effectiveness. In spite of its loss of the services of most of the young founding fathers of the *Globe,* it had no difficulty in recruiting able replacements. Guizot, of course, stayed on in a position of command.[14] There was still much to be done, none of it more important than carrying the vastly successful electoral operations over into the era of the forthcoming by-elections.

Before the end of May 1828 there would be forty-two of them. The multiple elections, as already noted, accounted for twenty-seven; there were another fifteen to fill seats made vacant by resignations, deaths, annulments, and the elevation of Villèle and Corbière to the peerage. In the by-elections of the spring many of the local electoral organizations which had first taken form months before and relaxed with the fall of the Villèle government resumed an active existence. In this they received stimulation and support from Paris. Their efforts produced a continuance of the political trends of November; the far right suffered a net loss of three seats, the old Villèlists of eight, while the constitutional left rewon all twenty-five seats it had had to vacate because of the multiple elections, and eleven more.[15] In short, the swing of the country continued to be away from the right and in Martignac's favor. From June till the end of the year another fifteen vacancies occurred in the chamber because

13. Aide-toi, no title. Text begins "M. Les elections sont terminées . . ." (Paris, 1827) BN Lb/49.796.

14. Pouthas, *Guizot pendant la Restauration,* pp. 380–401.

15. In the 25 I have counted 5 of the 6 surplus seats won by Royer-Collard; the sixth and last was not filled until later in the year.

of deaths, resignations, and the annulments of elections. The trend of the first half of the year continued. The counter-opposition had a net loss of one seat, the one-time Villèlists of five, while the constitutional left showed a net gain of six.

By now there were sitting in the chamber of deputies more than 200 of the 221 deputies who would soon defy their king in the dramatic vote on the Address of 1830. One hundred sixty-one had won election in the regular elections of November, and, in my count, another forty-six or forty-seven in the fifty-two by-elections of 1828.

During 1829 there were more vacancies – twenty-four of them – and more by-elections which further weakened the right and strengthened the constitutional left. The old counter-opposition had a net loss of two, the old Villèlists, a net loss of four, and the left side of the chamber a net gain of seven.[16] With the close of 1829, 220 of the 221 were in the chamber. The two hundred and twenty-first was none other than François Guizot who had arrived at age forty too late to run in 1827 and who on 23 January 1830 triumphed in a by-election at Lisieux (Calvados).[17] By the time he entered the chamber Martignac had fallen, and the king, in high disregard of the left-center and left majority in the deputies, had gone to the outstanding ultra-royalist of the day, Jules de Polignac, and formed a rightist government around him (8 August 1829). In the view of the leftist leaders, Charles had returned to his first principles of responsible government: responsible, yes, but above all to the crown, not to the elected legislature.

The antagonists of the king and his first minister did not have long to wait for an opportunity to show their displeasure. On 2 March the king opened the new legislative session with the traditional speech from the throne; its key passage contained an unequivocal statement of the royal prerogative as Charles and Polignac viewed it and couched in ominous terms. "If criminal maneuvers," began the key sentence. "If criminal maneuvers raise up obstacles against my government, which I hope will not be the case, I will find the strength to overcome them in my resolution to maintain public order, in the just confidence of the French people, and in the love that they have always demonstrated for their kings."

16. Seven, not six, because one deputy of unknown political affiliation – he was Bouchet – was replaced by a known adherent of Martignac. See Appendix IV.

17. There were three other by-elections in the first three months of 1830. All three were vacated by and refilled by men of the far right.

With these words the king threw down the challenge. It was straightway taken up. It was taken up as the opposition majority in the chamber named a like-minded committee to draft the Address, the habitual reply to the king's annual *Discours*. The outcome of these endeavors was a short and eloquent document which highlighted the fundamental disagreement between the sovereign and his elected legislature.[18] When the text came to a vote (16 March 1830) it received the affirmation of 221 of the deputies with only 181 opposed.[19]

Charles's immediate reaction was to prorogue the session until September; his second thoughts were to dissolve the errant chamber and summon the electoral colleges for June and July in a general election. In the weeks which separated the royal ordinance from the last days of the summer's balloting, the country once again went through a tempestuous campaign. Electoral organizations of the left, led once again by the Aide-toi, sprang back to life.

Irrespective of the efforts of the king, his ministry, and its bureaucracy, the *pays légal* reaffirmed, and more, the judgment it had first uttered in November 1827 and later in the by-elections of 1828, 1829, and 1830. It returned some 270 deputies committed to a leftist opposition to Polignac, including 207 of the 221. The old counter-opposition had, of course, largely disappeared; most of its one-time adherents were now in Polignac's corner. Clearly Charles could not live with this verdict. His attempt to undo it with his issuance of the July ordinances was what precipitated the Revolution and brought his reign to an end.

Thus it was that many of the very same men who had led the constitutional left in 1827 and mobilized its latent strength in the electorate — who won the election and caused the upset of the Villèle government — went on to set in motion another and far more important chain of events. This, beginning with the vote of the 221, led on to the fall of the Bourbon monarchy itself. Nor was their work over in the climactic days of July 1830; it continued. The first ministry of Louis Philippe, the successor monarch — a short-lived ministry to be sure — included Dupont de l'Eure, Casimir Périer, Dupin *aîné*, Laffitte, the duc de Broglie, Guizot, baron Louis, Gérard,

18. I have used Mr. Pinkney's translation of the sentence of Charles's *discours* (*French Revolution of 1830*, p. 18). His translation of the full text of the Address is on p. 20.

19. See Appendix VI about the 221. The balance of the chamber, 27 men, either were absent or refrained from voting.

and Sébastiani. All except Broglie, who was a peer, had been among the 221; all but Broglie and Guizot had been elected to the chamber in 1827; and Dupont, Périer, Dupin, Laffitte, and Guizot had played important roles in the mobilization of the electorate for that election.

In the second government of Louis Philippe, that which lasted from 2 November 1830 to 13 March 1831, were Laffitte (as president of the council), Périer, Dupont, and Sébastiani, joined by four men not elected in 1827. Of these, two had been important actors in the campaign: the young peer, Montalivet, who wrote one of the best-known pamphlets issued by the Friends, and the lawyer Mérilhou.

What of the chamber of deputies whence came most of these ministers and with which it worked in concord? For the first five months it was a rump assembly all of whose members (290-odd) had been elected in June and July of 1830. We have already seen that 207 of them were among the 221 and had come to the chamber either in the general elections of 1827 or in the subsequent bys. They were the men who played the pivotal role in seating the new king and in drafting and ratifying the revised constitutional charter. Later, after the special elections of October and November of 1830 which brought the chamber up to full strength, their influence continued on in the shaping of new legislation affecting local government, the national guard, and above all elections.

Here then in summary is the great significance of the election of 1827 to which this book is dedicated. The men it sent to the chamber of deputies became not only those who toppled Villèle and with whom the last of the Bourbon kings of France fought to his final defeat, but also those who survived the turmoil of the July Revolution to give much of the form and substance to the reign of Louis Philippe.

Appendixes, Bibliographical Note, Index

Appendix I / A note on the methodology of the use of the electoral lists

Working over electoral lists of the Restoration with an eye to discovering the composition of the electorate from the point of view of the occupation of the voters is more of a chore than first glance would indicate. What follows is a discussion of the principal methodological problems and my solutions to them.

First, there is the matter of the designators which appear in the "occupation" column of the lists. There are many more than 100 different ones. They range from the "sous prefet," "propriétaire," "marchand de vin en gros," and "notaire," which are readily grasped, to such as "courtier royal," "gourmet," and "employé," which were not – by me at least. It is not enough to understand the designators; clearly, they must be lumped under a few major categories. My predecessors had hit upon four: "public service," "propriétaires," "business," and "professions," and these I adopted both to make my findings compatible with theirs and, speaking pragmatically, to be able to use the results of Professor Adeline Daumard's analysis of the list for Paris.

The following shows what I included under each of the four categories:

1. Public Service

This category includes salaried (and usually career) officials and officers of the state.

a. Officers of the royal household.
b. Administrative: for example, prefects, subprefects, officers of the fiscal service, *ponts et chaussées, eaux et forêts,* customs, etc.
c. Foreign service: officers of the diplomatic and consular corps.
d. Judiciary: magistrates of all courts from the *juges de paix* up and non-judicial officers of the courts, i.e., members of the *parquet.*

e. Military: staff and line officers of the army and the navy. I also included in this group a relatively small number of high-ranking officers of the gendarmerie.

2. Propriétaires

This category includes those who derived the bulk of their income from their ownership of real property, most importantly land:

a. Men appearing on the lists simply as "propriétaire," or "prop."
b. Men designated as "cultivateur" or "fermier."
c. Men designated as "rentier." The *rente* at issue here must have been that derived from the ownership of real property. (The term "rentier" could, of course, also mean a man whose principal source of income derived from rentes, i.e., government bonds. But since such sources of income were not subject to any of the direct taxes, he would not have paid enough direct taxes to be a proper censeur and qualified voter.)
d. Men designated by title: (1) such as title of nobility (comte, duc); (2) membership in the *légion d'honneur* or cited only as chevalier de Saint-Louis; (3) holders of any of several unsalaried government positions (member of a prefect's conseil général, or a subprefect's conseil d'arrondissement, mayor or adjoint of a small commune) so long as they paid the bulk of their cens in the contribution foncière with negligible or no payment of the impôt des patentes.

3. Business

a. Men engaged in all manner of commercial enterprise: bankers, négociants, merchants of this and that, innkeepers, commission men, etc.
b. Men employed in industrial production: iron masters, textile mill operators down to small-scale brewers and millers.
   In those days of the beginnings of modern business, the gray zone between commerce and industry was wider and grayer than later. I began my count hoping to make the distinction, but abandoned it.
c. Men designated by title as in 2.d. above and who paid a substantial amount in the impôt des patentes.

4. Professional Men
   a. Law: *avocats, avouées, notaires,* professors of law, and an occasional law student.
   b. Medicine: doctors and professors of medicine, and surgeons – though the medical profession of the day would have disowned them.
   c. Other: a mixed bag which included architects, engineers, surveyors, clergymen, teachers, etc. If one of these performed his services, and for a salary, for one of the lay areas of government, I counted him in the public service category.

Some observations on the problem of categorization of callings as these occur on electoral lists of the Restoration:

1. Generally speaking, the identification of a man as a business enterpriser is likely to be easiest and done with most confidence. The overwhelming number of cases indicate in the occupation column that the man is an innkeeper or brewer or whatever. Furthermore the man's payment of an impôt des patentes which is noted in the appropriate column nails the matter down.

In some cases however the occupation column will mask the man's connection with the world of affairs. It will give him a title, for example, or call him "propriétaire": apparently some men were not all that keen to be known as "négociant" or "marchand de bois en gros" and did what they could to mute the matter. Another student of electoral lists, Jean George, noticed this quirk in some of the entries which he found in the lists for Marseille of the 1830's. In one for 1833 he found a number in which the occupation of certain men was listed as "Prop. et négociant," "Prop. et fabricant de savon." M. George was comforted to observe that no matter how much a négociant may have desired to conceal his business interests and be known simply as propriétaire, he did not succeed for in subsequent lists almost all of the men in question were noted for their business pursuits alone. (Jean George, "Le Pays légal de Marseille sous la monarchie de juillet . . . ," unpub. diss., Aix-en-Provence, 1956, pp. 23-24.)

I have followed M. George's pattern with all entries in which a man is listed with a dual occupation ("prop. et filateur," for example) when the man also pays a substantial *patente*. If the amount was only a few francs I classed him as a propriétaire. I did the same with others such as "maire et. . . ," "adjoint et. . . ," "membre du conseil general et [say] filateur."

2. "Ancien" this and that. In the absence of any other indicator I felt obliged to class an "ancien notaire," for example, among the practicing lawyers and an "ancien maître de forges" among the active businessmen. There is good reason to suppose that such men were on the electoral lists because they paid the bulk of their cens in the contribution foncière and were in fact a sort of propriétaire. I justified my classing them with the professions or business on the somewhat tenuous ground that their old callings would have left their psychological imprint.

Appendix II / Methodology of extrapolating from the sample to achieve an estimate of the national electorate

1. Subtract from the total electorate of 88,000 the 11,900 voters I tallied in the five large cities.

2. Apply to the remainder of the electorate (i.e., 76,100) the percentages derived from the lists of the 16 departments. One gets:

Public Service	9,132
Propriétaires	45,660
Business	15,220
Professions	6,088

3. Add to each of these categories the numbers of the matching group registered in the big cities. Add up the totals. The electorate is now back to full strength.

4. Recalculate the percentages on the basis of an electorate of 88,000.

Appendix III / Some statistics of the general election of 1827

A. Electoral success of the men endorsed as opposition candidates in the Paris press between 8 and 24 November 1827.

	No. of men endorsed	Winners	%	No. of men who ran well	%	Total	%
Lists of 8–9 Nov. 1827	286	108	37.8	47	16.4	155	54.2
Lists of 10–24 Nov. 1827	164	50	30.5	10	6.1	60	36.6
Totals	450	158	35.1	57	12.7	215	47.8

B. Outcome of the general election of 1827 (including the election in Corsica, January 1828), by colleges

Number of seats	Arrondissemental Colleges	Special Colleges	Departmental Colleges	Total
Seats won by candidates generally favorable to the Villèle government	89	10	96	195
Seats won by candidates of the left center and left	145	7	47	199
Seats won by candidates of the counter-opposition	10	0	21	31
Seats won by candidates of unknown political affiliation	3	1	1	5
Totals	247	18	165	430

C. Voting strength of the oppositions in the general election of 1827, by colleges

	Arrondissemental Colleges	Special Colleges	Departmental Colleges
Total inscribed electorate	88,000	1,670	21,600
Total voting	75,000	1,430	17,800
Total "ballots" cast	75,000	3,500	44,450
Votes received by winning candidates of the left center and left	34,500	1,000	13,100
Votes received by winning candidates of the counter-opposition	1,500	0	2,900
Votes received by the principal losing candidates of the left center and left	4,650	460	4,650
Votes received by the principal losing candidates of the counter-opposition	90	170	750

D. Number of deputies in each age-bracket

Age brackets	Just prior to the 1827 election	In the new chamber
40 - 44	10	55
45 - 49	83	97
50 - 54	86	88
55 - 59	90	73
60 - 64	84	74
65 - 69	45	22
70 - 74	21	11
75 and over	5	6
unknown	6	4

E. Occupations of members of the Chamber of Deputies[a]

	Chamber as it was just prior to the 1827 election		New chamber	
1. Holders of salaried government positions, including the military	197		165	
2. Propriétaires	180		148	
a. Men identified only as holders of unsalaried government positions, but whose livelihoods derived from the land		76		73
b. Men listed as propriétaires and holders of unsalaried government positions		55		44
c. Men listed simply as propriétaires		49		31
3. Men engaged in commerce or industry	32		61	
4. Professional men	17		46	
5. Occupation unknown	4		10	
	430		430	

a. The methodology of reducing many kinds of occupation to the four cited above is much the same as that which I used on the electoral lists. See Appendix I.

Appendix IV / Summary of the by-elections of 1828, 1829, and 1830

Summary of the by-elections of 1828, 1829, and 1830

	1828	1829	1830
Total number of vacancies to be filled	57	24	4
Losses to the chamber of deputies as a result of:			
1. Vacancies caused by 19 deputies who were elected by more than a single constituency	27	—	—
2. Vacancies caused by death of the incumbent	13	11	2
3. Vacancies caused by resignation	6	10	—
4. Vacancies caused by annulment	9	—	—
5. Vacancies caused by elevation to the peerage	2	3	2
Losses / Replacements, in political terms:			
1. Deputies of the counter-opposition (extreme right)	3/0	3/1	1/3
2. Deputies of the right center (one-time Villèle adherents)	16/8	11/7	2/0
3. Deputies of the left center and left oppositions	38/47	9/16	1/1
4. Deputies of unknown political leanings	0/2	1/0	0/0

which took care of the problem of the multiple elections, they would show nothing more than one small change in one department of Map #4 (the Nord, and that in favor of the oppositions). If they had been reconstructed at the end of the year on the basis of all the by-elections of 1828 they would show an appreciable growth in left-opposition representation in the chamber.

Appendix V / A word about the maps

The fact that there are almost exactly half of the 86 departn
each of Maps #1 and #2 is not by my design. My decision tc
arbitrary cut-off point at 20 percent opposition-wins turned
to be the point which dictated allocating 42 departments to
and 44 to Map #2. The choice of departments for Maps #3
then rested upon the decision made with respect to Maps #
#2.

As already noted, my calculations for Maps #1 and #2 re
large part on the findings of J. B. M. Braun (*Nouvelle Biogr*
pp. 26–52). The base against which I calculated the percen
opposition-wins is the total number of seats in contest in tl
lar elections (and the occasional by-elections) between 181
1824 inclusive.

My calculations for Maps #3 and #4 rest upon the sourc
cussed in the Bibliographical Note and in chapter 7 of the
principally archival material, the Paris press, the contempc
graphical dictionaries.

Since one of my primary aims was to show why the Vil
ernment fell – as opposed to merely chronicling electoral
of left-opposition candidates – the graphic representation
#3 and #4 take into account the wins of *both* opposition
of the left and those of the extreme right.

In those departments where I was unable to determine
cal orientation of an elected deputy (there were five of tl
just did not count the unidentified man. For example in
five deputies were chosen: one of them a ministerial supp
of them leftist opposition, one of the far right, and one u
I registered the situation on Map #3 as if the opposition
three out of four seats. This was one way of handling the
admittedly not ideal.

Maps #3 and 4 depict electoral wins and losses as of t
November 1827 – multiple elections and all. If these ma
been reconstructed on the basis of the bys of April and

Appendix VI / The 221

The 221 deputies who voted to affirm the Address of March 1830 were in many respects the human detonators of a train of events which led ineluctably to the Revolution of July. Since all were there in the chamber directly or indirectly as a result of the election of 1827 they are owing a word in this book.

What is most certain about the 221 is the number itself. Voting in the chamber on all important matters was accomplished by a deputy's dropping a ball into a box (a white ball for an affirmative vote, a black for one opposed). The count of the balls was official and final, and in this case the result, as formally announced, was 221 white and 181 black balls. There was, of course, no official cognizance of which deputies dropped which sort of ball. From this absence of an official accounting of those voting pro, those con, and those who did not vote because they were not in the chamber or because they were and could not make up their minds, some confusions have resulted. Accordingly, one will never know exactly which deputies made up the 221. One can however come close.

There are several contemporary and unofficial lists.[1] These were pieced together by newsmen and others from what they could learn by talking with deputies, friends of deputies, friends of friends, and out into the purlieus of political gossip. The main difficulty is that the names given in the various documents are not the same. The list in *Le Temps* contains 223 names, half a dozen of whom the editors were acknowledgedly not sure about. They set the names in italics to mark them as presumptive. But according to the writers of the *Biographie impartiale de 221 députés,* whose listing comes out at exactly 221, the issuance of *Le Temps* is in error not only in some of its presumptions, but in some of its flat-out attributions as well.[2] For its part the *Guide des électeurs* (BN Lb/49.1233)

1. Anon., *Biographie impartiale de 221 députés* (Paris, 1830) BN Ln/6.39; [*Le Temps,* Paris], *Tableau statistique des députés qui ont voté pour ou contre l'adresse* (Paris, n.d.) BN Le/65.428; Anon., *Le Guide des électeurs contenant . . . les députés qui ont voté pour ou contre l'adresse* (Paris, 1830) BN Lb/49.1233; *Quatrième Lettre d'un électeur parisien à quelques électeurs des départements.*

2. See pp. 234–240 of the *Biographie impartiale de 221,* "Documents généraux et conclusion."

does not include six names which do appear in the other publications. Looking over all the documents the total of men believed, for one reason or another, to have voted for the Address is well over the allowable number.

Part of the explanation for this embarrassing excess of claimants derives in the last analysis from the king's dissolution of the chamber and the consequent electoral campaign. The leftist opposition took as a goal the reelection of each and every one of the 221. Being known as one of them took on a political cachet of great importance; perhaps a score of men with highly dubious claims stepped forward. Others contented themselves with an out-loud assertion that only the accident of their absence from the chamber had prevented their being among the magic circle. In some tallies these earnests got counted as the real thing and the totals inflated.

In my personal census I rejected a number of this sort of claimant. This left me with 229 men, 217 of whom seemed to have solid credentials for inclusion. The claims of the remaining 12 were all dubious, some very dubious. But within the evidence I have had at hand there is not that which would lead me to a sure determination of the missing four. In the end I had to pick four to give me the 221 I needed for a statistical count. I am aware of the subjective nature of my choosing.

I have calculated that about 160 (about 73 percent) of the 221 were elected to the chamber in the general elections of November 1827. Another 27 (some 12 percent) might be considered as closely linked by virtue of their coming to the chamber to fill the seats left empty when 19 of November's deputies resigned their excess seats. Of this group 27 new deputies who won in the by-elections of the spring of 1828 had stood with the 221.

As already noted, more by-elections occurred in the summer and fall of 1828, and of the new deputies 24 were to be among those aligned with the 221. The continuation of the leftward swing of the electorate was in some measure a normal carry-over of the political momentum of the 1827 campaign. Constituencies which had returned left-oriented deputies only to lose them to death, resignation, or annulment, bestirred themselves to find new and like-minded candidates. In 24 different departments trends established in 1827 ran true to form. In nine constituencies of eight other departments where the winning candidate of 1827 was a Villèle adherent, future members of the 221 replaced them in the subsequent bys.

Whatever the momentum of the 1827 effort, it was not allowed to slow. Throughout 1828, 1829, and 1830 the organization of the Aide-toi gained in strength and political skill.[3] Largely through its efforts in 1829 the new crop of by-elections produced an increment of 9 to the future 221. In 1830, as already noted, Guizot himself, one of the Aide-toi's paramount leaders, won his first election to become the two hundred and twenty-first.

The 221 – Some Statistics

1. Elected in the general election of 1827	160
2. Elected in the subsequent by-elections	61
3. Elected from:	
a. Departmental colleges	57
b. Special colleges	4
c. Arrondissemental colleges	160
4. Titles of nobility including titles from the Empire	71
5. Ages	
40 - 44	12
45 - 49	42
50 - 54	42
55 - 59	50
60 - 64	36
65 - 69	20
70 - 74	11
75 and over	8

The median age falls within the 56th year, which (in the year 1830) is about the median age of the chamber as a whole.

6. Occupations		
a. Holders of salaried government positions		75 (34%)
1. Administrative, including one prefect	25 (11%)	
2. Officers of the judiciary	26 (12%)	
3. Military	24 (11%)	

3. See Pouthas, *Guizot pendant la Restauration,* pp. 383 ff.

b. Propriétaires (likely or certain)		49 (22%)
1. Unsalaried officials of the government	18 (8%)	
2. Men listed as Propriétaires/ unsalaried officials	10 (5%)	
3. Men listed as Propriétaires	21 (10%)	
c. Men engaged in commerce or industry		55 (25%)
d. Professional men		32 (14%)
e. Of unknown occupation		10 (5%)

One hundred twenty-nine had served in the chamber of deputies prior to the election of 1827; 92 came to the chamber for the first time as a result of the election of 1827 or of subsequent by-elections.

Looking down the road, about 200 of them stayed on in parliamentary life to serve in one or another chamber of the July Monarchy. Only about 40 of them swung far enough to the left to be associated with the "Mouvement" of Louis Philippe's day – as the opposition was known – while the other 160 lined up with the "Résistance," or the pro-government forces. Almost 50 of these were elevated to the peerage.

Bibliographical Note

What follows is a specialized bibliography of the basic sources for this book. For an essential listing of the many important printed materials, including the press, memoirs, monographs, etc., for the period under discussion, consult the splendid bibliographies in David Pinkney, *The French Revolution of 1830* (Princeton: Princeton University Press, [1972]), pp. 372-385, and in Vincent W. Beach, *Charles X of France* (Boulder, Colo.: Pruett, [1971]), pp. 456-474 and notes to chaps. 2-5.

Archival Sources

In the Archives Nationales (AN) the following series were of top importance:

C1164-C1323, a large series (pointed out to me by an anonymous well-wisher and dipped into for my account by Professor William Pruitt). These cartons contain copies of the procès verbaux plus the full documentation of the winners (birth certificate, certificates of payment of cens, etc.). They are also likely to contain a "liste de votants" which is a sort of check list of the voters for the use of the bureau of a given college. In a way these "listes" are also a kind of electoral list, but since they contain no data relating to the voter's occupation and cens, they are of little use to those who wish to study the composition of the electorate from the point of view of the callings of the individual voters.

F/1c/III series: *Esprit public et élections.* For specific dates within specific departments see the printed *Inventaire.* These cartons are, of course, the indispensable ones for devotees of elections. They contain a great deal of correspondence on the subject between prefects and the ministry of the interior, inter alia some of the prefects' replies to the questions raised in the minister's array of circular messages relating to the forthcoming election of 1827. Unfortunately it appears that the bulk of this correspondence has been lost or filed elsewhere. Beginning alphabetically with the Ain I encountered only a handful of the hoped-for reports until I reached the Tarn. There, and among the papers of succeeding departments all the way to the end with the Yonne, I found a bounty. I also found a few messages seemingly relevant to this special and classified correspondence in the cartons F/7 6767-6772, q.v. below.

Also in the F/1c/III cartons are copies of the procès verbaux for almost all the elections of 1827 and for most of the subsequent by-elections. It is the very very rare procès verbal that gives a hint of the political orientation of the winner and his opponents.

F/7 series: *Police générale.*

The 3600 group, a large number containing communications from local gendarme commanders, many forwarded to the director of police in Paris; principally useful for information about opposition electoral activities prior to the election of 1827.

6740–6741: *Affaires politiques, Elections,* 1820–1830.

6742: *Affaires politiques, Journaux,* 1814–1830.

6767–6772: *Affaires politiques, Situation politique des départements,* 1820–1830. This group of cartons was among the most useful; I will not cite individual ones with each reference. Know that carton #6767 has in it all departments which fall alphabetically between Ain and Bouches-du-Rhône; 6768, Calvados — Doubs; 6769, Drôme — Loir-et-Cher; 6770, Loire — Nièvre; 6771, Nord — Sarthe; and 6772, Seine — Yonne. Herein, for example, are the prefects' replies to the circular of the director of police of 5 July 1827.

Note: When you go to the AN to look up the series cited in this book as "F/1c/II" and "F/1c/III" and "F/7," you will find them in the catalogue as "F^{1c}II", and "F^{1c}III" and "F^{7}," respectively.

My only foray into the Archives privées (AP) of the AN was to consult the Guizot collection (letters to and from) for the years 1827–1830. As to this collection, the 42 AP series, I found disappointingly few documents which related to Guizot's leading role in the Société, Aide-toi and to his concern over the election of 1827.

I took great benefit from a number of the departmental archives. Generally speaking most of the documentation I sought is filed under the ADs' Série M, "Administration." In those cases where the *Inventaires* failed me, a kindly and expert archivist almost invariably had the answer. There were three groups of material of most importance to me:

1. The majority of the electoral lists which I used for my analysis of the electorate in chapter 3 — a few unofficial lists I found in the Bibliothèque Nationale (BN). The following cites the lists which I found and their call numbers whether in the ADs or the BN. I have deposited microfilm copies of these lists in the Yale and Harvard University Libraries.

a. Ain, *Première liste de service du jury pour 1828* (1827); AD Ain (U-7). This is a proper operational jury list. It contains 123 names drawn from the electorate which are not necessarily a random sample.

b. Aisne, *Liste générale des électeurs et du jury pour 1830* (Laon, Oct. 1829); BN Le/54.1, an unofficial list.

c. Bouches-du-Rhône. *Liste générale du jury pour 1831* (Marseille, 1830);

AD Bouches-du-Rhône (402 U 3), an official list. Note that this list, though post-Revolution (1830), is nevertheless based upon electoral law of the Restoration (i.e., the 300 franc cens, et al).

d. Côte-d'Or, *Liste générale du jury pour 1828* (Dijon, 1827); AD Côte-d'Or (2 M 19), an official list.

e. Doubs, *Liste des élécteurs du Doubs, 1827* (Paris, 1828); BN Le/54.1, an unofficial list.

f. Drôme, *Liste générale du jury pour 1828* (Valence, 1827); AD Drôme (6 M 25), an official list.

g. Hérault, *Liste générale du jury pour 1829* (Montpellier, 1828); AD Hérault (M), an official list.

h. Isère, *Liste du jury, 1829* (Grenoble, 1828); in the Archives Municipales of Grenoble, an official list.

i. Lot, *Liste générale du jury pour 1828* (Cahors, 1827); AD Lot (2 M 8-1), an official list.

j. Nord, *Liste des élécteurs composant le 3e arrondissement* (Lille) and *ibid., 4e arrondissement* (Lille), (1827); BN Le/54.1, an unofficial list.

k. Pas-de-Calais, *Listes électorales et du jury . . . pour . . . 1830* (Arras, 1829); in AD Pas-de-Calais (no call number), an unofficial list.

l. Pyrénées-Orientales, *Liste des électeurs . . . 1827* (Perpignan, Nov. 1827), AD Pyrénées-Orientales (II M/I/31).

m. Haut-Rhin, *Liste générale du jury pour 1828* (Colmar, 1827); AD Haut-Rhin (#634,266), an official list, lacks most of the rectification tables.

n. Rhône, an official list for 1828 (Lyon, 1827); AD Rhône (M?). Also *Liste des électeurs . . . Rhône* (Lyon, 1827); BN Le/54.1, probably an unofficial list, but with seemingly full data.

o. Seine, *Listes électorales et du jury du départment de la Seine en 1828* (Paris, [1828]); BN fol. Le/54.1, seemingly an unofficial list but with complete data as to occupation and cens.

I did not make my own count of Parisian voters according to occupation, but relied upon Professor Adeline Daumard's percentage figures (see her *La Bourgeoisie parisienne de 1815 à 1848* [Paris, 1963] p. 52), which I translated back into discrete numbers.

p. Seine-Inférieure, *Liste électorale . . . Rouen* (Rouen, 1827); AD Seine-Maritime (3M), an official list prepared for the spring by-election, and *Liste électorale . . . du Havre . . . pour 1828* (Le Havre, 1827); BN Le/54.1, an unofficial list.

q. Seine-et-Oise, *Liste générale du jury pour 1828* (Versailles, 1827); BN Le/54.1, an unofficial list.

r. Vendée, *Liste générale du jury pour 1828* (Bourbon-Vendée, 1827); AD Vendée (2 M 26 bis), an official list.

s. Vienne, *Liste générale du jury pour 1828* (Poitiers, 1827); AD Vienne (3 M 3-7), an official list.

2. The circular messages sent out to the prefects by the ministry of the interior in preparation for the election of 1827.

Note: The departments known for many years as the Charente-Inférieure,

Loire-Inférieure, and Seine-Inférieure are now known as the Charente-Maritime, the Loire-Atlantique, and the Seine-Maritime respectively. I will employ this usage in referring to their present-day ADs. The relevant liasses are: Bouches-du-Rhône M/2(III)-9, Cher 20 M 6, Drôme M 31, Gironde 3 M 206, Loire-Atlantique 1 M 51, Marne 7 M 7, Mayenne M 680, Tarn II M 3/8, Seine-et-Oise II M 11(2). I have deposited microfilm copies of these documents in the Yale and Harvard University Libraries.

a. Ministry of the interior to the prefects, 14 July 1827, signed by Corbière. AD Loire-Atlantique and Marne.

b. Min. int. to prefs., 18 Aug. 1827, signed by Corbière. AD Loire-Atlantique, Marne, and Tarn.

c. Min. int. to prefs., 3 Sept. 1827, signed by Villèle for Corbière. For the next 3 weeks Corbière was with the king's party making the tour of some northern departments; Villèle handled the affairs of the "interior" during his absence. AD Marne.

d. Min. int. to prefs., 4 Sept. 1827, signed by Villèle for Corbière. AD Bouches-du-Rhône, Loire-Atlantique, and Marne.

e. Min. int. to prefs., 14 Sept. 1827, signed by Villèle for Corbière. AD Bouches-du-Rhône, Loire-Atlantique, Marne, and Tarn.

f. Min. int. to prefs., 27 Sept. 1827, signed by Villèle for Corbière. AD Loire-Atlantique, Marne, and Tarn.

g. Min. int. to prefs., 9 Oct. 1827, signed by Corbière. AD Marne and Tarn.

h. Min. int. to prefs., 14 Oct. 1827, signed by Corbière. AD Cher, Loire-Atlantique, Marne, and Tarn.

i. Min. int. to prefs., 22 Oct. 1827, signed by Corbière. AD Cher, Gironde, and Loire-Atlantique.

j. Min. int. to prefs., 29 Oct. 1827, signed by [Franchet d'] Esperey, dir. of police in min. int. AD Bouches-du-Rhône and Gironde. This is a very different sort of communication. It is a letter transmitting monies from the secret fund for use in the election; its form for other departments may vary from these two examples.

k. Min. int. to prefs., 29 Oct. 1827, signed by Villèle for Corbière. The latter's illness, beginning about this time, kept him from his job until he was relieved at year's end. AD Cher and Marne.

l. Min. of finance to prefs., 3 Nov. 1827, signed by Villèle as min. of finance. AD Cher, Mayenne, and Tarn.

m. Min. int. to prefs., 5 Nov. 1827, signed by Villèle for Corbière. AD Cher, Loire-Atlantique, and Tarn.

n. Min. int. to prefs., 8 Nov. 1827, signed by Villèle for Corbière. AD Bouches-du-Rhône, Cher, Loire-Atlantique, and Marne.

o. Min. of finance to prefs., 9 Nov. 1827, signed by Villèle as min. of finance. AD Cher, Loire-Atlantique, and Marne.

p. Min. int. to prefs., 15 Nov. 1827, signed by Capelle for the min'y. of int. AD Bouches-du-Rhône, Cher, Mayenne, and Tarn. This was an instruction to prefects to report their election returns as speedily as possible. The message varies according to whether or not the prefect had access to the semaphore telegraph and how far from Paris his department lay.

q. Min. int. to prefs., 20 Nov. 1827, signed by Villèle for Corbière. AD Tarn. This message was a short exhortation to the voters of the departmental colleges. There is an unmistakable trace of its content in another document in the Seine-et-Oise.

r. Min. int. to prefs., 5 Dec. 1827, signed by Villèle for Corbière. AD Cher and Marne.

s. Min. int. to prefs., 26 Dec. 1827, signed by Capelle. AD Drôme, Marne, and Tarn.

3. Prefectoral correspondence.

In some of the ADs I found the first drafts of the prefects' messages to the minister of the interior when I did not find a trace of the clean copy in the AN. The best case was in the AD of the Bouches-du-Rhône. Throughout the ADs I often found correspondence relating to electoral matters between the prefects of different departments and between a given prefect and his subordinates within his department.

A single archival item worthy of special mention is the personal diary of Joseph de Villèle for the year 1827 which is among his papers in the family chateau at Mourville, near Toulouse. Through the kindness and generosity of the present comtesse de Villèle I have had access to the original manuscript of this document. It contains many entries which do not appear in the *Mémoires et correspondance du comte de Villèle,* ed. Jean Baptiste de Villèle (5 vols., Paris, 1888–1890).

The diary itself is a small book probably less than four by six inches. Each page has two daily entries, none of which runs much above a hundred words; many have less than half that number. Even the fullest entries seem cryptic, for Villèle was not the sort of man who would confide in detail matters he wished to be kept secret. Time and again, an entry has the character of a note which would recall something to the writer and little to an eavesdropper. And time and again there are whole sentences relating to small family matters such as, "Ecrit à ma femme et ma fille . . . ." Nevertheless, as the reader will have seen, the diary has much within it of highest importance to a devotee of France in the year 1827. Only a tiny fraction of it was incorporated into the printed *Mémoires*.

Neither Villèle's hand nor the pens that he wrote with, nor his spelling, nor his eschewal of capitalization and punctuation make for legibility. And when the humidity of the Paris spring and summer let the ink of one entry bleed through the page and appear in looking-glass upon the face of an already difficult passage, the resulting palimpsest is at first glance utterly impenetrable.

Printed Material

The principal collection of contemporary pamphlet literature dealing with elections are in the BN and catalogued fully in two volumes of its printed *Catalogue de l'histoire de France.* Within the Lb series Lb^{49}, which encompasses contemporary materials relating to "Charles X: Généralités de la vie et du regne . . ." and which appears in volume 3 of the *Catalogue,* there are a number of pamphlets dealing with electoral matters. Within the Le series Le^{54}, which lists other contemporary materials relating exclusively to "Elections à la Chambre des Députés . . ." and which appears in volume 6 of the *Catalogue,* there are the pamphlets devoted to specific elections, candidacies, etc.

Note: Pamphlets from these two series which appear in the *Catalogue* as, say, Lb^{49} 670 will appear in this book with the styling, Lb/49.670.

Actually the cataloguers did their best to keep the two series separate, but there is a certain amount of inevitable crossing-over.

One of the many electoral pamphlets which deserves special mention for the combination of its content and date is Anon., *Tactique électoral à l'usage de l'opposition* (Paris, 1821; 2nd ed., 1822; anr. ed., 1824 [same as 1822] : *Instructions électorales,* Lb/48.2494) BN Lb/48.2166. Few bits of printed evidence could tell more of the heights of sophisticated electioneering which the leftward opposition had achieved by the early 1820's.

The document carries no overt sign of having been prepared by a committee or having been specifically designed for the use of electoral organizations. Yet it is hard to believe that its very existence is not one of the outward signs of an accumulation of political wisdom in Paris among a group of political practitioners and that it was not put together with the sole aim of reaching old contacts in the departments and establishing new ones. In its mastery of the niceties of the electoral realm it seems to this reader the formal and unmistakable sign of the political coming of age of the left-wing opposition. It could have served as the model for many of the pamphlets put out by Chateaubriand's Friends and the Aide-toi in 1827, in fact there is good reason to believe that it did so serve.

In the BN there is another group of publications which are catalogued in the *Catalogue de l'histoire de France:* the Ln/6 series, which are the contemporary biographical dictionaries relating to members of the chamber of deputies upon which much of the essential *Dictionnaire des parlementaires français* of Adolphe Robert, Edgar Bourloton, and Gaston Cougny (5 vols., Paris, 1889–1891) rests. The best of these are: J. B. M. Braun, *Nouvelle Biographie des députés . . . 1814 à 1829* (Paris, 1830) BN Ln/6.38; J. Dourille, *Biographie des députés* (Paris, 1829) BN Ln/6.36; M. A. Larde, *Nouvelle Biographie pittoresque des députés* (Paris, 1826) BN Ln/6.31; Anon., *Biographie des députés de la chambre septennale de 1824 à 1830* (Paris, 1826) BN Ln/6.30; Anon., *Biographie des députés, session de 1828* (Paris, 1828) BN Ln/6.35; Anon., *Biographie nouvelle et complète de la chambre des députés* (Paris, 1829) BN Ln/6.37. Of these Braun's is the most ambitious and probably the best, but he does make errors, some of which are catchable by cross-checking with the others.

A last word – and that about the outstanding volume of Charles H. Pouthas, *Guizot pendant la Restauration* (Paris: Plon-Nourrit, 1923). Written during the period when he was arranging the Guizot papers, which he refers to as "Val-Richer Correspondance," Professor Pouthas had the first fruits of this rich collection, now in the AN. He also, of course, uses a wide range of other materials of the AN and BN. As I have remarked in the text, Professor Pouthas has written by all odds the best study of the Société, Aide-toi. His treatment has however raised two questions. The first is easily dealt with. For reasons given in the text I feel that he unduly slights the accomplishment of Chateaubriand's Friends, but after all Chateaubriand was not the focus of his concern.

The second is more worrisome, for I wish to believe with M. Pouthas that Guizot's role in the early days of the Aide-toi (say, from mid-July to the end of August) was of crucial importance. It is this very point that I have difficulty in accepting. For, as M. Pouthas himself knew well and so wrote, it was during these weeks that Guizot passed through the harrowing experience of tending his desperately ill wife, taking her to Plombières looking to the curative waters, taking her back to Paris to be present at her death on the first of August. With Mme. Guizot gone, Guizot absented himself from Paris and the center of the action until the end of September.

From the Guizot papers of this period one perceives a man in deep distress and crushing bereavement. I find it all but impossible to believe that he had room in his soul for much of anything other than this deep personal tragedy. Of course M. Pouthas, who knows more about the Guizot papers than any one since Guizot, may have the evidence to sustain his characterization of Guizot's political activity at this very time; I can only say that I did not find it.

Index

Family names are rendered in the text according to the style of Robert et al. except in those few instances which seem to depart from consistent common usage. In the index I have indicated in brackets their choice where it differs from mine.

Harvard Historical Studies

Out of Print Titles Are Omitted

33. *Lewis George Vander Velde.* The Presbyterian Churches and the Federal Union, 1861–1869. 1932.
35. *Donald C. McKay.* The National Workshops: A Study in the French Revolution of 1848. 1933.
38. *Dwight Erwin Lee.* Great Britain and the Cyprus Convention Policy of 1878. 1934.
48. *J. H. Hexter.* The Reign of King Pym. 1941.
58. *Charles C. Gillispie.* Genesis and Geology: A Study in the Relations of Scientific Thought, Natural Theology, and Social Opinion in Great Britain, 1790–1850. 1951.
60. *Robert G. L. Waite.* Vanguard of Nazism: The Free Corps Movement in Post-war Germany, 1918–1923. 1952.

62, 63. *John King Fairbank.* Trade and Diplomacy on the China Coast: The Opening of the Treaty Ports, 1842–1854. One-volume edition. 1953.

64. *Franklin L. Ford.* Robe and Sword: The Regrouping of the French Aristocracy after Louis XIV. 1953.
66. *Wallace Evan Davies.* Patriotism on Parade: The Story of Veterans' and Hereditary Organizations in America, 1783–1900. 1955.
67. *Harold Schwartz.* Samuel Gridley Howe: Social Reformer, 1801–1876. 1956.
69. *Stanley J. Stein.* Vassouras: A Brazilian Coffee Country, 1850–1900. 1957.
71. *Ernest R. May.* The World War and American Isolation, 1914–1917. 1959.
72. *John B. Blake.* Public Health in the Town of Boston, 1630–1822. 1959.
73. *Benjamin W. Labaree.* Patriots and Partisans: The Merchants of Newburyport, 1764–1815. 1962.
74. *Alexander Sedgwick.* The Ralliement in French Politics, 1890–1898. 1965.
75. *E. Ann Pottinger.* Napoleon III and the German Crisis, 1865–1866. 1966.
76. *Walter Goffart.* The Le Mans Forgeries: A Chapter from the History of Church Property in the Ninth Century. 1966.
77. *Daniel P. Resnick.* The White Terror and the Political Reaction after Waterloo, 1966.
78. *Giles Constable.* The Letters of Peter the Venerable. 1967.
79. *Lloyd E. Eastman.* Throne and Mandarins: China's Search for a Policy during the Sino-French Controversy, 1880–1885. 1967.
80. *Allen J. Matusow.* Farm Policies and Politics in the Truman Years. 1967.
81. *Philip Charles Farwell Bankwitz.* Maxime Weygand and Civil-Military Relations in Modern France. 1967.
82. *Donald J. Wilcox.* The Development of Florentine Humanist Historiography in the Fifteenth Century. 1969.
83. *John W. Padberg, S.J.* Colleges in Controversy: The Jesuit Schools in France from Revival to Suppression, 1813–1880. 1969.

84. *Marvin Arthur Breslow.* A Mirror of England: English Puritan Views of Foreign Nations, 1618–1640. 1970.
85. *Patrice L. R. Higonnet.* Pont-de-Montvert: Social Structure and Politics in a French Village, 1700–1914. 1971.
86. *Paul G. Halpern.* The Mediterranean Naval Situation, 1908–1914. 1971.
87. *Robert E. Ruigh.* The Parliament of 1624: Politics and Foreign Policy. 1971.
88. *Angeliki E. Laiou.* Constantinople and the Latins: The Foreign Policy of Andronicus, 1282–1328. 1972.
89. *Donald Nugent.* Ecumenism in the Age of Reformation: The Colloquy of Poissy. 1974.
90. *Robert A. McCaughey.* Josiah Quincy, 1772–1864: The Last Federalist. 1974.
91. *Sherman Kent.* The Election of 1827 in France. 1975.